£15.99

The origins of
Norfolk

Origins of the Shire

general editor
Nick Higham

already published in the series

The origins of Lancashire   *Denise Kenyon*
The origins of Somerset   *Michael Costen*

The origins of
Norfolk

Tom Williamson

Manchester University Press
Manchester and New York
Distributed exclusively in the USA and Canada by St. Martin's Press

Copyright © Tom Williamson 1993

Published by Manchester University Press
Oxford Road, Manchester M13 9PL, UK
and Room 400, 175 Fifth Avenue, New York, NY 10010, USA

Distributed exclusively in the USA and Canada
by St. Martin's Press, Inc., 175 Fifth Avenue, New York,
NY 10010, USA

British Library Cataloguing-in-Publication Data
A catalogue record for this book is available from the British Library

Library of Congress Cataloging-in-Publication Data
Williamson, Tom.
    The origins of Norfolk/Tom Williamson.
        p.   cm. – (Origins of the Shire)
    Includes index.
    ISBN 0–7190–3401–9 (cloth), – ISBN 0–7190–3928–2 (paper)
    1. Norfolk (England) – History.   2. Anglo–Saxons – England – Norfolk.
    3. Britons – England – Norfolk.   I. Title.   II. Series.
    DA670.N6W55   1993
    942.6′1–dc20   92-31522
                                                                                  CIP

ISBN 0 7190 3401 9 *hardback*
ISBN 0 7190 3928 2 *paperback*
Reprinted in paperback, 1994, 1997

Typeset by Best-set Typesetter Ltd., Hong Kong
Printed in Great Britain by Bell and Bain Ltd, Glasgow

Contents

List of figures		vi
List of plates		viii
General Editor's preface		x
Acknowledgements		xii
1	Topography and environment	1
2	Before the Angles	20
3	The coming of the Angles	49
4	The North Folk	73
5	An age of expansion	105
6	Pagans, saints, and churches	137
7	The Norman Conquest and beyond	162
	References	135
	Index	198

Figures

1.1 Norfolk: principal soil types   9
1.2 Norfolk: landscape regions   12
1.3 Norfolk: main topographic features   16
2.1 Early field patterns in the middle Waveney valley.
     The earliest boundaries in this area form a series of
     rough 'grids', orientated north–south, one of which
     appears to be slighted by the Roman Pye Road   26
2.2 The distribution of Iron Age hillforts in Norfolk   29
2.3 Iron Age and Roman landscape features in the area
     around Wells, north-west Norfolk   31
2.4 Major roads and nucleated settlements in Roman
     Norfolk   39
2.5 The distribution of all known findspots of Roman
     material in Norfolk (after Davies & Gregory 1991)   46
3.1 Early Saxon sites, and artefact findspots, in Norfolk 51
3.2 The distribution of major place-names incorporating
     elements referring to woodland   60
3.3 An early watershed boundary between Shipdham
     and Wymondham   71
4.1 The distribution of major place-names incorporating
     the element *hām*   86
4.2 The distribution of major place-names incorporating
     the element *tūn*   87
4.3 Forehoe Hundred: the pattern of ancient estates   98

List of figures

5.1 The distribution of major place-names incorporating Scandinavian elements (excluding *þorp*, and personal names) 109

5.2 Norfolk: population density in 1066 112

5.3 Norfolk: the distribution of woodland in 1066 115

5.4 Norfolk: the combined distribution of sokemen and free men in 1066 116

5.5 Norfolk: the distribution of sokemen in 1066 119

5.6 Norfolk: the distribution of free men in 1066 120

5.7 Domesday Norfolk: hundreds 127

6.1 Possible Middle Saxon monastic sites 147

6.2 The layout of parish boundaries in the area around North Walsham 153

6.3 The distribution of shared and adjacent churchyards in Norfolk 160

7.1 Tenurial organisation in medieval Norfolk: the number of manors per vill recorded in the *Nomina Villarum* of 1316 164

7.2 Isolated churches in Norfolk (*source*: Faden's map of Norfolk (1797); various early estate maps. A church is here defined as 'isolated' if it lies more than 200 metres from a settlement containing more than two dwellings) 171

Plates

1 Warham Camp, the most impressive Iron Age fort in Norfolk (Derek Edwards/Aerial Archaeology Publications)

2 Venta Icenorum, capital of the Roman *civitas*, five kilometres south of Norwich (Derek Edwards/Norfolk Landscape Archaeology)

3 Burgh Castle: the south wall of the Saxon Shore fort of *Gariannonum* (Jon Finch)

4 The Peddars Way Roman road near Harpley (Brian Horn)

5 The Bicchamditch: an aerial view of Norfolk's most impressive linear earthwork, probably constructed in the sixth or seventh century (Derek Edwards/Aerial Archaeology Publications)

6 William Faden's map of Norfolk, published in 1797, clearly shows the extent of commons and of common-edge settlement in the county before the impact of Parliamentary enclosure (Brian Horn)

7 Great Snoring: the migration of settlement to the margins of commons in the early Middle Ages frequently left churches marginalised or isolated in the midst of fields (Brian Horn)

8 Itteringham: an aerial photograph, taken in 1986, reveals an apsidal church, almost certainly the lost church of St Nicholas, one of two parish churches in the medieval vill (Derek Edwards/Norfolk Landscape Archaeology)

9 Great Melton: here, as at a number of other places in the

county, two churches stand in the same churchyard (Jon Finch)

10 Reepham: originally, the parish churches of Reepham, Hackford and Whitwell shared a single churchyard in the centre of this small market town; Hackford church was destroyed in the sixteenth century, although traces of it can still be found to the south of Whitwell church (Derek Edwards/Norfolk Landscape Archaeology)

11 North Creake: an early seventeenth-century map shows the arable open-fields around the village. In the middle ages the vast majority of land in Norfolk lay in open-fields of various kinds (Jon Finch)

12 New Buckenham: the castle and planned town established by the d'Albinis in the twelfth century (Cambridge Committee for Aerial Photography)

13 Castle Rising: the great keep of the d'Albinis' castle (Brian Horn)

14 Fritton Common: before the enclosures of the late eighteenth and nineteenth centuries, common-edge settlements were ubiquitous in Norfolk, especially in the east of the county (Jon Finch)

15 Egmere, one of a number of deserted medieval villages on the dry interfluve between the valleys of the Burn and Stiffkey in north Norfolk (Brian Horn)

16 Hales church, a particularly fine example of an early twelfth-century parish church with characteristic round flint tower (Jon Finch)

Plates appear between pages 104 and 105

General Editor's preface

The shire was the most important single unit of government, justice and social organisation throughout the Later Middle Ages and on into the Modern period. An understanding of the shire is, therefore, fundamental to English history of all types and of all periods – be it conducted on a national, regional or local basis.

This series sets out to explore the origins of each shire in the Early Middle Ages. Archaeological evidence for settlement hierarchies and social territories in later prehistory and the Roman period is necessarily the starting point. The shire and its component parts are then explored in detail during the Anglo-Saxon period. A series of leading scholars, each with a particular regional expertise, have brought together evidence drawn from literary and documentary sources, place-name research and archaeological fieldwork to present a stimulating picture of the territorial history of the English shires, and the parishes, estates and hundreds of which they were formed.

In some instances the results stress the degree of continuity across periods as long as a millennium. Elsewhere, these studies underline the arbitrary nature of the shire and the intentional break with the past, particularly where the West Saxon King, Edward the Elder, imposed his southern ideas concerning local organisation on the regional communities of the English Midlands.

These volumes will each be a great asset to historians and all those interested in their own localities, offering an open door into a period of the past which has for many so far been too difficult or obscure to attempt an entry.

Nick Higham

Acknowledgements

This book is, to a large extent, a work of synthesis. It draws on the research, both published and unpublished, of a large number of amateur and professional historians and archaeologists working in Norfolk. Many members of Norfolk Landscape Archaeology, the Norfolk Archaeological Unit, the Norfolk Archaeological and Historical Research Group, and others have contributed ideas and information. Thanks in particular are due to Chris Barringer, for information about Wymondham; Alan Davison, for a wealth of fieldwalking data; Kate Skipper, for the many hours she spent ploughing through Domesday Book; Mo Cubitt, for allowing me access to her unpublished research on Hempnall; Edwin Rose, for information about Reedham church; Alayne Fenner, for the *Liber Albus* reference; and to Peter Murphy, Bob Silvester, Ken Penn, Peter Warner, Derek Edwards, and (above all) Andrew Rogerson, for much advice and inspiration. Peter Wade-Martins and Andrew Rogerson read a draft of the text, and helped remove many of the more glaring mistakes; those that remain are, of course, entirely due to my own incompetence. Philip Judge provided the line drawings, and Vanessa Upton typed much of the text. Liz Bellamy read the text and turned it into English. Writing this book would have been difficult without the support and stimulation provided by colleagues and students at the Centre of East Anglian Studies, especially Cathryn Terry, Adam Longcroft, Jan Pitman, John Dean, Rosemary Hoppit, Ann Reeves, Jon Finch, Peter Murphy and Richard Wilson. It would have been impossible without the indulgence and support of my family: Liz, Matthew, and Jessica.

1

Topography and environment

Studying Norfolk

Most people in England are unfamiliar with Norfolk, for it is off the beaten track, reached by roads and railways that go nowhere else. The majority of visitors come to the coast, or to the 'Norfolk Broads', and it is the popularity of the latter destination which is responsible for the national image of the county as a flat land of reed-fringed lakes and rivers, with wide panoramas of marsh interrupted only by the ruins of the wind-pumps standing stark against a wide sky. Those who live and work in the county, however, know that Norfolk is not for the most part flat, and that the kinds of scenery experienced by visitors to Broadland constitute only a small part of a rich and varied repertoire. There are many Norfolks, ranging from the rolling chalk hills of the north-west, to the silent pine forests of the west, to the gentle claylands of the south.

Norfolk is the sum of its parts: yet it also has a character of its own which embraces all of its sub-regions. Today that character is predominantly rural: indeed, Norfolk is arguably the last truly rural county in south-eastern England. Lacking mineral reserves or significant sources of water power, the Industrial Revolution of the eighteenth and nineteenth centuries largely passed it by. It was, instead, the reputed birthplace of the Agricultural Revolution. Even today, the only significant towns are Norwich, Kings Lynn, Thetford, and Yarmouth, and – with the exception of the first – all occupy situations on the very margins of the county. All the other urban centres – Swaffham, Fakenham, Wymondham, and the rest – are still, despite modern expansion and peripheral industrial estates, essentially market towns.

But Norfolk was not always a backwater. At the time of Domesday Book Norwich was the second biggest city in England, and it was not to relinquish this position until well into the eighteenth century. During the medieval period the county was the most densely populated, the most prosperous, and the most economically precocious in England. In part, this explains one of the most striking features of the Norfolk landscape – the very high density of parish churches. There are now 700, although many of these are redundant or ruinous: others have disappeared entirely since medieval times. This prosperity was built on agriculture, for Norfolk farming methods were the most sophisticated in England, although in the later Middle Ages regional prosperity also owed much to the manufacture of textiles (Campbell 1983). Domesday Book shows us that another distinctive feature of the early medieval county was its weak manorial structure and tenurial complexity. Most vills contained more than one manor, and medieval documents reveal that these were not constrained by, but frequently cut right across, the boundaries of parishes. In many areas, and especially in the east, large numbers of free tenants existed. All this made for a county with a particularly idiosyncratic history. Individualism was deeply rooted in its culture: and both in the medieval period, and later, Norfolk men were famous for their litigiousness. As one seventeenth-century commentator put it: 'The inhabitants . . . are so well skiled in matters of the law as many times even the baser sort at the plough-tail will argue *pro et contra* cases in law, whose cunning and subtiltie hath replenished the shire with more lawyers than any shire whatsoever though far greater' (Hood 1938: 68).

The individualistic nature of Norfolk society was reflected in the landscape. Over great swathes of the county open-field systems existed which were so poorly regulated that they were only 'common' in the sense that tenants had the right to graze over each other's land during the fallow year; in many cases, only on the harvest aftermath (Campbell 1980b, 1981). Even the most regulated field systems, those in the west of the county, were generally more flexible in their cropping arrangements than was usual in the classic open-field systems of the Midlands. This absence of developed communal agriculture was mirrored in the county's pattern of medieval settlement. In much of the county, and especially in the south and east, villages were rare and farms were widely scattered across the landscape, often hugging the edges of commons and greens.

In the post-medieval centuries a society of competitive, individualistic, but essentially small-scale producers was gradually replaced by one with a more polarised tenurial and social structure. This was especially the case in the north and west of the county, where greater and greater quantities of land were amassed in the hands of large landed estates. But the process was a very gradual one, and the legacy of the county's individualistic past was never entirely lost. Over much of the county in-numerable seventeenth-century houses – large, prosperous-looking lobby-entrance farms – attest the wealth of the yeomanry, rather than the great landowner: the county was staunchly Parliamentarian in the Civil War.

The roots of Norfolk's social and tenurial idiosyncrasies go deep: they were already firmly in place in 1066. To understand Norfolk, therefore, we need to understand its history in the Saxon period. In fact, we need to delve even deeper into the past, for Norfolk was already an 'old country' at the time of the Anglian settlement. But here we are immediately faced with a problem. There are very few documentary sources which can tell us about the period before the Norman Conquest. Neither the historian Bede, nor the *Anglo-Saxon Chronicle*, have much to say about the county. Moreover, Viking raids obliterated Norfolk's monasteries and destroyed their records; not a single charter survives from the period before the 970s, and the few that have come down to us from the period thereafter do not have much of interest to tell us about landscape or territorial organisation.

Yet the situation is not quite as hopeless as it first appears. Some scraps of early history were incorporated in post-Conquest texts and traditions. Used with care and caution, these can be extremely informative. Moreover, like Suffolk and Essex, Norfolk is dealt with in the so-called *Little Domesday*, and we are therefore blessed with a particularly detailed picture of the county in the second half of the eleventh century. And, with no less than 726 separately named vills by 1066, Norfolk has an unusually large number of major place-names, which can tell us a great deal about its early history.

Other disciplines also have much to contribute. A number of important studies have been made of the pollen taken from sediments derived from the county's many meres and ponds, and these can provide much useful information about early vegetation history. But it is the evidence of archaeology which contributes most to our knowledge of early Norfolk. Excavations at places like Spong Hill and North Elmham have yielded vital information about the development of local society in the Early and Middle Saxon periods; thousands of aerial photographs have revealed much about prehistoric and Roman settlement; and even more evidence has been produced by fieldwalking surveys. Norfolk is a predominantly arable county, and is thus particularly suited to the use of the simple technique of systematically examining the surface of the ploughsoil for concentrations of pottery and other debris marking the location of settlement or other activities. The search for early settlements is helped by another distinctive feature of the region. Unlike many other areas of England, Norfolk has no 'aceramic' archaeological phases from the late prehistoric period onwards. Pottery production never died out here after the collapse of the Roman period, as it did, for example, in much of the West Country. In addition to this, the late Tony Gregory and others at the Norfolk Archaeological Unit pioneered the development of amicable relations with amateur metal-detectors – elsewhere often still regarded as the pariahs of archaeology – so that thousands of discoveries of early metalwork have been properly recorded, instead of disappearing for ever into the anonymity of private collections. Much about the early history of Norfolk remains frustratingly obscure: but by combining these various strands of evidence, we can begin to see some pattern in the county's early development, and go some of the way towards explaining its distinctive character in the Middle Ages and after.

Location and topography

In ways which are both complex and subtle, Norfolk's identity has been moulded by its location. It is the most easterly county in

England, and in common with adjacent areas is characterised by comparatively soft young rocks, rubbed smooth by glacial erosion and smothered by glacial and periglacial deposition (Larwood & Funnell 1961, 1970; Chatwin 1961). Soils, as we shall see, are very varied, but in most areas comparatively deep and fertile, and the terrain is gently rolling. It is also the driest county in England. Nowhere receives more than 27 inches per year: parts of the Breckland receive less than 23 inches (Grove 1961: 42; Edlin 1972: 5). It is this combination of deep soils, muted terrain, and dry climate which explains why most of the farmland in the county is devoted to the production of arable crops – and why, in consequence, much of the landscape has been laid bare in the last three decades, cleared of hedges and copses, to make the empty prairies most suitable for the combine harvester and other machinery. In earlier periods, too, the extent of arable land use was greater than in many other areas of England.

The climate is not always kind. The winters are cold, often ferociously so, and those who live here are only too familiar with the biting winds which blow – straight from Siberia, it often seems – on to the exposed coast, and into the interior. For Norfolk's second noteworthy characteristic is its long exposed coastline, stretching for some 150 kilometres from Lynn to Yarmouth, and more still if we were to count the innumerable indentations of estuaries and former estuaries. Such a coastline facilitated maritime trade – both longshore and foreign. It also, at times, invited settlement and raiding. For it does not look out across the narrow seas of the channel towards the civilised lands of France, but instead faces the wild North Sea, Norway, Denmark, and North Germany. Even in remote prehistory, the area did not develop in a hermetically sealed environment. Its economic and social system was affected by wider changes, not only in England but in northern Europe, and beyond. When England's connections were strongest with the areas immediately across the English channel, as in the late Iron Age, for example, Norfolk was a comparatively peripheral zone. But when, as in much of the Saxon period, the North Sea basin formed a focus for economic and cultural exchange, then the county had a more central role.

Lastly, we must take note of Norfolk's location in relation to the rest of England. The distinctiveness of any region owes much

5

to its degree of isolation: for it is isolation which encourages idiosyncratic, divergent developments in language, customs, and culture. To the west, the flooding of the Fenland basin in late prehistoric times, and again at the end of the Roman period, reduced contact with the Midland core of England. Although the marshes here were never quite the impassable, empty wilderness that are sometimes described, they nevertheless constituted an important barrier to everyday intercourse and communication. The Fens are long since drained. But even today, to reach Norfolk by car or train from the Midlands involves a long journey through flat, rather bleak, sparsely-inhabited terrain: through a landscape which, in the words of Graham Swift, 'of all landscapes approximates most closely to Nothing' (Swift 1983: 11). Norfolk people still refer (although these days in a somewhat self-conscious fashion) to the lands beyond the Fens as 'the Shires'.

The nature of Norfolk's historical connections with the area to the south, with the county of Suffolk, is a more complex matter. There are strong links between the two counties, and no sharp break between them, in terms of landscape, customs, and dialect. The Waveney and the Little Ouse form the boundary. These rivers share a common, east–west through-valley, formed in Pleistocene times, with the Waveney draining eastwards and the Little Ouse westwards. Their sources, lost in the wilderness of Lopham Fen, lie only a few hundred yards apart, and if we were to excavate a channel through the diminutive watershed between (as F. Mathew proposed in 1656, to create a 'Mediterranean Passage' between Lynn and Yarmouth), Norfolk would be an island (Mathew 1656). And yet, except to the east of Bungay, these are not wide rivers, and for most of history formed no significant barrier to contact. It is hardly surprising, then, that for much of the period covered by this book, the two counties were part of a single political unit, the Kingdom of the East Angles, and its successor, the Earldom. In later times, too, their fortunes were closely interwoven, so much so, indeed, that one might question whether it is really possible to write about the one in isolation from the other. The term 'Norfolk' first appears in documents as late as 1043. But it is probable that the division between the 'North Folk' and the 'South Folk' goes back, in some form, into Middle Saxon times. Moreover, in earlier periods, the northern and southern parts of East Anglia were culturally and politically distinct. In Iron Age and Roman times the former formed the territory of the Iceni, the latter, together with what is now Essex, that of the Trinovantes. This political and, later, administrative division did not, however, follow the unimpressive frontier of the Little Ouse/Waveney valley, a feature which, at this time, was perhaps as likely to unite as to divide the communities settled on opposite banks. Instead, it seems to have run a little further to the south, along the watershed between the Waveney and the Gipping.

The regions of Norfolk

Norfolk consists of a number of different regions, with distinctive landscapes, economies, and societies. The configuration of these relates to, although it was never simply 'caused by', the distribution of soil types, and the geological structure of the county. This structure is basically simple, and best envisaged as a series of sedimentary deposits laid down in sequence, and then raised and tilted in such a way that the earliest are only exposed in the north–west of the county, in a narrow strip of country between Hunstanton and Hilgay (Larwood & Funnell 1970; Chatwin 1961). Here a variety of sands, sandstones, and clays – including a distinctive building stone, called *carstone* – form an escarpment which is structurally a continuation of the Chilterns, although much less dramatic, having been levelled and smoothed by glacial action. The latest of these deposits, and the one which forms the main body of the escarpment, is the chalk. This dips towards the south-east and, buried ever deeper beneath later sediments, underlies the whole of the county. At Yarmouth, in the extreme east of the county, it lies more than 180 metres down, buried beneath a great thickness of pre-glacial deposits, which geologists term the Crag. These are a varied collection of Pliocene and Pleistocene clays, gravels, and shelly sands, which overlie the chalk to the east of a line drawn roughly between Weybourne and Diss, and thus form the basic 'solid' geology of the east of the county, as the chalk does in the west.

This essentially simple structure is, however, largely obscured by a highly complex series of superficial glacial deposits. In the centre and south-east of the county, chalk and Crag are buried under a mantle of boulder clay, in places as much as 250 metres thick. This forms a slightly tilted plateau, dissected by a number of streams and river valleys, which extends southwards into Suffolk, Essex, and Hertfordshire. It is not a homogeneous deposit. The level areas between the major valleys are, for the most part, occupied by the heavy, poorly-draining but fertile chalky boulder clay. Beneath this, and exposed in the sides of some of the major valleys, and on the fringes of the plateau, is the sandy boulder clay, which gives rise to more tractable soils (Hodge & Hellyer 1984: 117–23, 132–8). The extent to which the plateau is dissected is, therefore, a major factor in the evolution of landscape and settlement. In general terms, the degree of dissection is greatest in the north–west: the least dissected areas are in the south–east, especially between the valleys of the Tas and the Waveney, where wide flat interfluves carry particularly heavy soils.

To the north and west of the claylands, the glaciations had a very different effect on the landscape. Glacial meltwaters, and high winds blowing close to the ice front, deposited a wide variety of sands and gravels. A complex range of soils can be found in a great arc across the north of the county, associated with an equally complex range of landscapes. But one thing united these disparate districts. Whereas the soils of the claylands are, to varying extents, heavy and water-retentive, those in the north and west are freely-draining (Figure 1.1).

The geological distinction gave rise to a major economic division in the early modern period, between two broad economic zones in the county. In 1595 it was noted that 'Norfolk is compounded and sorted of soyles apt for graine and sheepe and of soyles apt for woode and pasture' (Skipper 1989: 51). The former, the areas of the so-called 'sheep-corn husbandry', corresponded with the lighter soils of the north and west: the claylands of the south, in contrast, were 'most apt and so employed to dayries and breeding of great cattel'.

To some extent this division is still etched on the modern landscape, in spite of the fact that the heavy clays are also now an area of intensive arable husbandry. They carry an 'ancient countryside', with field boundaries mostly created by gradual piecemeal change and enclosure over a long period of time (Rackham 1976: 16–17). The settlement pattern is highly dispersed: indeed, in many parishes there is no obvious 'village'

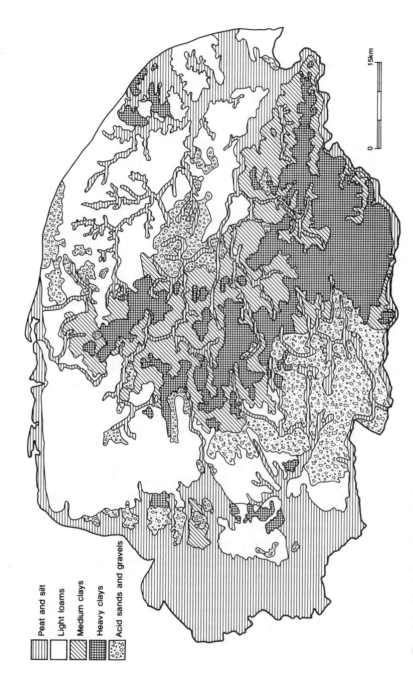

Fig. 1.1 Norfolk: principal soil types

Peat and silt

Light loams

Medium clays

Heavy clays

Acid sands and gravels

15Km

0

at all, and even the church stands isolated in the midst of arable fields. Many of the hamlets have names ending in 'green' or 'common' and indeed, before the last decade of the eighteenth century, most consisted of loose scatters of houses and farms around the periphery of common land. But the commons disappeared soon after, removed by Parliamentary enclosure, and only the names remain. The north and west, in contrast, have boundaries which, for the most part, originated in the period after 1650, often as a result of Parliamentary enclosure in the late eighteenth or nineteenth centuries. Arable farming provided less incentive to enclose the open fields and commons. There are other differences. The settlement pattern in this region tends to take the form of large nucleated villages, the outlying farms usually dating from after the enclosures of the eighteenth and nineteenth centuries. Moreover, while arable farming in the post-medieval centuries tended to favour the development of large landed estates, pastoral enterprises encouraged the survival of the smaller landowner. The majority of great country houses and landscape parks, and estate farms and villages, can still be found in the north and west.

But historians have tended to oversimplify the relationship between post-medieval farming systems and landscape. Many of the differences between the county's regions were already present in the early medieval period, long before the development of the specialised farming economies which supposedly engendered them. Thus, for example, historians sometimes see dispersed patterns of settlement as a characteristic of pasture-farming areas, nucleated villages as a feature of arable districts: but in Norfolk, the main regional differences in settlement patterns existed by the twelfth century. Moreover, on closer examination we soon find that the correspondence between landscape types and farming regions is less close than is sometimes suggested. The north-east of the county is an area of light soils, and was a sheep–corn country of predominantly arable husbandry. Yet it was already considered 'very old-enclosed' by William Marshall in 1787, with so many hedges that 'the eye seems ever on the verge of a forest' (Marshall 1787). It also has a settlement pattern which, instead of being like that of the north and west, shares the somewhat chaotic dispersal of the south–east.

The simple north-west/south-east division clearly needs to be broken down into more meaningful units of analysis. The areas of light soil, in particular, display much variation in their present landscape, and in their earlier history. Today the most distinctive is perhaps *Breckland*, in the south-west of the county (Figure 1.2). Its name is a recent invention, coined as late as 1894 by W. G. Clarke, although the term 'breck' is itself much older, the local term for an area of temporary 'outfield' cultivation farmed for a few years and then allowed to revert to heathland, beyond the areas of more regularly cultivated field land (Clarke 1894: 24). Such agricultural practices were related to the nature of the local geology: for here glacial sand lies directly on porous chalk, making for acid, infertile soils, whose inherent tendency to drought was exacerbated by the extremely low rainfall the area receives. The cultivation of short-lived 'breaks' sounds like an ancient, primitive practice, and it may have been widespread in the medieval period and earlier, although there are grounds for believing that it was, at least in part, a post-medieval innovation (Allison 1957: 28–30). Either way, settlement in this region in the Middle Ages largely took the form of loosely nucleated villages, surrounded by open field arable, strung along the river valleys cutting through the chalk, or sited on the margins of the area. Right up until the end of the eighteenth century, vast areas of rabbit warren and sheepwalk existed on the higher ground, away from the valleys. Little of all this survives today. Most of the heaths and open fields were enclosed in the nineteenth century, and, from the 1920s, much of this area was planted up as a vast conifer forest by the Forestry Commission.

To the north of Breckland is a different region, with a different landscape and history: a broad swathe of dry, rolling uplands, reminiscent in places of the Lincolnshire Wolds or the Berkshire Downs. Arthur Young called it the 'Good Sands', for the sandy soils could be improved by digging pits down to the chalk beneath, and assiduously spreading this across the fields, in order to improve the soil structure and neutralise acidity (Young 1809). This practice of 'marling' was known in the medieval period, but was adopted on a very large scale in the eighteenth and nine-teenth centuries, when the land was, for the most part, acquired by large landed estates (especially Holkham, Houghton, and Raynham), and both the open fields on the lower slopes, and the acid heaths on the higher ground, were enclosed into fields. The

11

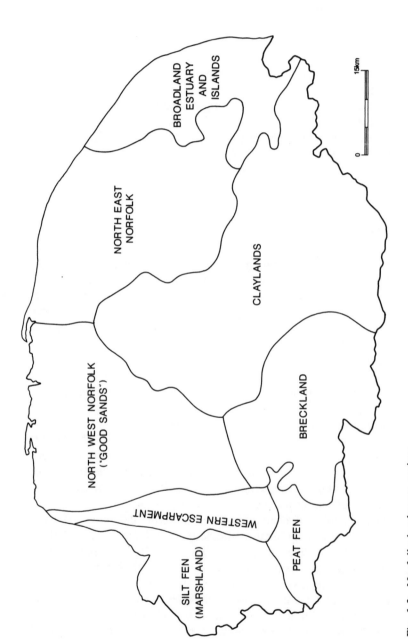

Fig. 1.2 Norfolk: landscape regions

BROADLAND ESTUARY AND ISLANDS

NORTH EAST NORFOLK

CLAYLANDS

NORTH WEST NORFOLK ('GOOD SANDS')

BRECKLAND

WESTERN ESCARPMENT

PEAT FEN

SILT FEN (MARSHLAND)

15km

0

settlement pattern consists of nucleated villages, often large, and widely spaced. Their location was largely determined by the availability of water, so that they occur in the lower reaches of the principal valleys; or where areas of water-retentive clays occur, on the margins of the region, or in small pockets on the higher ground.

This rolling landscape continues eastwards nearly as far as Holt: beyond, things are different and more complex. This is partly because the north-east of the county has a varied geology. There are areas of acid heathland, the more extensive of which – like those to the north-east of Norwich – today carry a conifer-dominated landscape reminiscent of the Breckland. But there are also districts of deep, extremely fertile and easily worked loams, especially on the former island of Flegg. The whole area is dissected by the wide, lush valleys of the Wensum, Bure, Ant, and their tributaries. The medieval settlement pattern was dispersed, with common-edge hamlets and many isolated churches.

To the east, this varied region is bordered by extensive areas of drained marshland, where before the Middle Ages the wide valleys of the Ant, Bure, Yare, Wensum, and Waveney merged in a vast estuary. The island of Flegg was, during the Roman and Early Saxon periods, a true island, lying on the northern edge of the estuary. This wide expanse of open water gradually silted up, as a great spit of land (now occupied by the town of Yarmouth) built up across the estuary's mouth, leaving Breydon water as its only remnant. But what was begun by nature was continued by local communities, who gradually embanked and ditched the marshes to create the stunning landscape of today. This area is often included, especially in the literature of the boat-hire companies, within 'the Norfolk Broads'; but this term, strictly speaking, refers to the lakes higher up the rivers feeding into the former estuary. These are artificial features, created by the extraction of peat in early medieval times and flooded by a rise in sea level during the thirteenth and fourteenth centuries (Lambert *et al.* 1960).

Two other regions need to be mentioned. On the other side of the county, to the west of the 'Good Sands', the western escarpment carries a landscape of considerable complexity, borne of its complex geology and topography. The escarpment itself rises in height towards the north; at Hunstanton it reaches a height of some 65 metres, while to the south, near Hilgay, it is only slightly above sea level. It is, moreover, cut through by a number of westward-draining rivers, creating a series of upland blocks separated by wide, and formerly marshy valleys. Villages stand on the ridges, which themselves have a very varied appearance. In places, acid gravels carry extensive conifer plantations established in comparatively modern times on former heaths; and especially towards the south, heavier soils give rise to fertile arable fields.

To the west of this escarpment lie the Fens, another former estuary – this time of the rivers Ouse, Nene, Witham, and a multiplicity of other Midland watercourses. This flat landscape of drained, and now unremittingly arable marshland extends into the neighbouring counties of Lincolnshire and Cambridgeshire; but closer inspection soon reveals that it is really two, quite distinct landscapes. Between Downham Market and the Wash lies the region known, traditionally, as *Marshland*; an area of deep silts laid down by marine transgressions in late prehistoric and Roman times, over a sequence of peat and clay deposits which had, earlier in the prehistoric period, accumulated in the mouth of the estuary. Changes in sea levels led, as we shall see, to colonisation of this area in Roman times, its subsequent abandonment, and recolonisation during the Middle Saxon period. Today this is a landscape of large, rather sprawling villages, linked by rather winding roads. It is, therefore, very different from the peat fen to the south, only a small part of which lies within the boundaries of the county. In early pre-history, much of this area was dry land, and its islands and fringes were intensively exploited; but it was later inundated and, because more low-lying than the silts to the north, was for much of the medieval period an area of marshland subject to seasonal flooding. Large-scale reclamation came only in the post-medieval period, and the result is a landscape devoid of villages, except for a few secondary settlements like Ten Mile Bank; a stark, open landscape of straight roads and dykes, few, mainly modern houses, and wide skies.

Valley and watershed

These divisions of the county, based on geology and soil-types, are useful and important. But they can also be misleading. Early farmers did not possess a map showing drift geology, soil-types, or agricultural potential. As clearance and colonisation expanded from certain points, it only leap-frogged over certain soils if these were particularly intractable or infertile. The last areas to be cleared during a period of demographic or economic expansion were not, therefore, necessarily the most agriculturally marginal. They might equally well have been the most *spatially* marginal. Moreover, early farmers did not only require soil in which to grow crops. They also needed adequate supplies of water for their livestock, as well as for their own consumption. Settlements needed to be near regular water supplies, and the larger the settlement, the larger the water source required. Furthermore, not all members of prehistoric, Romano-British, or early medieval societies were farmers. The needs of the ruling elite also had an important influence on the development of settlement and landscape. Proximity to communication routes and navigable water, with the access to prestige goods and the ease of mobility which these afforded, were also important to the rulers of society. So too, in certain periods, might be the needs of defence. The locations of the central places of local and regional societies – administrative centres, tribal strongholds, or whatever – were not necessarily determined by patterns of agrarian land-use. Yet the location of such sites would in turn have had an inevitable impact on the wider rural economy, determining where the greatest clusters of settlements were located: for dependent farmers had to be settled in places from where their surplus produce could most easily be transported to the homes of the rulers.

We therefore need to look beyond soils and geology, to the framework of topography within which early settlement developed, and in particular to the configuration of river valleys and watersheds (Everitt 1977) (Figure 1.3). These are the real key: the contrast between valley and watershed is deeply etched on the landscape of Norfolk, in spite of the rather muted nature of the county's topography. The earliest settlements tended to be in the river valleys, where water was freely available and soils generally fertile, tractable, and well-drained. When population levels were low the higher interfluves tended to be used for woodland and pasture, perhaps only on a seasonal basis. Even when they were opened up for agriculture, the largest settlements

Fig. 1.3 Norfolk: main topographic features

land above 60 metres

Peat and silty soils- estuary and marsh
in the early Saxon period

15Km

R.ANT

R.BURE

R.CHET

BROOME BECK

R.WAVENEY

R.TAS

R.WENSUM

R.TUD

R.YARE

R.REPPS

R.BLACKWATER

R.GLAVEN

CENTRAL WATERSHED

R.STIFFKEY

R.THET

R.LITTLE OUSE

R.BURN

R.NAR

R.WISSEY

R.BABBINGY

– and the most important – continued to occupy the older valley sites.

The precise nature of the valley/watershed contrast was, however, manifested in different ways in different parts of the county. On the claylands, the interfluves – especially where they were most level, or slightly hollowed – carry soils which, while fertile, were difficult to farm, so that they were only fully exploited when population levels were particularly high. The ready availability of water, however – from ponds dug in the water-retentive soils – ensured that when such expansion occurred, farms could spread freely across the interfluves. Some land was always impossible to cultivate, however, remaining as areas of pasture or woodland. Over much of the north and west of the county, in contrast, water could not be easily obtained on the interfluves, because of the porous nature of the soils. The frontier of cultivation might easily expand at the expense of woodland or pasture, but settlements tended to remain in the valleys. Of course, such a bald account tends to obscure a more complex topographic reality. In the 'Good Sands' region, in particular, pockets of boulder clay provided potential supplies of water, and therefore sites for villages and farmsteads, on the watersheds between the valleys. Massingham and Weasenham are good examples of such settlements; the traditional name of 'Dry' Docking suggests that settlements sometimes outgrew the reliability or capacity of the perched water table in this region.

Such anomalies might confuse and distort the overall pattern, but that pattern, nevertheless, is an important one. Moreover, the contrast between valley and watershed not only helped determine the progress of settlement, but also moulded the development of early social territories in the county. The sparsely-settled watersheds constituted zones of reduced contact, and thus tended to form boundaries between social groupings based on the principal valleys. It is possible that their status as 'buffer zones' might, in certain periods, have in turn retarded their colonisation and exploitation: Caesar noted of the Germanic Suevi that it was 'their greatest glory to lay waste the frontiers of their neighbours for as wide a distance as possible, considering this real evidence of their prowess' (*De Bello Gallico*, IV: 3).

In Norfolk, however, because of the complex pattern of the county's drainage system, and its muted terrain, the areas of contact engendered by valley and watershed were complex and often in the long term unstable. There was, if we can use the phrase, a *hierarchy of interfluves*. Where watersheds were narrow between the major rivers, as between the Wensum and the Yare immediately to the west of Norwich, they presented little obstacle to settlement or intercourse, and might be less important than soils, or routeways, in determining the development of territory and settlement. At the other extreme is the county's major watershed, which runs in a great arc through the centre of the county, between the rivers Yare, Wensum, Waveney, Tud, Tas, and others draining eastwards towards the former estuary at Yarmouth; and those – like the Nar, Thet, and Wissey – draining westwards into the Wash; or the Glaven, Burn, and Stiffkey draining northwards and discharging into the North Sea on the north coast of the county. I shall refer to this feature throughout the book – and it will appear, in many contexts – as the *central watershed*. This might seem rather a grand term for a feature which is, in some places, hardly perceptible on the ground. It is, however, at once the most important and the most neglected factor in the evolution of the county (Figure 1.3).

Yet it is a term, and a concept, which can only be used in a useful way if we cheat slightly. The central watershed, as the term will be used here, is a zone which is actually cut through, broken, by the valley of the river Wensum, just to the north of North Elmham. Here the high ground either side of the valley is capped with heavy boulder clay and patches of infertile sand and gravel, which in all periods seem to have repelled settlement. The true watershed, strictly defined, runs further to the west, in a twisting, contorted fashion, but here – on the edge of the good sands, where soils were tractable and there were enough patches of clay to provide sites for farms or villages – it had no major impact on the development of settlement.

Thus defined, the watershed was a feature of immense significance, a barrier of reduced contact between east and west, a remote area of woodland and woodpasture. Norfolk has no great uplands, no great areas of infertile soils like the Weald of Kent, which could provide significant barriers to settlement, major obstacles to movement of people and ideas. But this central zone, although its existence is scarcely noted today, stands apart, displaying in magnified form some of the features shared by the watersheds ranking further down our notional hierarchy.

It is on this watershed, as we shall see, rather than on the heavy soils of the south and east, that the greatest areas of woodland could be found at the time of Domesday, and before. The distribution of chance finds attest its sparsely-settled character in the early Saxon and Romano-British periods. The fact that two of the county's principal linear earthworks – the Launditch, and the Panworth dyke – run close to it hints that it may, at times, have also formed a political boundary.

Of course, watersheds in muted terrain like that of Norfolk were never more than a partial barrier to communication. And they were not the only topographical features to mould the configuration of early territories. While the higher or middle reaches of the major rivers might draw communities together, and form the centres of social groups, their lower reaches, especially in the east of the county, formed wide marshy tracts, which constituted important barriers to contact.

2

Before the Angles

In the beginning

Norfolk had been farmed and settled for millennia before the coming of the Angles. Indeed, the earliest clearances of the primeval 'wildwood' began early in the Mesolithic period. Evidence from the excavations at Spong Hill suggests that pine woodland was being cleared here in the early ninth millennium BC, presumably to improve the quality of grazing and thus encourage and concentrate game (Healy 1988: 104). Such events must, however, have been sporadic and small-scale, and did nothing to impede the development during the later Mesolithic of a densely wooded landscape. The precise composition of this woodland seems to have varied from place to place, although everywhere including a high proportion of lime, elm, hazel, and oak (Rackham 1986a: 161). The first major clearances seem to have occurred early in the Neolithic, at the beginning of the fourth millennium BC, and are marked in the pollen record by the sudden decline of elm. The precise significance of this 'elm decline' remains a matter of debate, although in Norfolk at least the phenomenon was certainly accompanied by an increase in the pollen of arable weeds and cereals, and must have therefore have been associated, in some way, with the impact of the first farmers (Murphy 1984a).

We must be careful not to exaggerate the scale of these early clearances in the county. Contrary to what was, until recently, received wisdom, the Breckland was not first deforested in the Neolithic but rather later, during the Bronze Age (Murphy 1984b). Even on the lightest, most easily worked soils, along the chalk of the western escarpment, large areas of woodland remained. Late Neolithic pits excavated at Redgate Hill, near Hunstanton, contained snails typical of wooded environments: the bones from the site came not only from cattle, sheep, and pigs but also from red and roe deer; while in addition to cultivating emmer, bread wheat, and barley the site's occupants also gathered hazelnuts (Murphy, forthcoming). Nevertheless, it is clear that settlements were being widely established during this remote period, appearing even on the heavier clay soils in the south-east of the county. In Loddon, for example, Alan Davison discovered two substantial scatters of Late Neolithic and Early Bronze Age flint, accompanied by scraps of pottery, indicating settlement of some kind close to the junction of the sandy and chalky boulder clays (Davison 1990: 12–15).

The extent of clearance increased during the Bronze Age, and on the poorer soils, especially in the north and west of the county, deforestation soon led to the development of the heaths which, for the next three millennia, were to constitute such an important feature of the county's landscape. Thus, for example, pollen recovered from the soil sealed beneath the barrow at Bawsey indicates an environment of open lime/hazel woodland; but after the mound's construction the area was dominated by open heathland, as the soil structure deteriorated and nutrients leached away (Murphy, forthcoming). Indeed, the Bronze Age probably saw a general increase in the diversity of the county's landscape. As well as tracts of uncleared woodland and woodpasture, the emerging heaths, and pockets of arable land, there were also – to judge from the species of snails entombed beneath the barrow at Little Cressingham – areas of open grassland (Lawson 1986: 16). The Bronze Age occupation at Grimes Graves had a faunal assemblage indicating an economy geared around dairying, while the Bronze Age settlement at Hunstanton appears to have functioned as a stock farm (Murphy, forthcoming).

The Neolithic and Bronze Age periods in Norfolk were not characterised by the construction of great ceremonial monuments. Norfolk has no Silbury Hill, no Stonehenge. Only a few substantial ceremonial features appear to have been constructed.

The most important was the henge at Arminghall, just to the south of Norwich. This consisted of a large circular earth and rubble bank, some 18 metres wide and flanked by ditches, surrounding a central space about 30 metres in diameter. A horseshoe of eight posts, each nearly 1 metre in diameter and sunk more than 2 metres into the ground, stood in the centre: whether these were free-standing, or supported some kind of superstructure, remains unclear (Clark 1936). On present evidence, this great monument appears to have been exceptional. The only other known henges – such as those excavated at Bixley and Witton – were very modest affairs, and substantial cursus are unknown. Even Neolithic long barrows seem to have been few in number and, to judge from the surviving examples at Ditchingham, Harpley, and West Rudham, comparatively diminutive features. It is unlikely that the ten or so others whose former sites are known or suspected in the county were any more substantial. Only from the early third millennium BC were large numbers of 'ritual' monuments erected in the Norfolk landscape: but these were the somewhat less impressive round barrows. Some 625 still survive, or are known from early maps and documents; aerial photography has revealed the sites of some 550 more which have long since been destroyed (Lawson 1986: 33–5).

This lack of large-scale early prehistoric monumental endeavour is a feature which Norfolk shares with a broad swathe of eastern England. It is something which marks this region off clearly from the 'text-book prehistory' of Wessex (Bradley, forthcoming). Other aspects of Norfolk's prehistory ally it with neighbouring areas of eastern England. Until the Late Bronze Age most of the artefacts used or monuments constructed in the county were similar to those to be found in a broad area all along the eastern seaboard, reaching as far north as Yorkshire. At certain periods – especially in the Earlier Neolithic, and again in the Middle and Late Bronze Age – there were also close similarities with the cultural material produced and used on the opposite shores of the North Sea. Wide distributions of artefacts and styles are a common feature of early prehistory, and in part reflect intensive, long-distance exchange of items, especially prestige goods. The societies living in Norfolk seem to have contributed amber, and flint tools from the mines at Grimes Graves and Whittlingham to these wide exchange networks: the former mines, still a striking feature of the Breckland landscape, were in operation soon after 1800 BC and continued in use for perhaps three centuries (Mercer 1976: 110; 1981).

Some Neolithic and Bronze Age distributions have boundaries which run through East Anglia, although they never correspond with those of the modern county. By the Bronze Age, the most important discontinuities in artefact distributions seem to occur along the line of the boulder clay watershed running through the centre of East Anglia, through Essex and Suffolk, and on into south Norfolk. Thus, for example, collared urns, or cremation cemeteries of the Ardleigh Series, only occur to the south-east of this watershed, while the distribution of food vessels is largely confined to the north-west (Lawson 1984: 168–9). We can see no sign in earlier prehistory of Norfolk as a coherent cultural zone, occupied by a society proclaiming a distinct identity through particular styles of stone, pottery, or metalwork artefacts. For much of the Bronze Age, the area of the county seems to have been a peripheral zone, marginal to the rich and densely-settled areas on the margins of the Fens.

None the less there must surely have been local societies, with their own recognised territories. The concentrations of Neolithic monuments around Arminghall, and perhaps Ditchingham, may represent 'central places' which retained their importance over long periods of time. These include large numbers of round barrows, or the 'ring ditch' cropmarks which indicate their former presence. In some areas of England, round barrows appear to have been constructed on watersheds, and were apparently employed to mark the boundaries of social territories. There is some evidence for this in the north-west of Norfolk, and to some extent in the north-east – areas which, we might expect, were more amenable to early agriculture, and therefore more densely settled, than the claylands of the south. But even in these favoured zones the the pattern is seldom clear, perhaps because even here population was not yet pressing hard on the available resources.

The Iron Age: tribes, territory and landscape

Most areas of Norfolk had seen some agricultural activity before the start of the first millennium BC. But pollen analysis and fieldwalking surveys leave little doubt that the scale of clearance and settlement accelerated thereafter. Intensive arable activity in later periods, coupled with the fragility of much Iron Age pottery, means that the sites of settlements of this period can be difficult to locate through fieldwalking surveys. Moreover, in abraded form such pottery is often hard to distinguish from that of the pagan Saxon period. Nevertheless, Iron Age settlements are known from most environments, including the heavier clay soils of the south-east. Pollen cores from Hockham Mere, Old Buckenham Mere, and Sea Mere suggest that deforestation was now taking place on an unprecedented scale (Bennett 1983; Godwin 1968; Sims 1972). These sites are all in, or close to areas of light, easily-worked, well-drained soils in the west of the county: the kind of environment which was particularly attractive to early farmers. But the pollen sequence from Diss Mere, in the valley of the river Waveney and surrounded by poorly draining boulder clay soils, seems to tell a similar story. Unfortunately, this important sequence has not been closely dated by radiometric methods, but it appears to indicate large-scale and sudden woodland clearance towards the end of the Iron Age, accompanied by the emergence of a landscape of open grassland (Peglar et al. 1989).

In this context, the layout of modern field boundaries in the area around Diss Mere is extremely interesting. Ignoring those boundaries which seem, on cartographic or documentary evidence, to be of medieval or post-medieval date, the basic framework of the landscape here appears to consist of a number of extensive, semi-regular grids. These form characteristic brickwork-like patterns, with long axes orientated roughly north–south, but with fewer boundaries running for any distance in a transverse direction. These systems run out of the Waveney valley, up on to the gently rolling clay plateau, and appear to have terminated at a long, continuous boundary running along the watershed to the north, a feature which, for much of its length, still survives, and is followed by the hundred and parish boundaries (Figure 2.1). The Roman road running south-westwards from the town of Venta Icenorum cuts obliquely through these systems, much as a modern motorway cuts through a pre-existing pattern of fields. This suggests that part, at least, of this relict landscape is of prehistoric, and presumably of Iron Age, date (Williamson 1986, 1987).

Such field patterns – called 'coaxial' systems in the jargon of prehistorians – are known from other areas of Britain, and from other periods (Fleming 1984, 1987). In particular, closely analagous layouts, dating from the Bronze Age, survive as networks of low, tumbled walls on Dartmoor. These south Norfolk examples share with these and other examples the characteristic of being 'terrain oblivious': that is, they ignore the dictates of the local topography. Their long axes run mindlessly across the claylands, ignoring the subtleties of terrain, the shallow minor valleys cutting through the boulder clay. This suggests that such grids were, indeed, the consequence of conscious planning, rather than the result of organic evolution. They were not simply created by the gradual expansion of cultivation, field by field, northwards out of the Waveney valley. It is, however, unlikely that they were all established at a stroke, but rather in a series of stages, each adding a further planned block on the edge of the existing framework. Not all the boundaries on Figure 2.1, of course, necessarily date to the time that these grids were first established. Centuries of piecemeal addition and alteration have modified, although not destroyed, the original pattern.

Such early landscape patterns are not confined to the central section of the Waveney valley. Other examples have been noted by Davison on the claylands arounds Hales and Loddon in the south-east of the county. Here, too, they appear to be stratigraphically earlier than a Roman road, and distorted or locally obscured by characteristic features of the medieval landscape. Thus the medieval park of Loddon *iuxta* Hales 'clearly interrupts the pattern suggesting that it is a later intrusion' (Davison 1990: 73). Similar organised landscapes may exist in other parts of the county. Around the town of Wells, for example, on the north coast, the pattern of furlong boundaries shown on the earliest maps seems to perpetuate traces of similar coaxial layouts: this furlong pattern, in turn, determined the street pattern within the town itself. Similar patterns may underlie the layout of much of the countryside to the west of here: but we need to be cautious. There are places where apparent regularities in boundary layout seem, in fact, to be the result of organic processes of development; and not all examples of planning need be of prehistoric date. The field boundaries in the noth-west of the county (and, indeed, in the north-east) urgently require detailed study.

Fig. 2.1 Early field patterns in the middle Waveney valley. The earliest boundaries in this area form a series of rough 'grids'. orientated north–south, one of which appears to be slighted by the Roman Pye Road

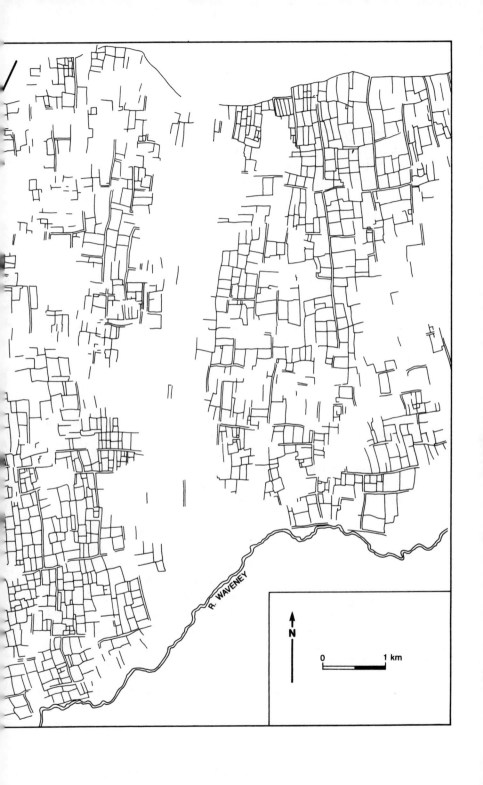

R. WAVENEY

N

0   1 km

On the southern claylands the establishment of organised coaxial field systems seems to have occurred at the same time as, or soon after, extensive deforestation occurred here. Perhaps as woodland was cleared for grazing, and as seasonal use of upland woodpastures gave way to permanent settlement, it became necessary to divide a formerly open, intercommoned landscape, and to allocate specific portions to the particular local communities, and their constituent lineages, who had formerly used it. Such large-scale planning suggests the existence of fairly sophisticated forms of social and territorial organisation in the county by the late Iron Age.

Yet the presence of such coherent social groupings is not reflected in the existence of dramatic, upstanding Iron Age monuments. Once again, the contrast with the 'text-book prehistory' of Wessex is marked, and also the similarity with other areas of eastern England. Norfolk has only two hillforts – at Thetford and Warham – which seem, on the basis of limited excavations, to date from this period (Gregory 1986; Gregory and Rogerson 1991). Three other defensive earthworks, at Holkham, Narborough, and South Creake, although unexcavated, are probably Iron Age (Davies et al. 1991). A sixth, that at Tasburgh, may be of Iron Age origin, but excavations suggest that part, at least, of the defences were constructed in the late Saxon period; whether we are seeing here the re-use of an Iron Age structure, or a fort built entirely de novo in the Saxon period, remains unclear (Rogerson & Lawson 1991).

All except the last of these sites are located in the west and north–west of the county, in areas of light, freely-draining soils (Figure 2.2). Warham is certainly the most impressive. Here, a pair of concentric ramparts and ditches enclose a circular area covering some 1.5 hectares beside the River Stiffkey. Unfortunately, the excavations in 1959 were restricted to the ramparts, and the scale and nature of occupation within the interior (if the area was, indeed, permanently occupied) remains unknown (Gregory 1986b). Thetford was once even more impressive, although now largely destroyed. This, too, was in origin a bivallate fort, probably covering an area of some 6 hectares. The ramparts were later re-used as the bailey of the Norman castle here (Gregory 1991b).

'Hillfort' is something of a misnomer for these defended

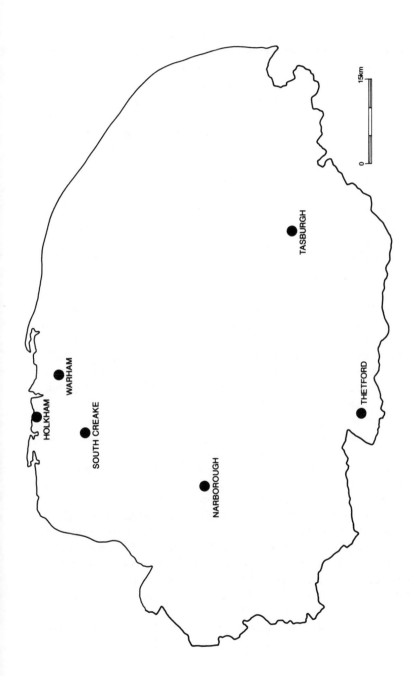

Fig. 2.2 The distribution of Iron Age hillforts in Norfolk

enclosures. All except that at South Creake are in river valleys or other low-lying situations; that at Holkham, for example, was built at the end of what was probably, at the time, a coastal sand spit, almost at sea level (it now stands within an area of drained coastal marsh) (Figure 2.3). Presumably, as Tony Gregory and Andrew Rogerson have suggested, the absence of dramatic, defensible hills in the county encouraged such a choice of location, which substituted 'a difficult approach across the river valley for a difficult approach uphill' (Gregory & Rogerson 1991).

The Norfolk hillforts raise important questions which, because they have been subjected to only limited excavation, we can do little to answer. Did they, as in Wessex, serve as central places, tribal strongholds, and contain permanently-occupied towns or villages? Warham is large enough to have defended a settlement containing, perhaps, 1,000 people. Or did they serve merely as temporary refuges, with no significant, permanent role in the hierarchy of settlement, as has, for example, been suggested was the case in Essex (Drury 1980: 47)? It is not only the absence of excavation which makes it difficult to answer such questions. Elsewhere, interpretations of the social role of hillforts have also relied on an analysis of their distribution and location (Cunliffe 1978), and the comparative paucity of such features in Norfolk may, in part, be due to later destruction; a reflection of the county's dense population, and the extent and intensity of arable land-use, in subsequent periods. Some Iron Age hillforts may have disappeared from the landscape in comparatively recent times. One might have been Warbury or Walbury, the 'fort of the Britons', an earthwork which survived in the north-western corner of the parish of Stiffkey until the end of the eighteenth century, although it has since disappeared without trace. Iron Age, as well as Romano-British material, has been found on its site. The sites of others may similarly be indicated by place-names incorporating the suffix 'burgh' or 'borough', some of which may derived from *burh*, the old English term for a defensive earthwork. This term does not automatically suggest a lost hilfort; it was used by the Anglo-Saxons for post-Roman earthworks, indeed, for structures in contemporary use. More-over, some of these names may incorporate the rather similar element *berg*, the Anglian term for a hill. But one or two may indicate the sites of long-lost Iron Age forts: in particular

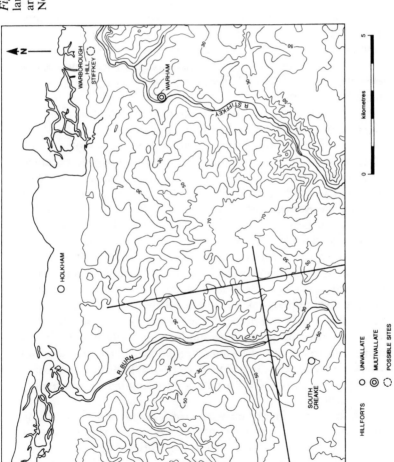

Fig. 2.3 Iron Age and Roman landscape features in the area north-west around Wells, Norfolk

HILLFORTS   O   UNIVALLATE

          ◎   MULTIVALLATE

          ⊙   POSSIBLE SITES

ROMAN ROADS   ———

WARBOROUGH HILL
STIFFKEY

WARHAM

HOLKHAM

SOUTH CREAKE

R BURN

R STIFFKEY

N

0   kilometres   5

Burgh by Aylsham, near to the Roman town of Brampton, and perhaps marking the site of its predecessor; and Aldburgh, 'the old *burgh*'. In this context, it is noteworthy that in Norfolk – as elsewhere in southern England – the distribution of surviving hillforts is closely related to areas in which chalk outcrops at or near the surface, providing a more durable construction material than was available elsewhere in the county, where similar features would, presumably, have been built of turf, wood, and earth. Such defences would have been much more prone to later destruction, either by deliberate levelling or by the action of the plough. Nevertheless, it is probable that the greatest concentration of hillforts was always in the north-west of the county (Figure 2.3), where competition for resources in a long-settled countryside may have encouraged warfare between rival social groups. Elsewhere, as in other areas of eastern England, power must have been exercised from open, or at least not massively defended, settlements.

The precise social and political context of Norfolk's hillforts, like that of its planned field systems, remains obscure: but from the century before the Roman Conquest we have, for the first time, some evidence concerning the social groups who occupied the county. We know from the Ravenna Cosmography, from Ptolemy's *Geography*, and from the Antonine Itinerary, that the name of the Roman administrative centre for the region, located as Caister St Edmunds, was *Venta Icenorum* (Allen 1970: 1). The second element of this place-name refers to a tribe called the *Iceni*, who are first referred to in Tacitus's *Annals*, written in 118 but describing events in AD 47. An earlier reference is probably contained in Caesar's *De Bello Gallico*, in the section describing his abortive military expedition to Britain in 54 BC. Caesar relates how the Trinovantes, a tribe occupying Essex and much of Suffolk, sought his protection, and how soon afterwards 'several other tribes sent emissaries and surrendered', including a group called the *Cenimagni*, presumably a rendering of the name Iceni. The extent of the tribe's territory is suggested by the distribution of their coins.

The first coins in Britain were struck by the tribes occupying the south-east of the country, and began to appear in the first or second decades of the first century BC. Their significance, and especially their economic role, is a matter of some debate among archaeologists. Coinage came rather later to the Iceni, first appearing in their area around 10 BC. The first coins were of gold, copies of Trinovantian and Catuvallaunian types; but silver soon became universal. All the coins carry a horse on the reverse, but the obverse takes three distinct forms: a wild beast (a boar?); a badly drawn head; and a design based on two conjoined, mirror-image crescents. Many also bear a name, or part of a name: the moneyer who struck them, or the dynastic ruler for whom they were minted. The latest of the 'pattern' series are inscribed with the letters ECEN, presumably a form of the word 'Iceni'. These coins do not occur in any numbers outside the northern parts of East Anglia, unlike the coins associated with the tribal groups of the south-east, which are found over wide areas. To the south, in particular, their distribution is defined by a comparatively sharp boundary. It is, moreover, one that is shared by the ornamental chariot fittings which are a characteristic feature of the late Iron Age in the area: bridle bits, terret rings, and hooks to hold traces. The horse appears to have had a particular significance for the Iron Age occupants of Norfolk – it is found as a symbol on all their coins – and although some of these objects were manufactured outside their tribal area (at Waldringfield in Suffolk), they seem to have been a particular feature of Icenian material culture. Both distributions suggest that the southern boundary of the Iceni ran through north Suffolk, along the interfluve between the Little Ouse and Waveney to the north, and the Gipping to the south (Martin 1988: 68–72). The majority of Suffolk thus looked southwards, towards Essex, and formed part of the territory of the Trinovantes.

To the west, the distribution of Icenic coins extends, in an intermittent fashion, into the Fenland. This was no longer, as in the Bronze Age, a core zone to which Norfolk was peripheral. A climatic deterioration had set in after 1250 BC, and by 850 much of the area was flooded, and thus constituted a major barrier to communication with the Midland heart of England. Icenic coins are found on some of the Fen islands, but do not penetrate into the Midlands. The territory of the Iceni thus seems to have approximated to the modern county of Norfolk. Norfolk, as it were, had arrived in history.

But we must be careful not to exaggerate the territorial cohesion, the political centralisation, of the 'Iceni'. They may, in fact, have been a loose group of tribes, rather than a centralised polity. When the Cenomagni surrendered to Caesar in 54 BC, they did so with a number of other tribes, the *Segontiaci*, the *Ancalites*, the *Bibracti*, and the *Cassi*. These groups are never mentioned by name again in classical sources; but subsequent references to the Iceni show them, once again, acting in association with unnamed allies or neighbours. Thus, according to Tacitus, when the Iceni revolted in AD 47 they carried a number of neighbouring tribes with them, while their revolt in AD 60 was supported by the Trinovantes and other, unnamed, neighbouring tribes. Moreover the suffix *magni*, 'greater', appended by Caesar to his rendering of the word 'Iceni' suggests the existence of more than one group bearing this tribal name. All this suggests that the Iceni were the dominant group within, and thus gave their name to, some kind of loose tribal hegemony; and that some of the other groups named by Caesar may have been their neighbours in late Iron Age Norfolk.

This kind of loose political structure seems to have been a feature of other areas of late Iron Age Britain. Caesar himself made a distinction between those regions nearest the Channel – comparatively civilised and settled (he believed) by recent immigrants from the Continent; and the more socially and economically primitive areas of the interior. In archaeological terms, a similar distinction is apparent, between the south–east of the country – which was actively involved in contact and exchange with Gaul and the Roman Empire – and the areas further to the north and west, which were marginal to or excluded from such contacts (Darvill 1987: 166–80; Haselgrove 1982). It was in the former region, in the Home Counties, northern Northamptonshire, and Essex that coinage was first used, and that the so-called *oppida* were developing in the late first century BC: large, sprawling, semi-urban agglomerations of settlement, usually defended by long stretches of linear earthwork. It is in this area, too, that foreign imports, especially amphorae which once contained wine, are most frequently discovered in graves or on settlements of late Iron Age date. Here the tribal groups who are named by Roman writers, or who gave their names to the administrative subdivisions of the Roman province of *Britannia*, were comparatively small and centralised polities. Their elites had grown wealthy and powerful through contacts with, and control of the exchange of luxury items with, the Roman world. Outside this core zone were less civilised, less centralised tribal federations. The line between these two broad zones runs through the middle of East Anglia. The Trinovantes belonged firmly to the 'core zone' of the south-east; they were a comparatively centralised polity with a great *oppida*, *Camulodunum*, at Colchester (Dunnett 1975: 18–27). The Iceni, in contrast, lay outside the main sphere of economic exchange; they had no true *oppida*, and no imported amphorae or other foreign luxuries.

Yet the Iceni, or at least their ruling elite, were not poor. The large number of torcs – heavy rings of gold, silver, or electrum, probably worn as neck ornaments – of late Iron Age date found in the county are evidence of this. Most have come from Snettisham, on the western edge of the county: more than 100 have been found here, many from a single field. Whether this was a place of manufacture, or of ritual deposition, remains unclear; but either way, somewhere near here there must surely have been a major centre of political power.

Allen, in a paper published in 1970, suggested that the three distinct series of Icenian coins – the face-obverse, boar-obverse, and pattern-obverse coins – each represented a separate tribe, or sub-tribe, of the Iceni (Allen 1970). The distribution of each type, he argued, although overlapping, tended to cluster in certain parts of East Anglia. The earliest of the boar-obverse silver coins seemed to be most numerous in the Norwich area. The earliest examples of the face-obverse series appeared to cluster in the north and west of the county, although the later ones seemed to have a wider distribution. The pattern-obverse coins seemed to be particularly numerous in the Breckland. Unfortunately, the large number of Iron Age coins discovered in the county since Allen wrote (largely as a result of amateur metal detection) do not seem to confirm this neat pattern. Instead, it now appears that the different series and their sub-groups are fairly evenly scattered across the territory of the Iceni. If the different types do, as Allen argued, represent different dynasties or tribal groups, then these must have made very free use of each others' coinage, and the coin distributions cannot – on present evidence – be used to identify the territories ruled over or occupied by them.

We can, however, speculate that a major political and social boundary may, at some time in the Iron Age, have run north–south through the centre of the county, along the central watershed. In the Roman and Saxon periods, as we shall see, this was a zone of fairly sparse settlement, and – although the evidence for the Iron Age is not so good – the same was probably true at this time as well. Recent excavations suggest that the linear earthwork known as the Launditch, generally considered to be of Dark Age date, is in reality of pre-Roman, presumably Iron Age, construction. This, significantly, runs for some 5 kilometres (the precise original length is unclear) north–south along the top of the watershed, to the north-west of East Dereham: to the west, the ground falls towards the river Nar, while to the east, the land is drained by the Blackwater, a tributary of the Wensum (Wade-Martins 1974). This, perhaps, represents the frontier of the Iceni with one of the obscure tribes mentioned by Caesar.

The *Civitas Icenorum*

Norfolk, with the rest of lowland Britain, was conquered by the Romans in the years after AD 43. Forts were established at Swanton Morley, Threxton, and Ashill, in a rough line through the centre of the county, perhaps to divide constituent groups of the Iceni and to control movement through the central watershed. These were probably established before the Icenian revolt of AD 47 – the 'first Icenian revolt' – which followed Ostorius Scapula's attempt to enforce the Roman law of *Lex Julia De Armes*, and remove battle weapons from the British tribes. This revolt culminated in a battle at an unknown fortification the description of which – in Tacitus's *Agricola* – could just fit the hillfort at Holkham (Robinson & Gregory 1987: 25). But peace was soon restored, and the Iceni – or at least, one section of them – were granted special privileges under a client king called Prasutagus by Tacitus, but whose name is rendered as 'Prasto' on a coin found in a hoard at Joist Fen, Lakenheath.

There are good grounds for believing that his power-base lay in the Thetford area. On Gallows Hill above the town of Thetford an unusual, probably ceremonial complex was constructed shortly before the Roman invasion, replacing an open settlement on the same site (Gregory 1991a). It consisted of a large square enclosure, defined by deep ditches, in which stood a large and elaborate timber building. Soon after the Conquest the enclosure was doubled in size, new buildings were constructed, and the whole surrounded by another ditch, enclosing in all more than 4 hectares. The space between the original enclosure ditch, and this outer line, was filled by a complex arrangement of close-set posts, perhaps carrying numerous concentric timber fences, perhaps free-standing. The purpose of this strange site is unknown. The marked absence of domestic refuse argues for some kind of ceremonial, 'ritual' function. The lines of close-set posts may have been intended to create a kind of artificial sacred grove (Gregory 1991a, 196). Moreover, a Romano-Celtic temple was later erected some 50 metres away; and, in its initial, square form the Gallows Hill enclosure is similar to a number of other embanked enclosures in Norfolk dating to the late Iron Age (at Warham, Wighton, and Thornham, for example), also apparently with a 'ritual' function (Gregory 1986a). But the sheer scale of the later expansion of the Thetford site puts it in a class apart. A major centre of political power, surely that of Prasutagus, must have been located no great distance away.

Many readers will know the familiar story, related by Tacitus, of how Prasutagus attempted to bequeath half his kingdom to his family, instead of leaving it to the emperor, as befitted his role as client king; of how, on his death, the Procurator Catus Decianus seized the entire estate; of how in the ensuing fracas the king's widow was beaten and his daughters raped; and of how finally that queen, Boudicca, led a revolt which – with most of the Roman army engaged in an assault on Anglesey – succeeded in sacking Colchester, London, and Verulamium (Webster 1978). The Iceni and their allies were finally defeated at an unknown location in the Midlands, perhaps near Mancetter, and their territory reconquered and absorbed into the empire.

This process was achieved in the time-honoured fashion of turning the former tribal territory into a *civitas*, or administrative subdivision of the province, ruled from a planned town bearing the tribal name, and transforming the former tribal elite into an *ordo*, or local council. That capital was Venta Icenorum, a few miles to the south of Norwich (Hawkes 1949; Frere 1971). Why the new centre of power should have been located here, rather than in the Thetford area, is unclear. With the Arminghall henge only some 2.5 kilometres to the north, this area had, of course, been a major focus for eastern Norfolk in early prehistory. It may have been an important centre of power in Iron Age times too; and it is possible that the choice of site was determined by a desire to support a group within the Iceni other than, if not hostile to, that represented by Prasutagus, and based in the east, rather than the west, of the county. Perhaps a major settlement of Iron Age date may await discovery in the locality; perhaps the Tasburgh hillfort, which after all lies only 8 kilometres to the south of Venta, has some significance in this context, although as we have seen there are doubts about its precise date. All this is speculation. Either way, Venta was provided with the normal grid-pattern of streets (rather irregular in this case), a perimeter bank and ditch, and a range of timber buildings. More substantial stone buildings were added in the second century, including a basilica, a forum, and public baths.

Venta stood at the northern termination of a major Roman road, usually referred to as the Pye Road, which is now followed for most of its course by the modern A140 (Margary 1973: 213–46) (Figure 2.4). This runs southwards across the claylands in a series of straight sections which in places still, today, visibly slight the grid-like mesh of earlier fields, leaving the county at Scole. The only other Roman road of classic form in the county which survives intact for most of its length is the Peddars Way, although this is now, for the most part, no more than a bridle-way. This road runs roughly parallel to and east of the line of the pre-historic Icknield Way, which follows a more meandering course through west Norfolk (Clarke 1914). The Peddars Way enters the county at Brettenham, crossing the Little Ouse at a ford, and runs north-westwards to Holme next the Sea, in 'the extreme north-eastern corner of the county. Thus, unlike the Pye Road, the Peddars Way has no obvious destination – there is no evidence that it terminated at a ferry crossing to Lincolnshire. Moreover, while the Pye Road runs in a number of short, straight alignments, Peddars Way runs dead straight for much longer distances: 35 kilometres without deviation between Woodcock Hill in Hockham and Massingham Heath (Rackham 1986b: 253–5) (Figure 2.4). These differences may be significant: Peddars Way looks like a military road, established in a hurry through the heartland of Prasutagus's territory in the aftermath

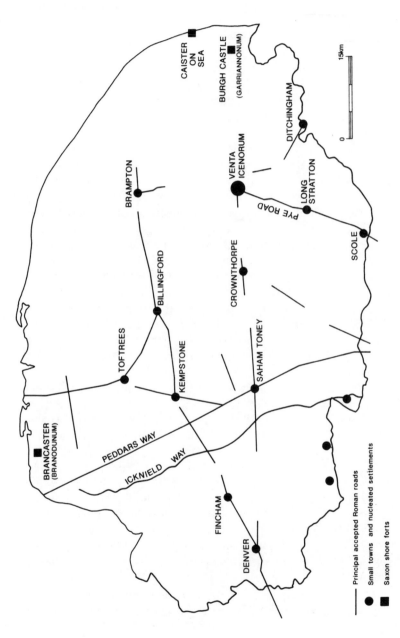

Fig. 2.4 Major roads and nucleated settlements in Roman Norfolk

of the Boudiccan revolt. The Pye Road, in contrast, may have been constructed principally for civilian and administrative purposes, at a more leisurely pace, following the establishment of Venta Icenorum.

These two roads are still striking features in the landscape. Elsewhere, straight Roman roads often survive only as short, disconnected stretches of road, track, or boundary, and their full course can only be reconstructed through archaeological field-work and aerial photography (Wade-Martins 1977) (Figure 2.4). A major road ran east–west through the centre of the county, from Brampton, through Billingford, Kempstone and Fincham, to Denver. Here it continued westwards as the 'Fen Causeway', a complex feature which began as a road, but was later followed by a canal. Another major road ran from Denver to Venta, via Threxton and Crownthorpe. A number of others have been suggested, but some short, straight stretches of Roman road may never have been anything more than just that: limited improve-ments to the local road network, analogous to modern bypasses.

Some of the county's Roman roads make little obvious sense as routes connecting towns and settlements. A striking section of straight road runs northwards from the Roman settlement at Toftrees, near Fakenham, to the North Sea coast near Holkham, a distance of some 15 kilometres. Like the Peddars Way, it has no obvious northern termination, or purpose. Around half-way along its length, at what is now Haggard's Lodge, this road is crossed – at almost exactly 90 degrees – by another dead straight track, almost certainly of Roman origin. This runs – in what was, originally, probably a single alignment – from the deserted village of Egmere, across the valley of the river Burn, to Barwick: a distance of nearly 10 kilometres. Here it may have turned north-west, towards Docking, but no link to the Peddars way can be suggested with any confidence, and there is no obvious eastern extension or destination. It is possible that both these roads never went anywhere at all. Both may have been like the Peddars Way, military creations, constructed to facilitate patrols and policing after the Boudiccan revolt, although the fact that they both pass within 2 kilometres of probable hillforts may be coincidental (Figure 2.3).

Venta Icenorum was not the only substantial Roman settle-ment in the county. There were, in addition, perhaps a dozen 'small towns', roadside settlements and large villages (Figure 2.4). These lacked the kinds of monumental public buildings erected at Venta (although many had temples, and Brampton was surrounded by defences in the fourth century) (Clarke 1935–37; Green 1977; Gregory 1982; Knowles 1977; Rogerson 1977; Smith 1987). Their prime function was probably as local market-places, but some were also involved in commodity production. Although excavations have been carried out at Brampton and Scole, and on a small scale at Denver and Brettenham, we still know little about the function of these places, although Scole and Kempstone seem to have been heavily involved in iron smelting, Denver in salt-production, while Brampton was a centre for pottery manufacture. Still less is known about the genesis of these places. Norfolk, as we have seen, had no real *oppida* in the pre-Roman period, and the Icenian coinage – lacking small-denomination 'potin' coins of the kind found in the south-east – was probably used for payments to or between elites, rather than for everyday market exchange. The Iron Age economy in this area was still, to use the conventional jargon, 'embedded': that is, goods changed hands through, and were a means of reinforcing, social relations, as gifts, or tribute (Hodder 1979; Polanyi *et al.* 1957). But with the arrival of the imperial economy 'disembedded' market trade began to develop: that is, the buying and selling of goods outside a social context for material profit. While some of these new market centres developed on or close to Iron Age settlements – those at Brampton and Brettenham have produced Iron Age material, while that at Woodcock Hall near Threxton seems to occupy the site of a large Iron Age settlement – others were on new sites, at the social margins. Some began beside Roman forts, whose garrisons constituted an important market of 'outsiders'; the settlements at Billingford, and perhaps at Brampton, may fall into this category. Others, as elsewhere in England, probably 'Grew up on tribal borders, where bartering and haggling can occur within a profit-making context – outside the inner sphere of social relations' (Hodder 1979: 191). These were often associated with religious sites, which were also often constructed on the frontiers of tribal territories. At Crownthorpe, a nucleated settlement associated with a Romano-Celtic temple occupies a fairly marginal situation around the headwaters of the river

Tiffey, close to the central watershed and, therefore, perhaps, on the boundary between territories based on the west and the east of the county. At Long Stratton, scatters of pottery and other debris along a 2.2 kilometre stretch of the Pye Road, on the watershed between the Tas and the Waveney, could similarly represent the boundary between sub-tribal groups based on the valleys of these two rivers. Others, like Ditchingham, occur beside major rivers which, because of their width, may have formed boundaries between social groups, at the point where these were crossed by major Roman roads.

Most of these small towns seem to have been in existence by the end of the first century AD, and by the late second century market relations had penetrated deep into local life (Davies & Gregory 1991: 71–5). Coins are found even on the most remote rural farmsteads, while a wide range of commodities was mass-produced, either locally, or brought into the county from elsewhere. One of the most important of these mass-produced items was pottery; and because this is well-made, durable, and present in large quantities, it is comparatively easy, through fieldwalking surveys, to reconstruct the pattern of rural settlement in Roman Norfolk.

Such surveys now suggest that in Norfolk, as elsewhere in England, settlement intensified in the first two centuries of the Roman period (Taylor 1983: 83–106). The discovery of eight small farmsteads within a fieldwalked area of just over 2 square kilometres at Witton in north-east Norfolk is, perhaps, hardly surprising, given the fertile, tractable nature of the loam soils in this area (Lawson 1983). But settlement was just as dense in the south–eastern claylands. Alan Davison's study of the Hales/Loddon/Heckingham area recovered no less than fifteen major concentrations of debris within an area of 20 square kilometres, and one of these, an almost continuous spread of debris stretching for over 1 kilometre either side of Transport Lane in Loddon, represents a number of separate farmsteads (Davison 1990: 15–16). Settlements now appeared, for the first time, on the heavy clay interfluves at some distance from the lighter, better-drained valley soils. Although these settlements were not all occupied at the same time, most seem to have been in existence at the end of the second century. If this area was typical of the southern claylands – and there is no reason to believe that it was not – then there can, at this time, have been few areas which were more than 2 kilometres from a settlement of some kind.

In the silt Fens of Marshland, in the west of the county, settlement also expanded, following a relative fall in sea level after *c.* AD 50. Because of a subsequent phase of inundation, which largely buried the Roman landscape under further deposits of silt, the full extent of settlement remains obscure: in the northern parts of Marshland, settlements have only been revealed where drainage dykes have cut through the silt to the old land surface beneath (Silvester 1988: 154–6). In the west of this district, however, recovery is more complete and, in addition to large numbers of settlements located by fieldwalking, aerial photography has revealed a complex landscape of fields, drains, and roadways, extending westwards into Lincolnshire. In the southern peat Fens, and in the south-eastern parts of Marshland, settlements are fewer and, in some places, absent altogether. Here the land is more low-lying, and where farms occur they tend to be restricted to the banks of former watercourses, the 'roddons', raised ridges of silt and gravel which provided firm, dry sites within the waterlogged peat. A notable example is at Welney, where a string of Roman settlements follows the roddon marking a former course of the Great Ouse. It is possible that the Fens formed, in part, an imperial estate, devoted to the production of wool and salt. Evidence for both has been revealed by excavation, but not for the wealth which such activities might, in normal circumstances, have been expected to generate for the local inhabitants. Coins are rarely found on Fenland settlements, suggesting that their occupants might have been imperial *coloni*, tied workers, rather than peasant proprietors (Gregory 1982; Salway 1970: 10–12; Gurney 1986: 146–8).

Other variations in the social and territorial organisation of Roman Norfolk can be detected in the archaeological record. Over most of the county, settlement seems to have taken the form of hamlets or single farmsteads, architecturally undistinguished, timber-framed and with thatched or tiled roofs. Many of these places continued the sites of Iron Age settlements, and it is probable that the existing tribal patterns of landholding, in which land was held by extended kin groups, was only gradually modified by the impact of the Roman economy, and by the triumph of the ideas of absolute individual property familiar to Roman law (Stevens 1966; Stevens 1947). In the north and west of the county, however, in the 'Good Sand' region and on the Western Escarpment, things seem to have been rather different. Here, a number of true 'villas' – elaborate country houses – occur. A particularly noticeable group is strung along the pre-Roman Icknield Way, from Gayton in the south to Hunstanton in the north. Norfolk villas were less elaborate than those in some other parts of England (such as the Cotswolds). But they were, nevertheless, sophisticated structures, constructed of chalk, flint and car stone, and with – in several cases – bath-houses, hypocausts, and mosaic floors (Gregory 1982). Each was probably supported by a sizeable agricultural estate. Here, apparently, a more hierarchical and polarised society had developed during the late first and second centuries AD. It is noteworthy that the north and west of the county were more heavily manorialised than the south and east in the Middle Ages, and that this same area saw, in post-medieval times, the development of a similar polarised social and tenurial structure of large estates, tenant farms and landless labourers. Perhaps the same kinds of economic factors were at work in all periods. These light soils were particularly suited to arable and sheep-farming, rather than to large-scale cattle-rearing; forms of husbandry which, in most periods, seem to favour a concentration of landholding in large units and the eclipse of small proprietors. Yet even in this north–western area, there are signs that proprietorship still resided with extended family groups, rather than with individuals, even if one branch of a kindred had prospered while economic forces had lowered the others to the status of bond cultivators. The villa at Gayton Thorpe consists of two buildings with similar plans, constructed side by side, linked only by a single small room. Such plans, which have been discovered elsewhere in England, suggest joint ownership of an estate by related families (Smith 1978, 1982).

Settlements of various kinds were thus widely distributed in Romano-British Norfolk. There are, however, grounds for believing that there were some areas of the county in which they remained comparatively thin on the ground. Few areas of the county have been fieldwalked as intensively as Witton, or the Hales/Loddon/Heckingham area. Any impression of regional variations in the intensity of settlement must, therefore, be based on a rather less satisfactory source of information: the many hundreds of sites and artefacts discovered by chance or, in particular, through the activities of amateur metal-detectors. To a large extent, the distribution of such finds will be a reflection, not of the original patterns of activity or settlement, but of patterns in the processes of discovery. Marked concentrations will, for example, often indicate no more than the presence on the ground of a prominent local fieldwalker, or metal-detector enthusiast. Nevertheless, it is probable that, viewed in *regional* rather than *local* terms, the distribution of such finds is significant, and that further discoveries would for the most part simply serve to 'darken up' the pattern of dots shown in Figure 2.5, rather than radically change their relative densities in different parts of the county.

Looking at this map it immediately becomes apparent that while settlement was widespread on the clay soils in the south–east of the county, and on the light soils of the 'Good Sands' and the Breckland in the west, these zones were separated by a broad swathe of much less densely settled country, running through the county from south to north, and then turning southwards again, extending along the north-eastern seaboard, through the hundreds of Tunstead, Happing, and Flegg, and so down to the margins of the great Broadland estuary. The core zones of settlement in the north-west and south-east of the county was thus separated by a great arc of less intensively settled land, not entirely unutilised and uninhabited, but exploited as woodland and grazing.

What is interesting about this pattern is that it does not relate, in any simple or direct way, to the distributions of drift geology or soil types. Indeed, looked at in these terms, the relative paucity of settlements on the fertile loams of Flegg is, in parti-cular, surprising. Instead, we need to interpret this pattern in terms of the models and processes briefly discussed at the end of the first chapter. We are probably looking here at a pattern of settlement and land-use which had been developing during later prehistoric times. The core areas of late prehistoric settlement seem to have been in the west of the county; and in the south-east, in the upper and middle reaches of the rivers Tas, Yare, Wensum, and Bure. The peripheral zone between was less densely settled simply because it was peripheral; remote, out-

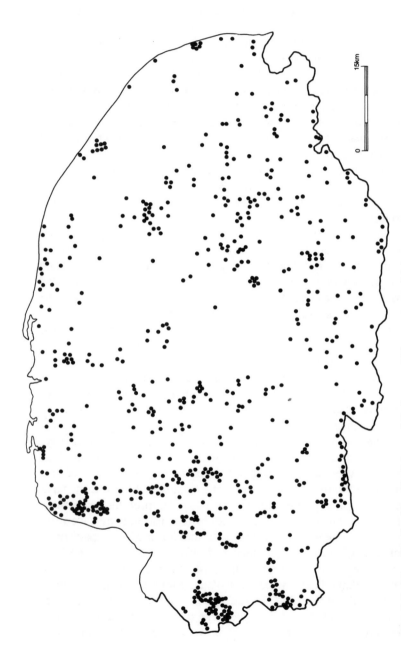

Fig. 2.5 The distribution of all known findspots of Roman material in Norfolk (after Davies & Gregory 1991)

lying, uninviting. The main north–south band of the sparsely-settled arc corresponds, not surprisingly, to the line of the central watershed. Its extension down the north-eastern seaboard takes in an area which, in the Iron Age and Roman periods, consisted of a number of islands or near-islands separated by bands of low-lying marsh. This area may have been fertile; but it was remote from the prime centres of power and settlement. It was also, in the later Roman period, particularly exposed to raiding from across the North Sea.

Such raiding seems to have begun in the third century. It was one symptom of a more general, and complex pattern of social and economic change in Europe. The whole of the Western Empire was, at this time, experiencing a profound recession, and in many areas urban life appears to have been in decline. This recession affected, not just the communities living within the Roman *limes*, but those outside, in southern Scandinavia and north Germany. Local elites which – like the tribes of south–eastern England in the late Iron Age – had grown rich and powerful through trading links with the Empire now found their position threatened: but 'a ready alternative to trading was raiding, for the acquisition of the resources necessary to sustain the political system' (Hodges 1989: 24).

Evidence of recession and insecurity abound in late Roman Norfolk. At Venta Icenorum the forum was destroyed by fire in the early decades of the century and lay derelict for at least fifty years before being reconstructed, significantly, on a much more modest scale. In the third century the town was provided with defences, but the new walls truncated the earlier grid of streets, enclosing no more than half the original area of the town. The small town of Brampton probably also recived defences at this time, but the most dramatic expressions of insecurity are the forts which were erected during the third century at Brancaster (*Branodunum*) on the north coast, and at Caister-on-Sea on the northern edge of the great Broadland estuary (Gurney 1990; Johnson 1980, 1983; Cunliffe 1977; Ellison 1969; Edwards and Green 1977). Even more impressive is the great fourth-century fortification on the southern shore of the estuary, at Burgh Castle, probably called *Gariannonum*, replete with all the latest in Roman military technology. These were part of a chain of forts gradually constructed all along the south-east coast of England,

and the north coast of France, in the third and fourth centuries. They were, by the second half of the fourth century, under the command of an official called the Count of the Saxon Shore.

Raiding must have compounded the effects of the region's economic problems, and by the second half of the fourth century the recession was biting deep. To judge from metal-detector finds, the number of coins in circulation in the county plummeted after the 370s; at the same time, the number of coin hoards being buried was increasing (Davies & Gregory 1991: 83–7). This presumably reflects not simply increased deposition, but an increasing failure of the hoarders to return and collect their savings. Industrial pottery manufacture came to an end around 400. Some time during the next few decades, Germanic raiding gave way to permanent settlement: but by this time the *Civitas Icenorum* had probably already ceased to exist.

3

The coming of the Angles

Graves and history

Early historical sources tell us little about the nature of the Germanic settlement in East Anglia. The *Anglo-Saxon Chronicle* provides an account – of dubious significance – of events in Kent, Wessex, and Northumbria, but does not concern itself with our area. Bede only tells us something of the ethnic origins of the settlers, in an oft-quoted passage in the *Ecclesiastical History*:

From the Jutes are descended the peoples of Kent and . . . the people who hold the Isle of Wight, and those in the province of Wessex opposite the Isle of Wight who are called Jutes to this day. From the Saxons, that is the country now known as Old Saxony, came the East, South, and West Saxons. And from the Angles – that is the country known as Angulus which lies between the province of the Jutes and the Saxons, and remains unpopulated to this day – are descended the East and Middle Angles, the Mercians, all the Northumbrian peoples . . . and other English peoples. (HE I: 15)

The most obvious evidence for ethnic change in the archaeological record is the appearance in the county, from the early fifth century, of distinctive cemeteries, similar to those found in the areas of northern Europe from which, according to Bede, the ancestral English migrated. Some, including all the earliest, consist of cremations, mostly buried in decorated urns. Others, of sixth- and seventh-century date, are mainly or entirely made up of inhumations, some but not all of which are accompanied by grave-goods – dress ornaments, tools, containers, and weapons. In a number of cemeteries, both rites are found, apparently in use at the same time. A large number of these pagan cemeteries have been discovered in Norfolk, together with several single burials, or small groups of two or three, some of which might represent the periphery of larger cemeteries, or their residual remains. Most were discovered accidentally, often during the extraction of sand or gravel. No doubt others await discovery, while others still must have been destroyed without record in the distant past. It is, however, unlikely that these would greatly alter the pattern of distribution exhibited by the ones we know about. This is largely confined to the major river valleys, and biased towards the lighter soils in the west of the county (Figure 3.1).

Some historians and archaeologists have tried to use the evidence of such cemeteries to illustrate and amplify the rather sketchy account of the English settlement provided by Bede and the *Anglo-Saxon Chronicle*. J. N. L. Myres, for example, argued that the earliest cemeteries represent the graves of Germanic mercenaries or federate troops who were settled in Britain before it ceased to be a part of the Roman Empire. The distribution of the later cemeteries, he believed, could be used to chart the subsequent revolt of these forces and the expansion of their territory; their defeat and containment by a sub-Roman counter-attack; and their eventual triumph, and conquest of lowland Britain (Myres 1969; Myres & Green 1973). But archaeologists these days are rather wary of this kind of simple linkage between the events related in early historical sources, and changing patterns of material culture. The historical accounts date from a long time after the events they purport to describe, and may be quite unreliable – exercises in story-telling only partially based on reliable traditions. Indeed, at least one historian has gone so far as to assert that 'the precise details of the German conquests in England' are 'irrevocably lost to us' (Simms–Williams 1983: 41). Partly because of this, some archaeologists have tried to interpret the evidence of the cemeteries quite independently of the historical sources, although still in terms of narrative history. Most recently, Bohme has argued that while there were Germanic troops in late Roman Britain, the critical development in the transition from Roman Britain to Saxon England was an influx of new peoples into East Anglia in the early fifth century (Bohme

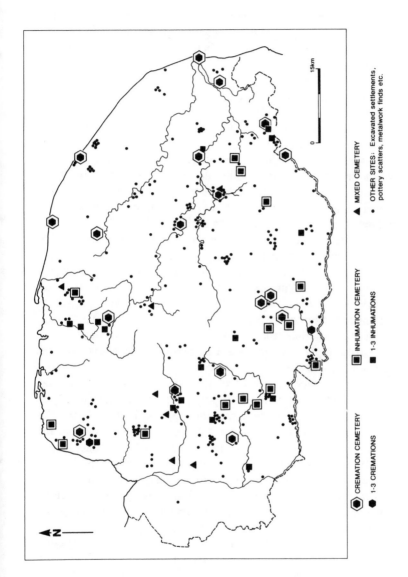

CREMATION CEMETERY   INHUMATION CEMETERY   ▲ MIXED CEMETERY

1-3 CREMATIONS   1-3 INHUMATIONS   • OTHER SITES: Excavated settlements, pottery scatters, metalwork finds etc.

Fig. 3.1   Early Saxon sites, and artefact findspots, in Norfolk

1986; Carver 1989: 147–8). Their arrival in Norfolk, Suffolk, and the adjacent counties is represented in the archaeological record by graves containing a range of distinctive continental metalwork, including equal-arm brooches, supporting-arm brooches, and early forms of cruciform brooch. Such items are also found not only in the 'Anglian' areas of Schleswig-Holstein, but also in the Lower Elbe region of north Germany, the traditional homeland of the Saxons. The East Anglian region in which these people established themselves was ringed by areas in which different kinds of metalwork deposited within graves – objects in the so-called Quoit-Brooch style, and late Roman military equipment – indicate the continuation of an essentially Romano-British society. In the middle decades of the fifth century, however, new contingents from Saxony and southern Denmark arrived, and settled in the Midlands, where – until then – Romano-British control had been maintained.

There have been other suggestions about patterns of immigration into Dark Age Norfolk based on artefact distributions. Hines, for example, has argued plausibly for substantial immigration into eastern England from southern Norway in the sixth century (Hines 1984). No doubt further attempts will be made to write history from graves. But some recent scholars have, in fact, questioned whether the cemeteries and their contents need necessarily imply any movement of people. Richard Hodges, in particular, has argued that new burial rites, and the new fashions in dress and equipment for which they are our best evidence, may not represent the movement of people at all, but the movement of objects and ideas. Continental influence on Britain during this period may have been largely through politics, religion, and trade, rather than through actual migration (Hodges 1989: 10–42). The immigrants were, according to Hodges, few in number, and the 'historical' accounts are largely inventions of the following centuries made by new elites attempting to identify with the heroic societies of the contemporary Germanic world whose culture and ideology they had come to adopt.

Hodge's ideas are challenging, but go too far. While it is quite possible, indeed probable, that some of the individuals interred in 'Anglian' cemeteries were people of British descent who had come to accept the fashions and beliefs of politically dominant immigrants, substantial numbers of newcomers clearly did settle in England in general, and in Norfolk in particular, at this time. The earliest cemeteries are dominated by the rite of cremation, a practice which had been going out of fashion in Roman Britain, as elsewhere in the Empire, for two centuries, and which is unlikely to have held much appeal for fifth-century Britons (Welch 1985: 14). Catherine Hills, moreover, has shown that the burial practices employed at the largest Norfolk cemetery yet excavated, at Spong Hill near North Elmham, are so close to those practised in parts of northern Europe that they must surely represent the graves of people of Continental origin or descent (Hills, forthcoming). More than this, she has demonstrated that the cemetery's closest parallels are with the Anglian, rather than with the Saxon, areas of the Continent. Hills compared the burials at Spong Hill with those at Suderbrarup and Bordesholm in Schleswig-Holstein, and at Westerwanna in Lower Saxony. The range of grave-goods found at all the sites was similar, but the closest similarities were consistently between Spong and the Schleswig sites. Thus, for example, 'The most characteristic late fourth and fifth century burials at Suderbrarup seem to be those which contain sets of miniatures with combs, in pots which either have no decoration or a horizontal/vertical bossed and grooved design. Very similar burials occur at Spong Hill' (Hills, forthcoming).

The Anglian affinities were not entirely clear-cut. In particular, the Spong pottery urns, with their use of stamped ornament, showed closest affinities with those from the Westerwanna cemetery. Nevertheless, Hill's conclusions – derived from a detailed study of the entire 'package' of grave-goods, rather than from an examination of individual items – challenges not only Hodge's extreme anti-invasionist arguments, but also Bohme's suggestions about the origins of the Germanic settlers in Norfolk: 'The people buried at Spong Hill owed many of their ideas about how to bury their dead to ideas current in Schleswig-Holstein, which is exactly where Bede said they came from' (Hills, forthcoming). But it is worth remembering that Bede, in another passage of the *Ecclesiastical History*, appears to include Danes, Frisians, the Frankish tribe of the Boructuari, and even the Huns among the Continental peoples from whom the English could trace their ancestry (HE V: 9). While the majority of settlers in Norfolk may well have come from Schleswig-Holstein, there were

c

some from other places, and some of these were buried at Spong. One of the graves here contained an assemblage suggesting that the interred individual was of south, rather than north, German origin or descent, and was perhaps a member of the tribal group called the *Allemanni* (Hills, forthcoming; Hills & Penn 1981: Fig. 139). Place-name evidence also hints at the presence of other Germanic peoples in the county. The name of Swaffham in the west of the county contains the element *swaefas* or *swaef*, the Old English form of the German tribal name *Suevi*, or Swabian (Ekwall 1960; Whittock 1986: 163).

Yet if large numbers of Germanic immigrants were arriving here in the fifth and sixth centuries, we need not necessarily assume that the indigenous population was exterminated. In a study based partly on Norfolk inhumation cemeteries, Harke has suggested that the distinction between burials with weapons, and those without, may be a manifestation of ethnicity. Burial with weapons was a sign of German origin as well as, perhaps, superior social status. Those buried without weapons represent the indigenous population (Harke 1990). There are, however, some problems with this interesting argument, not least the difficulty of identifying ethnicity on the basis of skeletal remains. Harke relied mainly on differences in height as an index of race, but not enough is known about the physical characteristics of the indigenous population, or about the ways in which long-term differences in diet, related to social inequalities, might produce height variations within an ethnically homogeneous population. Current work on the DNA of the buried individuals, as preserved in their bone, may well throw more light on these intriguing suggestions. Until then, we have to rely on more traditional lines of enquiry.

One is the study of place-names. The extinction of the vast majority of Romano-British place-names in Norfolk might, on the face of it, suggest an equivalent extinction of the indigenous inhabitants. But the relationship between linguistic and ethnic change is complex. The language spoken in a region can alter without a wholesale replacement of its population, as the case of Scotland clearly demonstrates. This change was, of course, a gradual one, but the same may have been true in Dark Age Norfolk. The Celtic inhabitants of Norfolk may only gradually have come to adopt the language of the newcomers, during the sixth and seventh centuries: and the old names of the county's settlements, estates, and topographic features may have been changed even more gradually. We simply do not know what most places in Norfolk would have been called in the Early or Middle Saxon period, for only three Norfolk place-names are recorded in documents before 800. Many, as we shall see, were coined as late as the ninth or even tenth centuries.

Some indication of the way in which the Celtic names were replaced is provided by the few examples which survive, and it is worth looking at these in some detail. Trunch, in the north–east of the county, probably incorporates the Old Welsh elements *trun*, 'nose, or promontory' and *ceto*, 'wood': hence, 'the wooded promontory', in the sense of hill (Ekwall 1960; Mills 1991). The parishes of North and South Creake, in the north-west, derive their name from Old Welsh *creic*, modern Welsh *craig*, 'a ridge'. Brancaster may incorporate the first element of the Celtic name for the Saxon shore fort here, *Branodunum*, while Lynn derives from the British *lindo*, 'lake', presumably referring to some kind of pool at the mouth of the Ouse. Some place-name experts would add to this list the two villages called Eccles – one in Shropham hundred, one in Happing – both of which may incorporate the British term *eglēs*, from the latin *ecclesia*, 'church', probably in the sense of 'a Christian community' (Gelling 1978). If this derivation is correct, these names *could* indicate the survival of organised Christianity into the period of the Anglian settlement: but, as we shall see, other derivations and interpretations are equally possible.

The only pre-Anglian river name still current in the county is that of the Ouse (Old Welsh term **ws*, 'water') (Ekwall 1928). But several others survived into the medieval period, or even beyond, and only then disappeared, often through the process known as 'back-formation'. This is where a river's name is changed to one derived from that of a settlement along its banks. Thus the river Nar is a back-formation from Narford and Narborough. Its original name was the Pante (Welsh *pant*, 'a valley'), preserved as the first element of the place-name Pentney. The river Chet takes its modern name from Chedgrave; but its earlier name, preserved in the adjacent settlement of Loddon, was the Ludne, derived from the British **Lutna*, 'muddy river'. The Yare is a post-medieval back-formation from Yarmouth. Its medieval name, first recorded in 1150, was the Gerne, derived from a British river name *Gariennos* or *Gariannos*. This gave its name to Gariannonum, probably the Saxon Shore fort at Burgh Castle, and means 'the loud one'. The Glaven in the north of the county is probably a medieval back-formation from the village of Glandford: but this place name may itself incorporate the earlier name for the river, derived from the Welsh *glan*, 'pure' (there are problems with the early etymology here, but the name seems particularly appropriate to the clear waters of this trout-stream). Other examples of Celtic river-names are indicated by modern place-names, or are mentioned in medieval documents. The Wimene, a tributary of the Bure near Wroxham mentioned in a Hundred Roll of 1275, is suspiciously similar to the Gaulish river name *Vimina*, from which La Vismes (a tributary of the Bressle in France) and the Wumne (a tributary of the Weser in Germany) both derive. The village of Carbrooke is named after the tributary of the river Wissey on which it stands: this probably incorporates a British word *caru*, 'pleasant', related to the Welsh verb *caru*, 'to love' (Ekwall 1928).

This is not to suggest that the county's Celtic river-names survived *en masse* into the Middle Ages. Some, certainly, were replaced very early. The Wissey takes its name from *Wissa*, an Old English term meaning, simply, 'river'. The British name, *Wigora*, 'the winding one', is preserved in the name of a village on its banks, Wereham (*Wigorham* in a charter of 1060) (Ekwall 1928). This change, however, occurred early enough for the Wissa to give its name to a tribal group, the Wissa, mentioned in the eighth-century *Life of Guthlac* (Courtenay 1981: 98; Colgrave 1940). Many Celtic river-names did, however, survive quite late into the Saxon period, and the implications are interesting. Celtic river-names survived better than Celtic place-names, while most of the latter refer to topographic features, like lakes and ridges, rather than to individual settlements. Names applied to large natural features would have been used by large numbers of people. They would have been slower to change than those given to individual estates or settlements, which might be altered, possibly more than once in the course of the Saxon period, as they passed through the hands of successive administrators or owners. The final disappearance of most of Norfolk's Celtic river-names in the post-Conquest period might thus represent the tail-end of a more general, and gradual, process of name-replacement. In terms of settlement and estate names, this process was almost entirely completed by the end of the Saxon period, but two centuries before we might well have found considerably more Celtic place-names in use in the county. The evidence of place-names can, in the final analysis, contribute little to our knowledge of the scale of Germanic immigration into the county, or the fate of the indigenous population. Whether substantial numbers of Romano-Britons survived in one sense matters little. In terms of language, and material culture, Norfolk was, by the seventh century if not before, a Germanic, rather than a Celtic region.

Continuity in the landscape

Excavations of pagan Saxon settlements at Witton in north–east Norfolk have clearly revealed the extent to which the post-Roman period witnessed economic recession and technological regression (Wade 1983a: 53–67). Both the quality, and the quantity, of the material culture of the sites' inhabitants were low. Here, as on contemporary settlements elsewhere in England, the pottery used was locally produced, poorly fired, and made without the use of a wheel.

Some historians argue that the collapse of the imperial economy was accompanied by large-scale abandonment of land and widespread woodland regeneration (Hodges 1989: 20–2). But there is little evidence for such a dramatic scenario in Norfolk. Rather, the evidence of place-names, pollen analysis, fieldwalking surveys, and chance discoveries suggests a more complex mixture of continuity and discontinuity. In his survey of Hales, Loddon, and Heckingham, Davison was able to show that a drastic thinning of settlement occurred at the end of the Roman period. In these clayland parishes there were, as we have seen, at least fifteen Roman settlements, scattered across all the principal soil-types, including the heavy chalky boulder clay of the interfluve plateau (Davison 1990: 16). The pagan Saxon period, in contrast, was represented by only four concentrations of pottery, although others could, in theory, be obscured beneath areas of modern settlement on the valley floors. The interfluve plateau was now entirely abandoned, at least as a location for settlements. Medieval documents show it as a landscape of woodland and woodpasture, interspersed with fields bearing names indicative of medieval clearance. And yet in one important sense, the settlement pattern displayed a marked degree of continuity from the fourth through to the seventh centuries. Not only did the four Early Saxon sites lie – like most of the Roman ones – in the 'boundary zone' between the two principal soil types. They all lay on, or immediately adjacent to, sites of Roman and Iron Age occupation, and it is hard to believe that some, at least, were not continuously occupied throughout this long period of time (Davison 1990: 66).

Contraction of settlement is apparent elsewhere. In Witton, on the light, fertile loams of the north-east of the county, the eight small Romano-British sites were replaced by only four main areas of early Saxon occupation (Wade 1983a). Surface collection and limited excavation were able to establish, moreover, that not all of these were occupied at the same time. Only the largest, site A, was in use throughout the fifth and sixth centuries. Of the others, one was occupied in the fifth century, one in the sixth, while the third could not be dated accurately. Equally interesting here is the distribution of stray sherds in the fields around the settlements, material which, for the most part, probably arrived in the soil with manure taken out from farmyards. Whereas Roman material was found in almost all the fields examined, sherds of early Saxon pottery had a much more limited distribution, suggesting that, perhaps, only some 40 hectares, or less than 25 per cent of the area fieldwalked, was under cultivation during the fifth and sixth centuries (Wade 1983b: 75). Some surveys suggest even more drastic contraction. Davison's current examination of the parishes of Mannington, Wolterton, and Wickmere has so far discovered only one major concentration of early Saxon pottery, compared with seven from the Romano-British period.

Yet reduction in the number of individual settlements was not necessarily accompanied by large-scale abandonment of land. Instead, we seem to have evidence for an expansion of the area under pasture, and therefore (presumably) an increase in the amount of meat being produced and consumed. Pollen cores taken from Hockham Mere, Saham Tony Mere, the Mere at Stow Bedon, Old Buckenham Mere, and Diss Mere, all provide little indication of woodland regeneration (Bennett 1983; Godwin

1968; Godwin & Tallantire 1951; Simms 1978). At Hockham, for example, the late Roman period seems to have seen some increase in the area under pasture, and a landscape of grassland continued through to the seventh or eighth centuries, when there was an increase in the area under cereal cultivation (Bennett 1983). At Seamere, similarly, there was no post-Roman upsurge in tree pollen, but again a continuation of the landscape of open grassland which had become established in the last centuries of the Roman period. These sites lie on or close to the light soils of the Breckland, where intensive settlement in the fifth and sixth centuries is anyway attested by the distribution of pagan cemeteries. Of more interest, therefore, is the evidence from Diss Mere, in the south-eastern claylands. Here the large-scale clearances effected in late prehistoric times were not reversed in the post-Roman period. There was a slight increase in the pollen of hazel and birch, probably dating to the third century, which might represent some development of scrub woodland (Peglar et al. 1989: 218). But for the most part, open pasture dominated the landscape within the mere's pollen catchment area until the Middle Saxon period when, as at Hockham and Seamere, the proportion of cereal pollen began to increase. If, as Jacobson & Bradshaw's arguments suggest (Jacobson & Bradshaw 1981), the pollen falling on a lake the size of Diss Mere is derived from an area within a radius of 10 to 20 kilometres, then there can have been little woodland regeneration on the south-eastern clays, for even a radius of 10 kilometres would embrace an area extending over the Waveney–Tas watershed and into the Tas valley. The modern field pattern in the area around Diss Mere appears to preserve, as we have seen, elements of late prehistoric systems of land division. The survival of such relict landscapes into the medieval period presumably suggests that some, at least, of their principal boundaries remained in use throughout the post-Roman period. Many of the minor boundaries could, however, have been created when regenerated woodland was cleared once again, their orientation simply replicating that of the dominant axes in the landscape (Williamson 1988).

This evidence, for at most only limited post-Roman woodland regeneration, is in broad agreement with that from other areas of lowland England (Bell 1989: 273–7; Fulford 1990: 30). Yet place-names leave little doubt that there was, in fact, a fair amount of

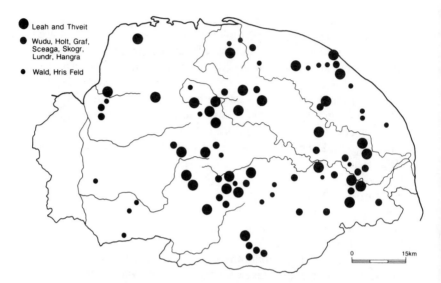

Leah and Thveit

Wudu, Holt, Graf, Sceaga, Skogr, Lundr, Hangra

Wald, Hris Feld

0   15km

Fig. 3.2 The distribution of major place-names incorporating elements referring to woodland

woodland in the early Anglian landscape. Figure 3.2 shows the distribution of all major place-names – those of medieval parishes, and Domesday vills – with woodland associations (Gelling 1984: 188–230). Some, like the Scandinavian *þveit* and the Old English *lēah*, both of which probably have the meaning 'clearing', presumably indicate substantial concentrations of woodland. Others, such as *wudu, holt, grāf, sceaga, skógr, lúndr*, and *hangra*, probably refer to individual woods. Others are of uncertain significance, especially *wald*, which probably refers to areas of fairly open woodpasture, or *feld*, which – meaning in this context 'open area' – refers to woodland only by implication, in that it suggests that adjacent areas were noticeably less open. Together, these major place-names have a highly structured distribution, and suggest that Anglo-Saxon woodland was concentrated in particular districts.

A major belt of wooded land ran through the centre of the county in a great arc, from Mundesley on the north-east coast down to Fersfield beside the Waveney valley. Another great concentration lay in the east of the county, around the fringes of the great Yare estuary. A smaller, but noticeable, area lay around Babingley, Rising, and Wooton in the area immediately to the north of Kings Lynn. What is interesting about this distribution is that it suggests that the greatest concentrations of Anglo-Saxon woodland lay, for the most part, in the same areas in which, to judge from the evidence of known sites and stray finds, settlement was comparatively sparse in Romano-British times. Figure 3.1, showing the location of all known pagan Saxon findspots, is – perhaps unsurprisingly – similar. We thus see in both periods the same contrast between the core areas of settlement, based on the west of the county and the river valleys in the south-east; and a broad corridor of more peripheral territory, corresponding to the central watershed, and the eastern marshes. No doubt there was some woodland regeneration, some expansion of the area under tree cover, but the overall pattern shows a remarkable degree of continuity. The only significant difference between the two periods was that the Fenland in the west had become, in Anglian times, a marginal, largely unoccupied zone, due to changes in sea level occurring at the end of the Roman period.

Major place-names – those of parishes and Domesday vills – indicate the main tracts of woodland in the Saxon period. Minor place-names – those relating, in particular, to areas of common-land – indicate more limited stands of trees. Such names tend to cluster on the principal interfluves between the major river valleys. This is noticeable in the claylands, but also, to some extent, on the lighter soils of the north and west. Thus, for example, a map of North Creake in 1600 shows the sides of the valley in which the village lies occupied by extensive open-fields, while the interfluves above carried areas of open commonland (Norfolk Record Office collection, NRO Diocesan T123A). These, however, are called 'The East Frith', and 'The Fold Course Called the Frith', names clearly derived from the Old English word *frið*, 'wood', and showing that these areas had, in the remote past, been wooded. Fieldwalking surveys suggest that pagan Saxon settlements were rare on the interfluves away from the major valleys. Romano-British settlements, on the other hand, do occur in such locations, especially in the south-east of the county, suggesting that the much of this woodland was the result of post-Roman regeneration, growing up over abandoned farmland. But the pollen evidence does not, at present, support such a suggestion, and these Romano-British interfluve settlements – which fieldwalking surveys suggest were, for the most part, small hamlets or single farms – may, in fact, themselves have been located within wooded environments, and were perhaps engaged in the specialised exploitation of woodland resources.

There were certainly major changes in the pattern of land exploitation and settlement in the post-Roman period, in Norfolk as elsewhere in lowland Britain. Reduction in the numbers of settlements, a contraction in the area under arable cultivation, expansion of the area under pasture, all suggest a substantial decline in population and continuing economic recession. But there is no evidence that the fields of Roman Norfolk were abandoned on a large scale, or that the landscape disappeared under a mass of regenerating forest.

Territories

It used to be thought that as the Roman Empire crumbled, the provinces of Britannia began to dissolve into their constituent tribal *civitates*; and that these were taken over by new Germanic settlers, and thus developed into the kingdoms which we meet with in Bede, and in the pages of the *Anglo-Saxon Chronicle*. The names of some of the early kingdoms might be taken as an indication of this kind of direct territorial continuity: Kent, for example, appears to preserve the name of the Roman *civitas* of the *Cantiacii*. Recent research has, however, tended to reject simple territorial continuity of this kind. Instead, scholars like Bassett have cogently argued that by the middle of the fifth century Britain was in an advanced state of political fragmentation (Bassett 1989). Bands of immigrants grabbed groups of contiguous Romano-British estates, creating territories much smaller than the *civitates*, each of which came to be dominated by particular families. The names of such dominant lineages are sometimes preserved in early place- and district-names, those with the suffix -*ingas*, 'people of'. Only later, and only gradually, did larger territories emerge, as population increased and neighbouring groups competed for resources. Defeated units were merged with successful ones, and the power of lineage head-men grew into that of chiefs. This process eventually led to the emergence of fully developed kingdoms like East Anglia or Essex, as the result of a kind of glorified Dark Age knock-out competition (Bassett 1989). The documentary and archaeological evidence from Norfolk, such as it is, would tend to support such a model of social and political development.

Wendy Davies has demonstrated the former existence of a lost chronicle which, unlike the *Anglo-Saxon Chronicle*, was particularly concerned with events in the eastern areas of England (Davies 1977). This chronicle was apparently based on, among other sources, entries in a seventh-century Easter table, and an early Mercian king list. It was still in existence in the twelfth century, perhaps in a monastic house in eastern England, for Henry of Huntingdon's *Historia Anglorum*, and the *Flores Historiarum* of both Roger of Wendover and Matthew Paris, all incorporate excerpts from it. In 527, according to the version preserved in the *Flores*, 'Pagans came out of Germany, and occupied East Anglia . . . from where some of them invaded Mercia and waged many wars against the Britons: but because their leaders were many, they have no name' (Coxe 1841–4; Luard 1890). Henry of Huntingdon adds, by way of qualification to the last phrase, the observation that 'they were not yet organised under one king' (Arnold 1879). The precise date assigned to this particular phase of the English settlement is, perhaps, not to be taken too seriously: but it is just possible that, in its description of an immigration into eastern England by fragmented, decentralised war-bands, the lost source preserved a reliable early tradition.

As we shall see, by the later decades of the sixth century a coherent kingdom of the 'East Angles' had begun to emerge, under the overlordship of a dynasty called the Wuffingas. Political coherence at this time is indicated by a document called the Tribal Hidage, a list of the tribute due from the various peoples of England to a Mercian overlord (Dumville 1989: 133; Hart 1971; Kirby 1991: 9–12; Davies & Vierck 1974). This document – variously dated by scholars, but probably drawn up in the reign of Wulfhere of Mercia (658–675) – gives a single large assessment to the 'East Angles', but shows that in the Fenland to the west they were bounded by a number of small tribal groups, including the North and South *Gwyre*, the *Spalda*, the *Sweorda*, the

Widerigga, the *Willa*, and others (Davies & Vierck 1974; Courtenay 1981; Darby 1934). These may have survived as independent entities because of their political context – in a kind of political buffer zone between East Anglia and Mercia – and because of the fragmented topography of the Fenland basin (Darby 1934). Either side of the Fens, such groups had, by the late seventh century, coalesced into larger territorial units, but some of their names have come down to us. The eighth-century *Life of Guthlac* describes how Guthlac's sister Pega was visited on Crowland by a sick man 'from the province of the Wissa', a name which, as we have seen, incorporates the name of the river Wissey (Courtenay 1981). The names of other early territories and folk-groups may be preserved in the names of hundreds. Happing, in the north-east of the county, takes its name from the 'people of Haep', an individual who also gave his name to Happisburgh, 'Haep's fort'. Loddon hundred appears in Domesday as *Lodningas*, 'the people of the *Ludne*', the early name, as we have seen, of the river Chet. Clavering hundred appears under a variety of spellings in Domesday, but many are variations on *Cnaveringas*, 'the people of Cnava', a name of some significance to which we shall return shortly.

It is noteworthy that in two of these cases, a tribal group seems to have taken its name from a river. Everitt has suggested that early tribal territories often corresponded with river valleys, being separated from their neighbours by less densely-settled watersheds (Everitt 1977, 1979). Such a pattern would accord well with the evidence of Romano-British and pagan Saxon artefact distributions, and 'woodland' place-names, already discussed. It would also fit in well with the distribution of early Saxon cemeteries, and especially the cremation cemeteries, which tend to be located within the major river valleys.

Indeed, the social, territorial significance of the early cemeteries is crucial here. Arnold has suggested that large cremation cemeteries were 'centralised depositories, not belonging to individual settlements': and that there was a relationship between the rite adopted for the disposal of the dead, and the distance between cemetery and settlement (Arnold 1988: 41). That is, inhumation was favoured where burial took place close to the cemetery, cremation where the body needed to be taken to a centralised depository. 'If cremation took place near the settlement it would be more practical to take the remains to a distant cemetery' – assuming, of course, that the precise rite to be adopted was a matter of some indifference, as the frequent appearance of both, side by side, in the same cemetery would seem to suggest.

Hill's excavations at the Spong Hill cremation cemetery near Noth Elmham have thrown considerable light on all this (Hills & Penn 1981; Hills, Penn, & Rickett 1987). The cemetery was entirely excavated, and found to have contained at least 2,300 cremations and fifty-seven inhumations (Hills 1989). This total includes a large number of burials badly damaged by earlier urn-digging, rabbiting and ploughing, but an unknown number must have been destroyed or removed completely in the past. The eighteenth-century historian Blomefield describes how labourers removed thirty urns in 1711; and how this encouraged 'other persons to make further trial, who found several near to one another. One person employed in the search is said to have taken up about 120' (Blomefield 1805, Vol 9: 409).

The 2,357 interments must, therefore, be considered a minimum. Yet even on the basis of this figure McKinley has argued that, assuming the cemetery was in use for between 150 and 200 years, it must have served a community which at any one time numbered between 500 and 850 people (McKinley 1989). A contemporary settlement lay adjacent to the cemetery. This contained only three post-built structures, together with a number of sunken-featured buildings: although it was not entirely excavated, it can hardly have housed more than a fraction of this figure.

It is interesting to compare the size of this inferred community with the Domesday population figures for this area. In 1066 the survey ascribes to the large vill of North Elmham, in which the cemetery lies, a total recorded population of 132, suggesting a real population of around 550. Elmham at this time included not only the entire area of the present parish, but also the greater part of Brisley, and at least half of Bilney. The adjacent vill of Beetley was, at this time, a dependent berewick of Elmham, and had a recorded population of eight, representing, perhaps, a further thirty-five individuals. In 1066, therefore, North Elmham and its dependencies had a population probably less than that of the community using the Spong Hill cemetery in the fifth and sixth centuries. The cemetery can, therefore, hardly have served an area smaller than this. Population densities were unquestionably much lower in the Early Saxon period, and we might reasonably infer that Spong Hill served a territory perhaps twice this size, possibly corresponding to the eastern half of the Launditch hundred, in which it lies.

Anglian cremation urns are decorated with patterns made up of lines of small stamped designs, pressed into the wet clay from bone dyes. The same stamps often appear on more than one pot, and this, until recently, was thought to indicate the existence of specialised workshops, marketing their wares over often wide areas (Myres 1969). Petrological analysis has, however, shown that in some cases, the same stamps occur on pots which were made from clay coming from very different geographical locations, suggesting that it was the *stamps* that moved, rather than the pots. Many archaeologists now believe that stamps may have had some kind of totemic, perhaps quasi-heraldic significance, being passed down through families and combined and recombined on cremation urns as lineages intermarried (Arnold 1983; Arnold 1981; Arnold 1988: 76–80).

Hills and her co-workers painstakingly grouped the excavated urns at Spong according to the stamps which they shared in common (Hills & Penn 1981: 4–22). This revealed forty-two separate groups, of which some contained only two or three pots, but the largest, group 7/12, contained no less than thirty-one. The pots in each group were found to cluster in particular areas of the site. The pots in some of the smaller groups were buried close together, within a few metres of each other; the larger groups, while more scattered, were nevertheless generally restricted to one broadly defined zone of the cemetery. Only a handful exhibited a more randomly dispersed pattern, and Hills noted that some of these were groups which have been identified in other cemeteries, and which might, therefore, represent individuals from other communities marrying in to that interring at Spong (Hills 1980).

A number of cremations were buried in pots which lacked any stamped decoration, and these again were clustered, occupying a large area in the centre of the cemetery. In addition, Spong contained a number of inhumations, some under barrows (Hills & Penn 1981: 3–4; Hills 1977; Hills 1980). It is clear that inhumations were still being made while the rite of cremation was being practised on the site, because a number of the cremation burials had cut into the grave-pits. Again, the inhumations were closely clustered, forming a group on the northern edge of the cemetery.

It seems reasonable to conclude that the stamp-linked groups represent families or lineages occupying farms or small hamlets scattered across the territory of the community using the cemetery. The cremations in undecorated urns are less easy to interpret. They may represent bond lineages, whose status did not merit the mark of 'heraldic' devices. The inhumations, in contrast, would be most plausibly interpreted as the burials of people living in the small settlement adjacent to the cemetery. The fact that some of these burials were elaborate, in wooden chambers or beneath barrows, may suggest that this group was, or was becoming, socially dominant. The Spong Hill community does not seem to have been a simple egalitarian tribe, but a more complex and ranked society.

Spong Hill lies less than four kilometres from the Romano-British 'small town' at Billingford. This close relationship of a fifth-century cremation cemetery with a place of Roman importance is not unique (Myres 1969). Most dramatically, the great cemeteries at Markshall, and Caistor St Edmund, lie within 300 metres of the walls of Venta Icenorum, while a probable fifth-century cemetery lies just outside the walls of the Saxon Shore fort of Burgh Castle. The relationship of pagan cemeteries to Roman small towns and similar nucleations of settlement is also noticeable. The cemetery at Kettlestone lies less than 6 kilometres from the Roman settlement at Toftrees, while Earsham lies less than 4 kilometres from that at Ditchingham. The cemetery at Great Walsingham less than 3 kilometres from a substantial Roman settlement which extends into the adjacent parish of Wighton, while the Brettenham cemetery is little more than 1 kilometre from the settlement beside the Peddars Way in the same parish. That at West Acre is only 2 kilometres from the substantial late Roman site at Narford. This recurrent pattern implies that these major Roman settlements continued to function as central places into the fifth century, and perhaps later, and that the small tribal territories which succeeded the *civitas* continued to have their main focus at or near to them. Some slight indication of the nature of this transition may be provided by Wighton. Here, the fifth-century cemetery lies only 1 kilometre from a substantial embanked enclosure which was destroyed in the eighteenth century. Excavations here in 1974 were on a small scale, but sufficient to show that the structure had been constructed in the late or post-Roman period, presumably as a central place for a tribal group (Lawson 1976). Perhaps similar features once lay at the heart of other early Anglian territories: the Haeppingas, for example, clearly once had their own fort at Happisburgh.

The fifth- and sixth-century cremation cemeteries thus appear to represent central burial grounds for tribal territories based on the principal river valleys and which, in some cases at least, were focused on places which had been of administrative or economic importance in the late Roman period. The predominantly inhumation cemeteries of the sixth and early seventh centuries, however, are rather different. In general, these do not exhibit the same kind of relationship with the decaying geography of late Roman Britain. Moreover, they seem, for the most part, to have served smaller, more local communities. Bergh Apton, for example, contained only sixty-three interments, and although it was not entirely excavated it is unlikely that the total number of burials was more than twice or three times this number (Green & Rogerson 1977). That at Morningthorpe was bigger – around 365 inhumations and nine cremations – but while again the entire cemetery was not excavated, these were clearly much more modest repositories than Spong (Green, Rogerson, & White 1987: 5).

It is not entirely clear how we should explain these apparent differences. Some historians have seen the inhumation cemeteries as evidence for the influx of new people, in the sixth century, perhaps the 'pagans from Germany' whose arrival in 525 was apparently referred to in the lost Anglian chronicle (Morris 1973: 283). While this is, perhaps, possible, it is more likely that their appearance is a manifestation of important social changes. Perhaps, as population density increased and local societies became more stratified, members of senior lineages chose to bury their dead, and those of their social dependants, in more localised burial grounds. If Arnold is right in seeing a connection between the mode of disposal, and the distance which human remains were to be brought for burial, then it might well follow that a shift to more localised burial would go hand in hand with the adoption of inhumation, rather than cremation, as the dominant rite. We would, therefore, see something akin to the observed pattern: the proliferation of small inhumation cemeteries between larger cremation or mixed cremation/inhumation ones. But there is another possibility. Comparatively few Romano-British burials are known from the county: the rite of disposal current in the third and fourth centuries, unlike that of the fifth-century immigrants, is archaeologically invisible. It is just possible that the appearance of the inhumation cemeteries in the sixth century represents the adoption by the *indigenous* population of a new, more 'visible' form of disposal, perhaps in line with fashions sweeping across northern Europe from the territory of the Franks (Hodges 1989: 30–1). It is, at present, impossible to decide between these two interpretations – and there are, indeed, others. What does seem clear, however, is that it is the cremation cemeteries, rather than those dominated by the rite of inhumation, which represent 'central places' for large social territories; and that some of these are associated not only with places of importance in Roman Britain but, as we shall see, with those of significance in the Middle and Later Saxon period.

Some of the county's linear earthworks must relate to this fifth- and sixth-century period of political fragmentation. Unfortunately, we do not know when most were constructed: few have been dated by excavation, and arguments based on their relationship with other archaeological features can be misleading. Thus the Launditch, long thought to be a post-Roman monument because it lies across a major Roman road, has recently been dated, by excavation, to the Iron Age. The Fossditch, however, is certainly post-Roman. Excavations in 1954 revealed that it was cut through a settlement occupied into the fourth century (Clarke 1957). The Panworth Dyke and the Bicchamditch also *appear* to be post-Roman, as they were erected across Roman roads, although the recent evidence from Launditch advises caution here. The Fossditch faces eastwards, and runs for 6 miles in a north–south direction, each end terminating at marshy ground, in the valleys of the Wissey and the Little Ouse. The Bichamditch, more substantial, is positioned so that it cuts across the main Roman road leading east-west through the county from Denver to Billingford and beyond: it too faces eastwards and runs across high ground to terminate in areas of former marsh (Wade-Martins 1974). These two earthworks should, perhaps, be viewed as part of a single system, defining a territory embracing what were once, in effect, two promontories extending out into the marshes of the Fens. The Panworth Dyke (locally known as Devils Ditch) is less impressive than the two Breckland dykes, and face westwards rather than east, lying astride the Roman Road running eastwards from Ashill near to the place, significantly, where it passes over the central watershed (Wade-Martins 1974; Reid & Wade-Martins 1980). A number of other linear earthworks once probably existed in the county, but were destroyed during the medieval and post-medieval periods. Thus, for example, an earthwork called the 'Laundyche' is referred to in medieval documents relating to Holme and Thornham, in the extreme north–west of the county (Gregory 1986a: 3).

Rather than see these earthworks primarily in terms of military strategy, we should perhaps interpret them as attempts to regulate exchange at the boundaries of petty kingdoms; partly perhaps to allow tolls to be charged, but mainly to control the passage of elite goods, in order to prevent them falling directly into the hands of rival lineages, who could use them to bolster their power and prestige, and thereby challenge the rule of the territory's leader. We should also, however, remember the symbolic role of such features, as demonstrations of the power and prestige of princes, and of their control over their subjects (Hinton 1990: 42–4).

It is always tempting to suggest some 'historical' context for linear earthworks. The Biccamditch, for example, could have been the eastern boundary of the territory of the Wissa, while the location of the Panworth Dyke might suggest that during the sixth century the central watershed had appeared – or reappeared – as a political frontier, with the dyke marking part of the western frontier of a territory embracing much of eastern Norfolk. Wade Martins has pointed out that for much of its length the Panworth Ditch was little more than a substantial hedge-bank (Wade-Martins 1974). In this context it is, perhaps, worth noting the existence of a prominent, near-continuous boundary which runs all along the central watershed in a series of great arcs from Shipdham to Wymondham – a distance of nearly 30 kilometres (Figure 3.3). Running from north–west to south–

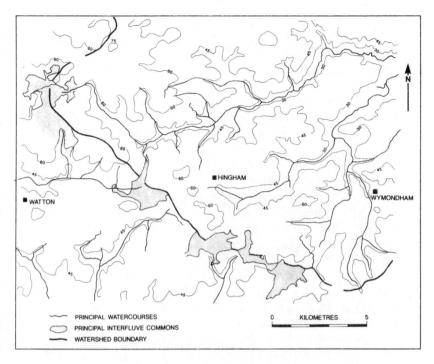

Fig. 3.3 An early watershed boundary between Shipdham and Wymondham

east, this forms, successively, the boundary between the hundreds of South Greenhoe and Mitford, Mitford and Wayland, Wayland and Forehoe, and finally Forehoe and Shropham. This may simply have been created when the hundreds themselves came into existence, in Late Saxon times: but it could well have originated much earlier in the Saxon period.

We know nothing about the dynasties who ruled over the tribal territories of fifth- and sixth-century Norfolk. There are hints – but no more – that one may have been called the *Iclingas*, 'the people of Icel', whose name is preserved in the place-name Hickling. Icel is an archaic personal name which occurs in several other place-names in Norfolk and the adjacent counties. Possible examples include the two Eccles in Shropham and Happing hundreds, and Icklingham, just over the county boundary into

71

Suffolk. These names have been the subject of some speculation because Icel is the name of the person from whom, by the seventh century, the kings of Mercia claimed descent (Martin 1976). The epic *Beowulf* recites the names of Icel's ancestors, rulers in continental Angeln, down to Icel's father, but no further. Some historians have suggested that Icel migrated to England, perhaps during the early sixth century, and that his family achieved some prominence in East Anglia before establishing themselves in Mercia (Morris 1973). Such speculative pseudo-history might hardly be worth mentioning were it not for two interesting coincidences, both pointed out by Edward Martin. According to the Mercian genealogies, Icel's 'great-grandson' was Creoda, a figure who died, if we can believe the *Anglo-Saxon Chronicle*, in 593. The genealogy of the kings of Lindsey also mentions him, making him the kingdom's first ruler, and describing him as *Cretta Vinting*, 'son of Vinta'. Now Vinta is not a personal name that appears in any Old English or even British text: it is, however, very similar to the name of a place, *Venta Icenorum*. Moreover, the name of Icel's son in the Mercian genealogies, Cnebba, looks suspiciously like a hypochoristic (that is, shortened) form of the archaic dithematic name Cnobhere. This again is a name with Norfolk connections. In the 630s, according to Bede, the East Anglian king Sigeberht gave the Irish monk Fursa a place, almost certainly the Saxon Shore fort at Burgh Castle, called 'Cnobheresburg, that is, the urbs Cnobheri'. And just the other side of the Waveney, in Norfolk proper, lies the hundred of Clavering, which preserves the tribal name of the *Cnaveringas*, 'the people of Cnava', almost certainly the same name, if not the same person, as Cnebba. It is doubtful whether too much should be made of all these coincidences, but it is just possible that we have here a dim, garbled memory of a powerful dynasty in sixth-century Norfolk. But it is with the rise to power of a different dynsty, the *Wuffingas*, that East Anglia first emerges, fitfully, into the light of history.

4

The North Folk

To understand the development of Norfolk during the Middle Saxon period – roughly from the middle of the seventh century, until the end of the ninth – we need to look beyond its current boundaries. The area occupied by the modern county formed, at this time, the northern part of the kingdom of the East Angles, one of the petty states which emerged out of the political chaos which followed the collapse of the Roman Empire. The fortunes of its kings, their relationships both with their own nobles and with the leaders of neighbouring kingdoms – Mercia, Northumbria, the East Saxons – were of vital importance in moulding the region's character. Yet at times we must look still further afield, across the North Sea and even beyond. For the inhabitants of Middle Saxon Norfolk – kings, nobles, peasants, slaves – were, whether they knew it or not, part of a wider world. The ramifications of political, social, and economic changes in areas as far away as the Mediterranean could be felt in the most remote farmstead of the North Folk.

The kingdom of the Wuffingas

The first East Anglian king about whom we have any information is Raedwald, who died around 624 (Kirby 1991: 63–6). He is mentioned both in Bede's *Ecclesiastical History*, and in the *Anglo-Saxon Chronicle*. Raedwald got a bad press from Bede.

Converted to the Christian faith in Kent, he returned to East Anglia where, 'seduced by his wife and certain perverse teachers', he set up in the same temple a Christian altar, and a heathen one (HE, II: 15). Raedwald was the fourth in a series of kings whom Bede describes as exercising *imperium* over the kingdoms and peoples south of the Humber. He is listed after Aelle of the South Saxons, Ceawlin of Wessex, and Æthelberht of Kent. Raedwald in his turn was followed by Eadwin and Oswiu, kings of Northumbria. The *Anglo-Saxon Chronicle* adds Egberht, king of the West Saxons in the early ninth century, to the list, and describes all these rulers as *Bretwaldas* in version A of the *Chronicle*, or *Brytenwealdas* in all the other versions. The former title is the one which usually appears in the history books, but it is almost certainly a misreading of the latter, so that the epithet means, not 'Britain-ruler', but 'wide ruler' (Kirby 1991: 17–18). The extent of Raedwald's power is demonstrated by Bede's account of his relations with the Northumbrian king Æthelfryth. The previous king of Northumbria, Edwin, had been forced into exile at Raedwald's court. Æthelfryth offered Raedwald a substantial sum if he would betray him but he refused, and instead marched against him, defeating him 'on the east bank of the river that is called Idle' (HE, II: 12).

Bede tells us that Raedwald was 'the son of Tytil, whose father was Wuffa, after whom the East Angles are called Wuffingas' (HE, II: 15). Further information is given in a list of early kings of East Anglia preserved in a ninth-century Mercian document, generally if somewhat prosaically known as *Cotton Vespasian B vi*, which may have been first written down as early as 725 (Dumville 1976; Stenton 1959). This does not mention Raedwald. It was written to establish the descent, and therefore the legitimacy, of the early eighth-century king Ælfwald, and he was descended not from Raedwald, but from his brother Eni. According to this genealogy, Eni was the son of Tyttla, Tyttla the son of Wuffa, and Wuffa the son of one Weha, whom Bede does not mention.

We must not assume that all these names necessarily represent real people (Dumville 1977). In particular, the name *Wuffa* may well be an invention, to explain the family name Wuffingas, which might, in fact, have a very different derivation. As Sam Newton has pointed out, the patronymic Wuffingas is a phonological variant of Wulfingas, 'the offspring of the wolf', an ancient folk-name which may, originally, have entailed a totemic affinity with the wolf (Newton 1990). Interestingly, a group called the Wulfingas are mentioned in the Old English poem *Widsith*, in a context which suggests that they lived in or near Denmark. It is possible that the ultimate origins of the dynasty were indeed in southern Scandinavia for, as we have seen, the archaeological evidence suggests that there were close contacts between this area and East Anglia in the sixth and early seventh centuries, and perhaps even some migration of people. Not only were forms of metalwork of closely comparable form in circulation in both areas at this time. The rite of ship-burial used at Sutton Hoo, the great cemetery in south–east Suffolk which may well have been the burial ground of the Wuffingas, has close parallels with practices in contemporary Scandinavia (Carver 1984; Wilson 1983; Bruce-Mitford 1984).

The rapid rise to prominence of the Wuffingas was followed by an equally rapid decline (Kirby 1991). The Northumbrians were now the dominant power in England, and following Raedwald's death East Anglia was wracked by internal strife. Raedwald's son and successor Eorpwald struggled with his half-brother, Sigeberht. The latter was driven into exile in Gaul, but a few years later Eorpwald was killed 'by a heathen called Ricberht: and for three years from then the province was given over to error, until the brother of Eorpwald, Sigeberht, succeeded to the kingdom, a man most Christian in all his ways and learned' (HE, III: 18). It was Sigeberht who, as we shall see, brought Christianity to the kingdom. He himself retired into a monastery before being dragged out of holy retirement by his joint king, Ecgric, to face the invasion of the pagan Penda of Mercia, in 635/6. Both men were killed. The kings of the Mercians were now vying with those of Northumbria for hegemony over eastern Britain, and East Anglia was a territory to be dominated and exploited, rather than a force to be reckoned with. The new East Anglian king, Anna, Raedwald's nephew, was expelled from the kingdom by King Penda of Mercia in 650, and although he soon returned and defeated him, he was in turn defeated and killed by the Mercian forces in 654 or 655.

Anna's brother Æthelhere, the next king, was probably a dependent client of the Mercian king. He was killed at the great battle of Winwaed in 655, fighting alongside the Mercians 'with his own men'. It was here that the Northumbrian king Oswiu defeated the Mercians and established a short-lived hegemony over southern England, which even involved the direct rule of Mercia through governors (HE, III: 24). But this was a mere interlude in the growth of Mercian power. Mercian independence was re-established following a coup by Penda's son Wulfhere in 658 or 659, and under his successors the rise of Mercia commenced once again. Under Æthelbald (716–757) and especially under Offa (757–796), Mercia came to dominate all of England south of the Humber (Fisher 1973: 162–73).

Nevertheless, under the successors of king Æthelhere – Æthelwald (c. 655–644), Aldwulf (c. 664–713), and Ælfwald (c. 713–749) – East Anglia maintained some degree of independence. The kingdom was not absorbed into Mercia, and may even have enjoyed a measure of authority over the neighbouring kingdom of the East Saxons: the East Saxon king Swithelm was baptised by bishop Cedd at Rendlesham, near Sutton Hoo in Suffolk, with king Æthelwald as his sponsor (HE, III: 22). The coins minted in East Anglia in this period, moreover, retained their distinctive designs, escaping Mercian influence (Metcalf 1984: 58–9).

On Ælfwald's death in 749, according to one source, the East Anglian kingdom was divided between three kings, Hun, Beonna, and Æthelberht. This account, however, seems to be based on an early misreading of a regnal list, and it is more likely that these obscure kings reigned in succession, with Beonna reigning between c. 758 and 779, and Æthelberht from 779 into the 790s (Kirby 1991). There seems to have been some reassertion of full East Anglian independence, which perhaps coincided with the assassination of Æthelbald and the early years of Offa's reign. Beonna minted coins bearing his own name, as for a short while did his successor Æthelberht: but Mercian hegemony was soon restored.

We can, for the moment, leave this slightly tedious catalogue of the deeds of Dark Age kings, and concentrate instead on the nature of their kingdom. It has become customary to associate Raedwald and the Wuffingas firmly with the Sandlings area of Suffolk, and to see Norfolk as a peripheral part of their kingdom. This is partly because of the presence here of the cemetery of Sutton Hoo, with its two great boat burials, but also because of Bede's reference to the baptism of Swithelm 'in the province of the East Angles, in the royal estate which is called Rendlesham' (HE, III: 22). Whether the early Wuffingas can be tied down quite so neatly to this district is unclear. Even if Rendlesham was an important royal residence as early as Raedwald's reign, others must have existed in the northern parts of the kingdom. Indeed, Raedwald's original power-base could have been anywhere in Norfolk or Suffolk: the name Tittleshall – which has as its first element the archaic *Tyttel* or *Tytla*, the name of Raedwald's father – could, conceivably, associate the dynasty with west-central Norfolk (Dymond 1985: 67).

For we must be very careful not to draw too tidy a boundary around the domain of the early Wuffingas. Bede gives the impression that England in the early seventh century was already divided into neat kingdoms with definable boundaries. He may, however, have been reading back into an earlier period the more stable political circumstances of his own era. In the early seventh century, the political geography of England was probably still in a state of flux, with smaller territorial groupings being absorbed by larger ones, and 'kings' like Raedwald may, in reality, have exercised only a loose overlordship over smaller political groups. While for Bede Raedwald was king of the East Angles, it is doubtful whether this term would have had much meaning in the early seventh century. At times, certainly, the overlordship of the early Wuffingas seems to have extended over a wider area than Norfolk and Suffolk. The small tribal groupings described by the Tribal Hidage in the area to the west of the kingdom were certainly sporadically under their influence. Bede at one time describes the Isle of Ely as part of East Anglia, and it may be significant that the second bishop of the kingdom, Thomas, was a member of the Gwyre, one of the obscure Fenland tribes mentioned in the Tribal Hidage (HE, III: 20).

Bede includes in the *Ecclesiastical History* two probably reliable transcripts of ecclesiastical councils held at Hertford in 672 and at Hatfield in 679 or 680 (HE, IV: 5; HE, IV: 17). The preamble to the latter mentions Bisi, 'bishop of the East Angles', and the conference is itself dated by the regnal year of Aldwulf, 'king of the East Angles'. These are the earliest references to the East Angles by name, and the term may have been a new one at this time. It has, in fact, been suggested that names like East Saxons and West Saxons were replacing earlier folk or dynastic names in the middle decades of the seventh century, and that far from being determined by indigenous concepts of ethnicity, they may have been moulded by the needs of the English church (Kirby 1991: 20–33). As bishops came to be established within each of the emerging kingdoms, it may have become necessary to define more rigidly the territory over which both king and bishop had jurisdiction. In other words, Aldwulf's territory 'was being defined for him in terms of the diocese of his bishop as perceived by the metropolitan church' (Kirby 1991: 22).

Christianity may well have been of importance in the emergence of kingdoms and kings, but it was, arguably, as much a consequence as a cause of the formation of coherent, centralised states. The increasing dominance of the Wuffingas over other local leaders was the result of a complex nexus of social, economic, and demographic changes. In the last analysis, however, their monopolisation of political power in the region rested on their success in war. Warfare with neighbouring polities, in a parallel state of development, was not an occasional occurrence. As Stenton pointed out, Æthelhere, the brother of Anna who came to the throne in c. 664, was the last of six male Wuffingas who were either murdered, or killed in battle, in the space of less than eighty years (Stenton 1959). Nor was war an inconvenient distraction in the lives of dynasties like the Wuffingas: rather, it was their *raison d'être*. Success in war depended on an ability to maintain a sizeable retinue of loyal warriors. Dark Age kings like Raedwald did this by rewarding followers with prestige goods, obtained either through plunder, or through contacts with distant trading partners. The objects found in the Sutton Hoo ship burial, and other archaeological discoveries, make it clear that the early Wuffingas maintained trading contacts with the northern world: but increasingly, in the seventh century, trade was concentrated with the Franks and the Frisians.

Control of long-distance trade with foreign elites was essential to dynastic security. If prestige goods fell directly into the hands of aristocratic groups, they could use them to establish rival networks of gift-giving and alliance, and therefore rival power-bases (Hodges 1989: 69–71). Thus it was that trading came to be concentrated at a few entrepôts, *wics*, where foreign exchange could be controlled and regulated (Hodges 1989: 69–114; Hodges 1982). The West Saxon kings had Hamwih, the predecessor of Southampton, while York served as the entrepôt for the Northumbrians. The East Anglian kings established theirs at Ipswich, in the early seventh century (Wade 1988). Initially this was a modest affair, a periodic landing-place on the northern bank of the Orwell, visited by traders from the Merovingian Empire and elsewhere (the cemetery excavated here included the graves of people from the Allemannic areas of southern Germany). But this nucleus was expanded considerably in the middle decades of the eighth century, when facilities for tradesmen and craftsmen were laid out immediately behind the original trading area and, further to the north, an extensive planned area was established. This development may have occurred in the reign of Beonna, perhaps reflecting the intensified exchange with the Carolingian Empire which provided the basis for that king's brief measure of independence from Mercia (Hodges 1989: 101). Long before this, however, Ipswich seems to have developed as a centre for controlled production, as well as for controlled exchange, with facilities for weaving, metalworking, and the production of leather goods. It has been argued that such a role may have become increasingly important as the seventh century progressed, because the supply of gold from Byzantium and the Mediterranean was drying up (Hinton 1990: 37–40). There was a gradual decline in the availability of prestige goods from abroad with which kings could reward their retinues, and monopolisation of internally produced commodities may thus have become important. Pottery is the most archaeologically visible of these products, although presumably not the most important at the time. *Ipswich Ware* was produced here in large quantities, probably from the 640s, and widely distributed throughout East Anglia. This pottery was far superior to the crude wares current in the region during the previous two centuries, in that it was produced on a slow wheel and fired in kilns, rather than bonfires.

It is possible that a secondary entrepôt was established during the eighth century at Norwich, to serve the northern parts of the kingdom. The nature and extent of Middle Saxon occupation within the city remain imperfectly understood. A number of Middle Saxon settlements have long been known, or postulated, within the area of the medieval city, largely on the basis of stray finds: at Needham, Conesford, and Westwick, on the south of the River Wensum, and at Coslany to the north (Ayres, forthcoming). But all seem to have been small affairs, probably rural hamlets: the largest, Conesford, occupied no more than 2 hectares, and the negative results from recent excavations at the Castle Mall site have reduced the possible size of one of the putative settlements, Needham, drastically (perhaps calling its very existence into question). In 1985, however, excavations by the Norfolk Archaeological Unit in Fishergate, to the north of the river, uncovered evidence of Middle Saxon occupation on a much more impressive scale. Large quantities of Middle Saxon pottery were excavated from a comparatively small area: an area, moreover, that lies within a part of the city which was given substantial defences in the tenth century. There is nothing to suggest a settlement on the scale of Ipswich. But this may well have been the 'North Wic' from which the medieval city took its name. This term may simply signify that the settlement lay to the north of the other farms and hamlets in the area. But it may indicate that this was the north *wic* of the kingdom, as opposed to the south *wic*, at Ipswich. More excavations in and around Fishergate are urgently needed to test the nature of Middle Saxon occupation here.

Military power, the monopolisation of commodity exchange and production, together with the influence of the church, ensured the increasing consolidation of the Wuffingas' power. Raedwald may have exercised a personal leadership over a shifting collection of disparate, semi-autonomous groups: by the second half of the seventh century, firmer political boundaries were being drawn. By the time of the Tribal Hidage, the tribute list probably drawn up in the reign of the Mercian king Wulfhere, the kingdom of the East Angles was a recognisable political unit, with a definable capacity for raising tribute and therefore, by implication, with recognised boundaries. The East Angles were assessed at 30,000 hides, considerably more than the 7,000 assigned to the East Saxons (Davies and Vierck 1974). Although historians do not have the foggiest idea what these figures really mean, they do suggest that the East Anglian kingdom was one of the richest in England, in spite of its subordinate political position.

In the seventh century the economy of the kingdom seems to

have been largely of an 'embedded' nature, with the distribution of goods being used to reinforce patterns of social alliegance and political power. By the middle of the eighth century, however, there are signs that in East Anglia, as elsewhere in England, royal control over the economy was beginning to break down, and incipient market exchange was developing (Hodges 1989: 105–6). Coins appeared again in East Anglia, probably in the second quarter of the century (once again, as in the Iron Age, rather later than in Kent and Essex). Initially these were of gold or gold/silver alloy, but from the 680s *sceattas* – small silver coins – made their appearance. The complex development of these coins in England has been intensively studied by archaeologists and numismatists (Metcalf 1984). Those belonging to 'series C' and 'series R' seem to have been struck in East Anglia, perhaps produced (like so much else) at Ipswich, although only those struck by Beonna, at the very end of the coin series, bear a king's name.

The earliest Middle Saxon coins seem to have been used for high-level exchange between elites, for the payment of tribute or the purchase of foreign commodities, but the *sceattas* appear to have been more widely employed (Metcalf 1984: 58–9). Large quantities recovered from outside the walls of the Roman forts of Burgh Castle and Caister-on-Sea perhaps indicate the sites of fairs established beside prominent local landmarks. *Sceattas* have also been found on a large number of rural sites, including Tibenham, Cockley Cley, Watton, Harling, and Costessey: a substantial hoard, consisting almost entirely of issues of Beonna, was discovered at Harling. Nevertheless, we should not exaggerate the extent to which market exchange impinged upon Middle Saxon society in Norfolk. At North Elmham, the excavations of the Middle Saxon settlement produced only two *sceattas*. At a local level, at least, the movement of goods and services was probably still organised largely around the payment of customary renders: and even at higher social levels, many goods appear to have moved through the medium of social relationships, rather than by market exchange, until well into the ninth century.

One indication of this is the curious distribution of Ipswich Ware. In most cases, the distributions of items of material culture in Middle Saxon England do not correlate closely with the political divisions referred to by documentary sources. That of Ipswich Ware, however, is rather different. Although small quantities have been found at London, Canterbury, and as far west as Northamptonshire, it is virtually absent from Essex (Wade 1988: Figure 4). In Norfolk, its distribution in the Fenland is particularly interesting (Silvester, forthcoming). Middle Saxon sites occur in some numbers in the northern silt Fenland. The quantities of Ipswich Ware recovered from the surface by field-walking here can be considerable: the 104 sherds collected from a site in Tilney St Lawrence, the 125 from Bristoe field, Walpole St Peter, are typical quantities, but over 1,000 were recovered from the extensive occupation area at Hay Green, Terrington (Rogerson & Silvester 1986; Silvester 1988). With the exception of a site at West Walton, the assemblages collected from these sites are characterised almost exclusively by Ipswich ware. Other kinds of pottery prevalent in areas further to the west, especially the rough, shelly, 'Maxey-type' ware of the East Midlands, are either absent altogether or present in very small quantities. It is a remarkable fact that 'on the further side of the river Nene the percentage of Ipswich-type Ware in contemporary assemblages drops off rapidly'. Thus on the neighbouring Cambridgeshire siltlands, at Tydd St Giles, less than 10 per cent of the material collected from the surface of two Middle Saxon sites is of Ipswich Ware. The Nene, to quote Silvester again, appears 'To reflect an economic boundary. More than this it might perhaps mark a political border as well, in which case the tribal boundary of the Middle Saxon kingdom of East Anglia would be by far the most likely candidate' (Silvester, forthcoming).

The East Anglian kingdom had thus, probably by the later seventh century, become a recognised political and territorial unit. But what of Norfolk? Not one of the historical sources which we have so far mentioned make any reference to it. Indeed, the term first appears as late as the 1040s, in a will in which one Thurstan bequeathed all his possessions 'in Norfolke' (Hart 1966). This absence of early references is surprising, given the rather archaic flavour of the terms 'North Folk' and 'South Folk'. It is possible, of course, given the very limited nature of the documentary evidence, that this division of the kingdom existed from an early date, defined by the Waveney–Ouse line or – just as plausibly – by the Waveney–Gipping watershed. It may be that such a division is reflected in the dual kingship of Ecgric and Sigeberht, mentioned by Bede, which followed the death of Eorpwald (HE, III: 18). But it is also possible that the division had a rather different origin.

In the 680s, during the reign of Aldwulf, the East Anglian diocese was divided in two. The old see of *Dommoc* (probably Dunwich in Suffolk) continued in use, and a new see was established – according to William of Malmesbury – at a place called Elmham (Wade–Martins 1980a: 3). But at which Elmham? Although by Late Saxon times, as we shall see, the bishopric was located at North Elmham in Norfolk, several historians have suggested that it was originally at *South* Elmham, in Suffolk (Rigold 1962; Woodward 1864; Harrod 1874; Howlett 1914). We need not rehearse the various arguments here: most historians would probably agree that the see was, from the start, located at North Elmham (Wade–Martins 1980a: 3; Rigold 1962; Heywood 1982, Howlett 1914). Apart from anything else, we should surely expect a new see to have been located in a position in which it could most effectively serve the needs of the northern parts of the kingdom (Whitelock 1972: 5).

We have seen how the needs of the church may have helped to define and name the emerging kingdoms in seventh-century England. In a similar way, the division between 'North Folk' and 'South Folk' could have been created, or at least encouraged, by this division of the East Anglian see. The North Folk may not, in origin, have been an archaic folk grouping so much as a concept moulded by the establishment of the bishopric at North Elmham.

Settlement and territory

As the power of the Wuffingas grew, so the independence of local tribal leaders declined. A pattern of independent tribal territories was replaced by one of large royal estates. Such estates are better documented elsewhere in England, where early charters survive. Sawyer describes these as 'Large units variously called federal, discrete or multiple estates by modern scholars. These large estates contained the varied resources needed to sustain life: arable, pasture, woodland, and probably fisheries as well' (Sawyer 1979: 7). Some of these large estates were used as endowments for warriors in the king's retinue, or royal administrators, and were thus temporarily alienated from the Crown.

Such endowments may have become more important in maintaining political power as the supply of prestige goods dwindled in the course of the seventh century (Hinton 1990: 37). Only gradually did permanent alienation of these estates occur, first as monasteries were endowed, later through gifts to leading nobles. Once alienated in this way, they could be divided by inheritance or sale. Even when they were not formally alienated, however, many individuals or families seem, over the centuries, to have usurped rights of ownership over portions of such estates. The end result of all this can be seen in the pages of Domesday: by 1066, most of England was divided up into much smaller units, 'manors', and even the largest landowners held scattered rather than discrete estates.

Yet there was another fundamental difference between systems of territorial organisation in Middle and in Later Saxon times. The vills and manors described by Domesday were, for the most part, economically independent agrarian units, involved in mixed farming (although with an arable bias) on their own account. The great estates of the Middle Saxon period, in contrast, seem to have contained economically specialised sub-units, farms or hamlets which produced some specialised commodity, or provided some particular service, for the estate centre. Traces of such economic specialisation abound in Norfolk place-names: Horsey, 'the horse island'; Hempstead (near Holt), 'the place where Hemp is grown'; Horstead, 'the place where horse are kept'. Other names suggest tenurial dependence on some other settlement: Guestwick, for example, was probably the *þveit*, or clearing, attached to Guist, some 7 kilometres away. Sandringham was once 'the sandy place belonging to Dersingham', the adjacent parish (Ekwall 1960; Mills 1991).

In most areas of Britain, these archaic estates seem to have shared a common pattern of spatial organisation. They had a core area of arable and meadow land, near to the estate centre. This was occupied by both bond cultivators, dwelling close to the estate centre; and, at a slightly greater distance, by lineages of semi-free status, who owed less onerous services. The peripheral areas of such estates were occupied by tracts of woodland and pasture (Jones 1971, 1979). An analysis of the different kinds of prefixes most frequently used to qualify particular kinds of place-name element suggests that such a pattern once existed in Middle Saxon Norfolk.

The two most common place-name suffixes in the county are the Old English *hām*, usually translated as 'village or settlement'; and *tūn*, 'settlement or farm'. Together, these make up more than 48 per cent of the places recorded in Domesday Book. The most noticeable difference between these two kinds of name is that *tūn* names are frequently qualified by terms which suggest some kind of specialised agricultural function, whereas this is seldom, if ever, the case with *hāms*. Thus we have two *beretūns* (Bartons), 'outlying farms', and a *meolc beretūn* (Mulbarton), 'outlying milk farm'. There are no less than four Swantons (the *tūn* of the *swanna*, or herdsman); a *tūn* where mules were kept (Moulton); a bee-keeper's *tūn* (Bickerston); *tūns* used on a seasonal basis (Somerton and Winterton); *tūns* attached to meadow land (Metton), *tūns* for growing rye (Roughton), and even for growing leeks (Letton) (Mills 1991). Unlike settlements with names incorporating *hām*, moreover, many in *tūn* have prefixes which suggest that they were involved in the exploitation of woodland resources. Thus we have Wood Norton; Ruston, Sco Ruston, Ryston (all from *hris*, 'brushwood'); Woodton & Witton (*wudu*, 'wood'); and East Walton (*wald*, 'forest') (Mills 1991; Schram 1961).

Hāms can be long (Langham) or broad (Bradenham), but they are never – in Norfolk – described in terms of the direction in which they lie from another place, a characteristic which is, in contrast, frequently displayed by *tūns*. These can lie to the north (Norton Subcourse, Wood Norton, Blo Norton, Pudding Norton); east (Easton in Forehoe, Easton in South Erpingham, and Testerton, *Estretūna* in Domesday Book); west (Weston Longville); and south (Sutton in Launditch, Sutton in Happing); as well as lying in the middle of something else (Middleton in Freebridge; the lost *Middeltūna* in Depwade; Melton Constable (Old Norse *meðal*, 'middle') (Mills 1991).

These features strongly suggest that most *tūns* were, in origin, subsidiary and often outlying settlements, sometimes with specialised functions. *Hāms*, in contrast, tended to be *areas* rather than individual settlements, the core zones of estate arable, or the estates themselves. This general interpretation is supported by

Fig. 4.1 The distribution of major place-names incorporating the element *hām*

the differing location and distribution of the two kinds of place-name. With few exceptions, *hām*s are found in areas most suitable for arable agriculture during the Early and Middle Saxon period. They are numerous in the 'Good Sands' region of the north and west, in places where there are good supplies of water, either near the junction with the boulder clay (with its perched water table), or in the lower reaches of the minor streams of the district (Figure 4.1). Elsewhere, in the south-eastern claylands or in the Breckland, they are largely confined to the principal river valleys. *Tūn*s, in contrast, are much more widely distributed (Figure 4.2). While they do sometimes occur in the same kinds of location as *hām*s, they are characteristic of more marginal and peripheral locations: they are numerous on the level clay interfluves away from the principal valleys, or in the upper reaches of the minor tributaries of the Breckland rivers.

The distinction is also brought out by the character of the places bearing these different kinds of name at the time of Domesday. Many *hām*s were important royal estates, manors to which hundreds were attached, or places which had given their

Fig. 4.2 The distribution of major place-names incorporating the element *tūn*

names to hundreds: examples include Hingham, Earsham, Buckenham, Mileham, Foulsham, South Walsham, Saham, Aylsham, Taverham, and Shropham. In contrast, most *tūn*s were small places, several of which – like *Alcmuntūna* in Loddon hundred, or *Narvestūna* in Clavering – are now lost. Conversely, a number of present-day settlements containing this element do not appear as Domesday vills, presumably because they were still dependent settlements in some larger territorial unit: examples include Coston, Morton, Doughton, Ovington, and Whitlington. Lastly, whereas *hām* names are often shared by several contiguous parishes, each identified by the addition of some epithet like 'North' or 'Great', this is rarely the case with names ending in *tūn*. There are, of course, exceptions to all this. Wighton, for example, was an important royal and hundredal manor. But the broad distinction is clear enough.

Many of these names – 50 per cent in the case of *tūn*, 53 per cent in the case of *hām* – have as their first element the name of an individual or a group. Of names ending in *hām*, twenty-eight per cent have as their first element an *ingas* compound, a formation usually translated 'people of', and indicating a tribal group or a lineage. This is never the case with *tūn* names. Moreover, the personal names associated with *hām*s are often obscure and archaic, and in some cases it is difficult to tell whether they are personal names at all, or terms for wild animals and birds. *Tūn*s, in contrast, are usually associated with personal names of more familiar Late Saxon type, the kind which we encounter in the pages of Domesday Book: names like Aslac, Osmund, etc. More significant still is the fact that a third of these names are Scandinavian, compared with a mere one per cent in the case of *hām*. In other words, well over a third of the county's *tūn* names must have been coined in the period after *c*. 870, when the county was occupied by the Vikings, whereas *hām* names appear to be much older. The relatively recent nature of our *tūn*s is also indicated by the fact that no less than six are expressly described as 'new' (Newton by Castle Acre, Newton in Henstead, Newton Flotman, West Newton, and the lost *Neutūna* near Holt).

It is sometimes suggested that *tūn*s were places first cleared and settled at a later date than *hām*s, especially as the latter feature in greater numbers in early charters and chronicles than the former (Cox 1972; Dodgshon 1973; Cox 1975). In reality, however, this is probably because *hām*s tended to be more important places. The difference, that is, is primarily one of status rather than chronology. The 'late' personal names attached to many *tūn*s do not necessarily indicate that the settlements to which they refer were first established as late as the ninth or tenth centuries, although some may have been. Most had probably been settled for centuries, but received their present name when they first became separate estates, severed from more ancient territorial units. The names of their new owners replaced some older descriptive or functional prefix like 'north' or 'wood'.

Other kinds of place-name in the county seem to fall into the kind of pattern displayed by the *hām*s and the *tūn*s. Many places with topographic names (other than those indicating areas of woodland) display similar characteristics to the *hām*s. They occupy areas of tractable soils in major valleys, and are often shared by two or more adjacent parishes. Thus, for example, we have North Creake and South Creake (from the Old Welsh *creic*, 'a ridge'); or Castle Acre, South Acre, West Acre (OE *œcer*, 'an area of cultivated ground'). Place-names containing the elements *wīc*, *worð*, and *stede*, on the other hand, seem to have much in common with those ending in *tūn*. This is especially true of those containing the element *wīc*. Thus, of the settlements bearing this suffix which appear in Domesday, two are lost, Godwick was deserted in the later Middle Ages, and Keswick, Westwick, and Oxwick all suffered drastic shrinkage. Conversely, several do not appear in Domesday, but exist today as single farms or hamlets: places like Wicken Farm near Castle Acre, Bolwick Hall near Aylsham, and Dudwick near Buxton. When used as a term for a rural settlement, *wīc* often seems to have had the sense 'grazing farm'. Keswick is the cheese farm, Oxwick the ox farm, Hardwick the herd farm (Mills 1991). Settlements bearing such names tend to occur in areas where we might expect to have found extensive areas of pasture land in the Middle Saxon period, on the high watersheds (Godwick, Oxwick, Hardwick) or on the edge of the Broadland marshes (Postwick, Wickhampton, Woodbastwick, Bastwick). Names incorporating *worð*, usually translated 'an enclosure', also seem to occupy watershed or marsh-edge locations, and may again have been some kind of specialised grazing establishments.

The development of a more coherent East Anglian kingdom, and the emergence of royal estates in place of primitive tribal territories, seems to have had a dramatic effect on the pattern of settlement. As a result of a number of fieldwalking surveys, we now have a fairly clear idea about the nature and extent of Middle Saxon settlement in the county. Whether or not the distribution of Ipswich Ware really can be used to define the boundaries of the kingdom of East Anglia, it is certainly of immense significance in identifying the pattern of settlement within it. Archaeologists in Norfolk are lucky: unlike their colleagues in most other parts of England, they work in a region in which, thanks to the widespread dissemination and use of this durable and diagnostic pottery, settlements of Middle Saxon date can be easily discovered and recognised from scatters of sherds on the surface of the ploughsoil.

Alan Davison's study of Hales, Loddon, and Heckingham is once again of particular interest (Davison 1990: 16, 66). In these three parishes, as we have seen, early Saxon settlement continued, albeit in a highly attenuated form, the pattern of the Roman period. In the early or middle decades of the seventh century, however, there was a dramatic change. The older sites were all abandoned. Occupation moved away from the 'junction zone' between the chalky and sandy boulder clays, abandoning the higher ground altogether and relocating in the main valleys. These new sites are close to medieval parish churches. One, represented by a concentration of fourteen sherds, was found some 400 metres to the north-west of Loddon church, on the edge of and probably extending beneath the modern settlement surrounding it. In Heckingham, where the church stands isolated from modern housing, a number of concentrations of Middle Saxon pottery were discovered around it: several Middle Saxon coins have also been discovered here by metal-detectors. As a result of this 'Middle Saxon shuffle', settlements now lay far from the chalky boulder clay of the interfluve plateau, and for the most part occupied sites adjacent to both the valley-floor meadow land and the well-drained, tractable soils of the sandy boulder clay. These were clearly, to judge from the distribution of stray sherds, being farmed as arable.

The changes in settlement in this area were typical. Few Middle Saxon settlements in Norfolk continued the sites of those occupied in the Early Saxon period. The latter, both in their distribution and in their specific locations, often relate quite closely to settlements of the Roman period. The former, in contrast, tend to be fewer, larger, and usually lie close to parish churches, and on the same sites as settlements of the Later Saxon period. The close association of church sites and Middle Saxon settlements was first noticed by Wade-Martins in his study of the Launditch Hundred in 1970s (Wade-Martins 1980b). Here, in a selective rather than systematic fieldwalking exercise, Middle Saxon settlements were discovered beside parish churches in twelve of the sixteen parishes examined. In all these cases, such occupation was visible because, as at Heckingham, later changes in the pattern of settlement left the church isolated in the midst of arable fields. In two of the four cases in which Wade Martins failed to find evidence for Middle Saxon occupation beside the church, this was probably because, unusually for the area studied, it was surrounded to some extent by modern housing, or by other forms of non-arable land-use.

In Norfolk, as elsewhere in England, the decisive break in the pattern of settlement thus seems to have occurred in the seventh century, rather than at the end of the Roman period. Why such a dramatic change occurred is unclear. We can speculate that, in some way, it was related to the changes in society incident upon the transition from tribal territories to royal estates. The increasing power of the Wuffingas, and of the nobles who constituted their retinue, may have encouraged a determination to maximise the productive potential of land (Hodges 1989: 62). In the case of Hales, Loddon, and Heckingham, effort was concentrated on the arable potential of the lighter clay soils, probably because of the proximity of a major estate centre at Loddon. In other places, as we have seen, place-name evidence suggests that settlements concentrated on other kinds of specialised economic production.

So far we have talked only of large, economically self-sufficient estates. In some parts of the county, however, extensive areas (rather than individual sub-units of estates) seem to have been devoted to the production of specialised commodities. The silt Fens of Marshland are one example. Here, settlement dwindled (without perhaps disappearing altogether) at the end of the Roman period, but reappeared during Middle Saxon times. Seven definite and two possible sites were discovered as a result of Bob Silvester's fieldwalking survey here, 'spread in an arc across the width of Marshland'. 'The regular spacing of these spreads of debris is evident: for the six sites between West Walton and Hay Green, intervals of 1.5–2 kilometres indicate that this distribution was to some extent ordered' (Silvester 1988: 157).

Large amounts of bone debris recovered from these sites suggests that they were probably exploiting the rich grass of the new marshland. Another area of specialised grazing estates might have existed on the edges of the Broadland estuary, on the former island of Flegg and on the adjacent marsh islands and peninsulas. These areas have not, to date, been subject to systematic fieldwalking surveys but, as we have seen, chance finds suggest that they were sparsely inhabited in Romano-British and pagan Saxon times. The pre-Danish place-names and elements here hint at their function as specialised grazing areas: Horsey, 'the horse island'; Bastwick, 'the grazing farm where lime-bark is stored'; Winterton, the winter *tūn*, and Somerton, the summer *tūn*. The first element of Stokesby is *stoc*, 'an outlying grazing farm' (Mills 1991).

In the absence of excavations on Middle Saxon rural settlements in the county we know little about the estate centres, still
less about their outlying dependencies. Only North Elmham has
been excavated on a large scale, and as this was the probable seat
of the bishopric it may be atypical. Excavations in the area to
the south of the church revealed a number of phases of Saxon
occupation (Wade-Martins 1980a). The first, consisting of two
small buildings and a possible bakehouse, may date to the late
eighth century; the major phase of Middle Saxon occupation,
however, was more impressive. It was represented by parallel
ditches defining unmetalled roads, and by a number of small,
two-roomed buildings and wells. The regular layout of the
property-boundaries suggests that the settlement may have been
planned. A timber from one of the wells gave a dendrochrono-
logical date of 794, while two *sceattas* also imply an eighth-
century date. Surprisingly, other artefacts were few in number,
but included a number of silver objects (including a decorated
strap, perhaps from the edge of a box or shrine, and a fragment
of a mount, probably from a book) and sherds of imported
pottery. There was, however, little Ipswich Ware. The bones
excavated from this phase included those of cattle, sheep, and
pigs, the latter presumably fattened in the extensive woods still
attached to the estate in 1066. The fact that three quarters of
the sheep were fully grown suggests that part of the estate was
involved in large-scale wool production.

In search of the great estates

In the absence of early charters it is very difficult to reconstruct
the pattern of early estates in Norfolk. In a few cases, their
presence is suggested by the names of parishes and the configuration of their boundaries. The Burnhams – a group of seven,
formerly nine, parishes in the north-west of the county – are
the most striking case. There can be little doubt that Burnham
Overy, Burnham Thorpe, Burnham Deepdale, Burnham Ulph,
Burnham Westgate, Burnham Norton, and Burnham Sutton once
formed a single territorial unit, covering an area of nearly 40
square kilometres. At the time of Domesday, their combined
recorded population was 133, implying a real population of at
least 600. These parishes lie in the lower reaches of the river

Burn, the name of which is almost certainly a back-formation from Burnham, which itself means, simply, 'river estate' (Mills 1991). The names Norton – 'the north *tūn*' – and Sutton – 'the south *tūn*' clearly suggest subsidiary establishments within the larger *hām*. The name Overy – *ofer ie*, 'over the water' – also implies a settlement subsidiary to somewhere else. Overy lies on the eastern side of the river Burn. In medieval times, the largest settlement in the Burnhams area lay on the opposite bank, where a sizeable nucleation – now known as Burnham Market – developed between the churches of Burnham Westgate and Burnham Ulph, probably following the establishment of a market some time before 1209 (Dymond 1985: 159). But field-walking has revealed the presence of a substantial Early and Middle Saxon settlement some 400 metres to the east of Burnham Ulph church: the suffixes 'Norton', 'Sutton', and Overy probably relate to this, rather than to the present village nucleus at Burnham Market.

The Burnhams are unusual: in most cases the process of estate fission led to the loss of such shared estate names. We can, however, often detect traces of early estate organisation in medieval documents. One useful approach is to examine Domesday for evidence of connections between manors, or vills, which might represent residual survivals of more ancient relationships. Sometimes, Domesday describes a holding as a 'berewick', that is, an outlying estate, attached to somewhere else. In some parts of the country such connections are very ancient, the berewick representing a specialised farming establishment still attached to the parent *caput*, but isolated from it by the alienation of intervening territories (Stafford 1985: 30). In Norfolk, however, few such connections seem to be ancient. Often the berewick is too far away to have ever formed a functioning economic sub-unit of an estate: Caston was a berewick of Fakenham, but lay more than 30 kilometres away and separated by three hundreds. Many berewicks, and especially those attached to royal manors, seem to have been relatively recent attachments, for administrative purposes. Such connections were still being forged in the late eleventh century: Alfsi added Blo Norton to Lopham 'as a berewick' after 1066.

More interesting are the Domesday entries that tell us that the soke, *soca*, of a vill or its inhabitants lies in another place.

Usually the soke centre is a hundredal manor, the principal royal vill in a hundred. *Soc* in this context seems to have meant the right to exercise justice over a person, and to receive any profits accruing from this. In origin, however, it included a wider range of obligations, customs, and duties which had originally been due to the king, but which – as estates had been alienated by the Crown – were often now owed to someone else (Scammell 1974: 524–7). Such archaic dues were owed by a category of individuals Domesday calls *sochemanni*, 'sokemen', peasant farmers who were listed as the inhabitants of a manor, but separately from the bond tenants – the villeins, bordars, and slaves. These people seem to have been descendants of the broad mass of the semi-free cultivators of the great Middle Saxon estates (Stafford 1985: 158–61). As these had been alienated from the Crown, such people had often passed with the land on which they dwelt out of direct royal control, into other hands, and now owed their 'customary dues' – to use the phrase repeated *ad nauseam* in the pages of the Domesday Survey – to some local landowner, although some residual duties might still be rendered to the old estate centre. Thus, for example, at Little Snarehill six sokemen were held by Ailwin with all customary dues, but 'each one has always paid 4d for carrying services in the king's manor of Kenninghall and the king has the six forfeitures of them'.

In some cases, it appears that more complete authority had been maintained over the sokemen dwelling in outlying, alienated areas of estates. In such cases, the individuals in question might well appear in the entry for the old estate centre, although they actually dwelt in some other vill. This is seldom immediately apparent from a reading of Domesday, and is usually only revealed in later documents. One interesting and instructive case is Gimmingham, in North Erpingham hundred in north–east Norfolk. The only connections between Gimingham and other vills in the vicinity expressly stated in the survey are those with Knapton and Sidestrand, but in both cases the association is evidently a recent one. Of Sidestrand we read that 'Waleran delivered this to make up the manor of Gimingham'; while Knapton was 'delivered to make up Gimingham'. But later medieval documents make it clear that the 'soke of Gimingham' was a functioning economic and jurisdictional entity embracing several neighbouring settlements. Thus, for example, a Crown

Plea Roll of 1288 refers to 'all the free tenants of the soke of Gimingham, in which is contained the eight villages of Gymingham, Monesle [Mundesley], Southrepps, Sidestrand, Trunch, Northrepps, and Trimmingham' (Rye 1883: 229). Now Trimingham is absent from the pages of the survey and was, therefore, presumably still part of Gimingham, its tenants and other assets listed there. But North and South Repps, Mundesley, Sidestrand, and Trunch all appear as separate vills in Domesday, each with its own church. Domesday records that in 1066, Gimingham had been held by 'Rathi, one free man', as two carucates of land. Its population was listed as twelve villeins, forty bordars, two slaves, together with twenty-three sokemen: in all, seventy-seven recorded individuals. North and South Repps, Mundsley, Sidestrand, and Trunch together contained only sixty-eight individuals. Significantly, no sokemen were recorded in any of these vills and we may confidently assume that they were all entered under Gimingham. Later in the Middle Ages a large number of manors could be found in these vills: Colmans in Gimingham and Trunch, Spriggs in Mundesley, North Hall in Repps, and others. Yet all continued to owe suit of court, and sometimes services and renders, to the Gimingham manor (Hoare 1918).

Medieval documents show that the Gimingham soke had an elaborate organisation. The reeve of the soke presided over eight *wickeners*, *wigners*, or *wigeners*, elected annually by each vill. These were responsible for collecting the rents, amercements, and other dues owed by the tenants, and the village or part of the village for which each *wigener* was responsible was called the *shift* (Hoare 1918: 130–5).

There are other places in which medieval and even post-medieval documents suggest the existence of territorial connec-tions which Domesday largely passes over in silence. Domesday tells us that the vill of Long Stratton – which was, by 1066, divided between a large number of separate landholders – contained twenty-seven sokemen. Later documents indicate its archaic importance more clearly. In the medieval period, two superior leet courts were held at Stratton each year, and – if an account of events in April 1644 is any indication of medieval practice – these were attended by the churchwarden and four men from each of the parishes of Stratton, Morningthorpe,

Carleton, Tibenham, Moulton, Wacton, Tasburgh, Fritton, and Bunwell. In all these places, moreover, Stratton had important rights over the common land, and superior jurisdiction over the manorial lords (Blomefield 1805, V: 187–9).

We can use a combination of later documents, Domesday, and place-names to reconstruct, in some detail, the pattern of early estates in the hundred of Forehoe in central Norfolk. This contained Wymondham, by Norfolk standards a massive parish of 4,243 hectares. At the time of Domesday this vill comprised a single manor (with one separate listed 'holding' consisting of a group of attached free men), and contained no less than eighty-eight sokemen. The total recorded population of the vill, at least 350, implies a real population of around 1,500. The configuration of parish boundaries strongly suggests that the small adjacent vill of Crownthorpe had once been a part of Wymondham, but otherwise it appears to have been an early estate which had not undergone any significant degree of fission, in part due to the fact that it had remained in the hands of the Crown. In the Middle Ages Wymondham was reckoned a half-hundred in its own right, jurisdictionally separate from the rest of Forehoe hundred (Blomefield 1805, II: 498–534). The hundred itself was attached to the royal manor of Hingham, some 9 kilometres to the west of Wymondham, and Domesday explicitly tells us that the *soca* of Deopham and Wicklewood lay there. The survey does not explicitly mention the *soca* of any other place or group in Forehoe, but later medieval documents show that the jurisdictional arrangements of the hundred were complex. An inquest of 1242 found that the manor of Costessey, in the extreme north-east of the hundred, had the same liberties and exemptions as Wymondham, and that a number of local lords did their suit to Costessey rather than to the hundred (Blomefield 1805, II: 406).

Costessey manor, and its various appendages, is discussed in some detail by Domesday. It was held by Count Alan in 1086, but before the Conquest had formed part of the holding of Gyrth, along with its berewicks of Bawburgh and Honingham Thorpe. Domesday tells us – as it often does – that forty-four sokemen 'lie in' (*iacent*) the manor. Unusually, however, it expressly states that these men did not actually live in Costessey, but that 'The land of the sokemen . . . is Easton; and Honingham, which a certain one of these sokemen holds.' Domesday also informs us that one of Gyrth's sokemen held Wramplingham; that seven dwelt in Barford and two in Marlingford; and that six sokemen in Brandon Parva, four in Runhall, three in Carleton Forefoe, and one in Honingham were in the valuation of Costessey. But it is later medieval and post-medieval documents which clearly reveal the importance of Costessey as, in Blomefield's words, 'one of the largest manors in the county, extending itself into most of the adjacent villages, over which it hath the superiority, in as ample a manner as the lord of the hundred hath over the rest' (Blomefield 1805, II: 406).

The places mentioned in medieval documents as dependent on or attached to Costessey duplicate, for the most part, those mentioned in Domesday: in 1547 the dependencies of Costessey were listed as Bowthorpe, Easton, Colton, Marlingford, Bawburgh, Honingam, and Honingham Thorpe (Blomefield 1805, II: 415). In the reign of Edward I several inhabitants of Wramplingham were impleded for cutting down wood 'as what they could not do, it being parcel of the manor of Costessey, and a member thereof' (Blomefield 1805, II: 409).

These archaic, residual connections suggest that the hundred of Forehoe originally consisted of – perhaps we should say, was constructed out of – three large estates, each covering an area of more than 40 square kilometres, based on Hingham, Wymondham, and Costessey (Figure 4.3). Their boundaries appear to correspond to extensive areas of commonland which survived into the eighteenth century, and to clusters of place-names indicating the former existence of woodland. Thus a great string of vills bearing names with woodland associations ran along the watershed between the Wymondham and Hingham estates: Morley St Peter and Morley St Botolph (*mor lēah*, 'the wood on the moor'); Kimberley ('Cyneburg's wood'); and Wicklewood (*wice, lēah, wudu*; 'the wood by the clearing with the wych-elms') (Mills 1991). The southern boundary of the Hingham estate, which coincides with the southern boundary of the hundred of Forehoe, is similarly marked by a string of woodland names, running from Morley St Peter through Hockwood Common and Deopham Stolland (*lúndr*, 'a grove') to White (probably from *þveit*, 'clearing') Green.

Traces of Wymondham's archaic system of organisation survived into the medieval and post-medieval periods, despite the

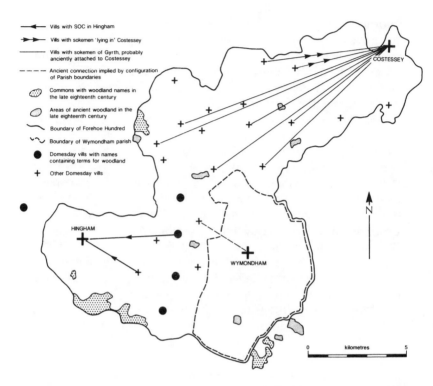

Vills with SOC in Hingham

Vills with sokemen 'lying in' Costessey

Vills with sokemen of Gyrth, probably anciently attached to Costessey

Ancient connection implied by configuration of Parish boundaries

Commons with woodland names in the late eighteenth century

Areas of ancient woodland in the late eighteenth century

Boundary of Forehoe Hundred

Boundary of Wymondham parish

Domesday vills with names containing terms for woodland

Other Domesday vills

COSTESSEY

HINGHAM

WYMONDHAM

N

0   kilometres   5

Fig. 4.3   Forehoe Hundred: the pattern of ancient estates

progressive fragmentation of the main manor in the decades after the Norman Conquest, the founding of Wymondham Abbey in 1107, and the early development of the vill as an important urban centre (the market was established by 1137). The vill was divided into four divisions called, as in Gimingham, 'shifts': Norton, Suton, Silfield and Wattlefield. These divisions cut right across the system of manorial organisation, so that the records of the eight principal manors all operated within this basic fourfold structure (Barringer, forthcoming).

Suton, Silfield, and Wattlefield still survive as hamlets: Norton no longer appears on the map, and probably occupied part of the present urban area of Wymondham, as perhaps did Downham, another settlement referred to in medieval documents, and sometimes equated with Norton. Place-name evidence suggests that other settlements in the vill, which survive today as farms or hamlets, already existed by the end of the Saxon period. Burfield and Stanfield both sound like Old English settlement names which, like Silfield and Wattlefield, incorporate the term *feld*. The name of Brathwayte Hall, 2 kilometres to the east of the town, clearly incorporates the Danish term *þveit*, 'clearing'. All suggest settlements in a wooded environment, and medieval and later documents make it clear that there were indeed sizeable areas of woodland, woodpasture, and commonland all around the southern periphery of the parish, on the level clay plateau in which these places were located. In medieval times all had arable open fields adjacent to them. In the Middle Saxon period, while they may have farmed on their own account, their main function may well have been the exploitation of the estate's woodland and grazing resources. Wattlefield, probably 'the *feld* by the coppice', may suggest one of the ways in which this wooded fringe was exploited. The other settlements within the estate – Norton, Suton, Downham – occupied the lower ground, adjacent to the better drained soils on the side of the valley of the Tiffey and its tributaries. These, we might suppose, were more geared to arable production.

Once the archaic structure of the hundred of Forehoe is recognised, it is possible to see, albeit indistinctly, the configuration of neighbouring estates. Thus the area to the north of the Hingham estate was probably occupied by a territory based on East Dereham, in the adjacent hundred of Mitford. This, as we shall see, was apparently the location of a nunnery established by Withburga, the daughter of King Anna, in the seventh century. By the time of Domesday, it was in the hands of the Abbey of Ely. Post-Conquest tradition asserted that it had obtained the estate in 976, at which time it was assessed at $40\frac{1}{2}$ hides – implying a much more extensive area than that occupied by the vill at the time of Domesday (Blomefield 1805 II: 431). In 1066 the hundred of Mitford was attached to it; Hoe, immediately to the north, was still reckoned its dependency. Further north, the next great estate – over the watershed into Launditch hundred – must surely have been centred on North Elmham, where the bishopric of the North Folk was established in the 680s. Elmham was still a large estate in 1066, and contained twenty-four sokemen. All or most of the neighbouring parishes of Brisley and

Bilney, which are not mentioned in Domesday, seem to have been included within it. Worthing, too, is omitted from the survey, and may have been part of Elmham, while Beetley was its berewick, or outlying estate.

Large numbers of sokemen attached to manors and vills are, in most of the cases so far discussed, an important clue to their former role as major estate centres. But they are not an infallible guide, because fair numbers of such people can often be found dwelling in the vills immediately adjacent to such places, occupying the former core areas of estate arable. Thus, for example, the existence of twenty-five sokemen in Deopham is really an indication of the early importance of the adjacent vill of Hingham. Nevertheless, combined with other scraps of evidence, concentrations of sokemen do allow us to suggest more possible early estate centres. Most of the manors to which, by 1066, hundreds were attached contained significant numbers of sokemen, and must surely represent ancient estate centres: Buckenham (hundredal manor for Shropham) had 71; Mileham (Launditch) 20; Wighton (North Greenhoe) 19; Foulsham (Eynesford) 30; and Saham (Wayland) 51 (Cam 1944: 75–6). The royal manor of Southmere is perhaps a similar case. This is now lost in the vill of Docking, but was probably the main manor in the hundred of the same name: it contained fifty-two sokemen. Earsham (hundredal manor for Earsham) and Kenninghall (for Guiltcross) had fewer – eleven and twelve respectively – but there were, significantly, large numbers in the adjacent vills. Thus Denton contained a further twelve owing 'customary dues' in Earsham, while Banham, the vill next to Kenninghall, contained twenty-eight and, as we have seen, those dwelling in Snarehill still owed carrying services there.

Another interesting group of vills with large numbers of sokemen comprises those which, while not hundredal manors in 1066, seem nevertheless to have been of early administrative importance because they gave their names to hundreds. Thus South Walsham contained 43 sokemen, Blofield 48, Happisburgh (Happing) 21, Taverham 25, Tunstead 24. Loddon contained only 16, but a further 6 dwelling in neighbouring vills were included in its valuation.

Some places do not fit in to this pattern. Holt, for example, gave its name to the hundred in which it lay but had no listed sokemen. It was, however, an important royal manor, with out-lying berewicks containing small groups of sokemen. Shropham also gave its name to a hundred yet contained only two sokemen, probably because its role had been taken over at an early date – along with its sokemen – by Buckenham. Wimbotsham, to which the hundred of Clackclose was attached, had none, while East Dereham – which we have already discussed – had only twelve. In both these cases, the hundred had been granted to ecclesiastical houses (Ramsey and Ely respectively) at an early date, and we might suspect here some systematic policy of downgrading the status of cultivators to the level of bondmen. Certainly, there is some evidence that on ecclesiastical estates in the later Saxon period sokemen might be obliged to render services little dif-ferent from those of villeins or bordars: on the Abbey of Ely's estate at Feltwell forty-five sokemen were obliged to plough, weed, and harvest the abbot's land 'as often as he commanded' (Blomefield 1805, II: 188).

There are a number of other places where large numbers of sokemen seem to indicate archaic estate centres. Hethersett, for example, contained no less than eighty sokemen: Blomefield states (although he gives no supporting evidence) that this was the chief manor for the hundred of Humbleyard (Blomefield 1805, V: 23–4). The great royal manor of Aylsham contained sixty sokemen, and the Domesday entry for Tuttington informs us that its *soca* 'was in Aylsham in the time of King Edward'. Richard I confirmed to the monks at Bury an income from rents 'in the soke of Aylsham', and in 1272 the hundreds of North and South Erpingham were attached to it (Blomefield 1805, VI: 283). Cawston contained ten sokemen but a further twenty-three were 'held before 1066 in . . . Marsham and Blickling': a 1222 Patent Roll refers to the *hundredum de Kaustun*, the 'hundred of Cawston', a territorial unit never mentioned again (Anderson 1934: 64). Ludham contained no less than 135 sokemen: a grant of *c.* 1180 refers to land held 'in the soke of Ludham' (West 1932: 117). Stow Bedon contained twenty-nine sokemen: in 1086 there were disputes concerning the church at Griston and land at Breccles, both claimed 'as part of Stow Bedon'. Creake, a vill with a name (as we have seen) which incorporates a probable Old Welsh element, contained no less than thirty-one sokemen.

Other possible examples of early estate centres include the

Acres (19 sokemen), Wroxham (21), Langley (25, but others in outliers); Brooke (47); Waxham (25); Marham (27); Ringstead (28); Feltwell (75); Heacham (35); Lopham (23); Massingham (25 or more); and Snettisham (13, but others in outliers of this great royal estate). Fakenham, too, is a probable example: a royal manor with few listed sokemen, but with large numbers dwelling in adjacent berewicks of Dunton (16) and Pudding Norton (7). The reader will have observed that almost all these places have names which are either of a topographic nature, or incorporate the element *hām*.

Further research in medieval and post-medieval documents would, no doubt, throw further light on the extent and organisation of these putative estates, and bring others to light. At present, all we can say is that there is abundant evidence for the existence of large 'multiple estates' in the county; and that every hundred seems to have contained two or three, giving a probable total of between fifty and a hundred large estates, each embracing an area of between 40 and 100 square kilometres.

These estates seem to have replaced, as suggested above, an earlier pattern of largely independent tribal territories. Not surprisingly, some seem to have developed directly out of them, either as their chief lineages became members of the Wuffinga's retinue, or as they were conquered and absorbed as functioning units into the Wuffinga's patrimony. The evidence for this is archaeological. We have already argued that the close relationship of fifth-century cremation cemeteries to the decaying geography of Roman Britain suggests some measure of territorial continuity. But many of these Early Saxon 'central places' also relate closely to Middle Saxon estate centres. Spong Hill not only lies within 4 kilometres of the Roman settlement at Billingford: it is also within the same parish as, and some 2.5 kilometres to the south of, the probable site of the cathedral established to serve the North Folk in the 680s. The pagan cemetery in Great Walsingham not only lies next to a large Romano-British settlement: it also lies within 1,500 metres of the royal manor of Wighton, the hundredal manor for North Greenhoe. The hundred of Shropham was, by 1066, attached to the royal manor of Buckenham, but its name suggests that it may have developed out of a territory based on the eponymous vill; this contains a substantial fifth-century cemetery. In the south of the county, the half-hundred of Earsham had its jurisdictional centre at the vill of the same name: this lies only 4.5 kilometres from the early cremation cemetery at Ditchingham. Gimingham lies 3.5 kilometres from the cremation cemetery at Mundesley, Fakenham only 3 kilometres from that at Pensthorpe, Taverham 2.5 kilometres from that at Drayton. Sometimes, and not surprisingly given the uneven and haphazard nature of the survival and discovery of the archaeological evidence, the pagan Saxon link is lost, but the proximity of estate centres to important Roman settlements – nucleated villages and small towns – remains suggestive. Thus, in particular, Saham Tony, the hundredal manor for Wayland Hundred, lies little more than a kilometre from the large settlement at Woodcock Hall; Aylsham, hundredal manor for South Erpingham, lies some 4 kilometres from the town at Brampton; Diss, which gave its name to the eponymous hundred, less than three from the important settlement at Scole; while Long Stratton lies less than a kilometre from the roadside settlement in the south of the same parish.

The evidence is not conclusive, but it is suggestive: and what makes it particularly so is the fact that the inhumation cemeteries of the sixth and seventh centuries display a very different pattern of association. Not only are they less closely related to sites of late Roman importance; few seem to be close to the centres of our Middle Saxon estates. Those at Thetford and Kenninghall certainly break this general rule: but most of the others, places like Morningthorpe, Grimston, North Runcton, Tottenhill, Northwold, Mundford, and Foulden, were always of peripheral importance.

The extent of continuity over this immense period should not be exaggerated. Some cremation cemeteries display a relationship with probable Middle Saxon estate centres, but not, apparently, with significant Romano-British sites: Sedgeford, close to Heacham, is one example. A few show no clear association with either: those at Saxlingham, Wolterton, Smallburgh, and East Walton, for example. Patterns of territorial organisation no doubt went through many changes during the Early and Middle Saxon period, first as tribal groups were extinguished or amalgamated, later as royal administrators altered the boundaries and organisation of estates. Nevertheless, there does seem to be some thread of continuity running through this long period. In ways which we do not, as yet, fully understand, the cremation cemeteries of the fifth and sixth centuries seem to represent the stepping-stones from the world of late antiquity to that of the early Middle Ages.

1 Warham Camp, the most impressive Iron Age fort in Norfolk

2 Venta Icenorum, capital of the Roman *civitas*, five kilometres south of Norwich

3 Burgh Castle: the south wall of the Saxon Shore fort of *Gariannonum*

4 The Peddars Way Roman road near Harpley

5 The Bicchamditch: an aerial view of Norfolk's most impressive linear earthwork, probably constructed in the sixth or seventh century

6 William Faden's map of Norfolk, published in 1797, clearly shows the extent of commons and of common-edge settlement in the county before the impact of Parliamentary enclosure

7 Great Snoring: the migration of settlement to the margins of commons in the early Middle Ages frequently left churches marginalised or isolated in the midst of fields

8 Itteringham: an aerial photograph, taken in 1986, reveals an apsidal church, almost certainly the lost church of St Nicholas, one of two parish churches in the medieval vill

9 Great Melton: here, as at a number of other places in the county, two churches stand in the same churchyard

10 Reepham: originally, the parish churches of Reepham, Hackford and Whitwell shared a single churchyard in the centre of this small market town; Hackford church was destroyed in the sixteenth century, although traces of it can still be found to the south of Whitwell church

11 North Creake: an early seventeenth-century map shows the arable open-fields around the village. In the middle ages the vast majority of land in Norfolk lay in open-fields of various kinds

12 New Buckenham: the castle and planned town established by the d'Albinis in the twelfth century

13 Castle Rising: the great keep of the d'Albinis' castle

14 Fritton Common: before the enclosures of the late eighteenth and nineteenth centuries, common-edge settlements were ubiquitous in Norfolk, especially in the east of the county

15 Egmere, one of a number of deserted medieval villages on the dry interfluve between the valleys of the Burn and Stiffkey in north Norfolk

16 Hales church, a particularly fine example of an early twelfth-century parish church with characteristic round flint tower

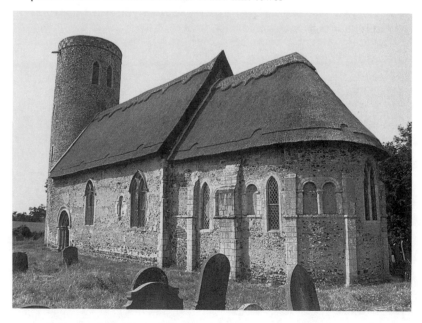

5

An age of expansion

The Viking incursions

The Mercian domination of East Anglia came to an end in 825, when King Æthelstan successfully rebelled against his overlords (Kirby 1991). He was supported by the West Saxons, now the rising power in England. Whether the East Anglian kingdom would, in time, have fallen under their domination we cannot say, for the political history of England was thrown on to an entirely new course by the arrival of the Danes.

According to the *Anglo-Saxon Chronicle* Viking forces first raided Norfolk in 865: they were probably led by Ivar the Boneless, as Aethelweard, writing in the late tenth century, referred to them as 'the fleets of the tyrant Ivarr' (Campbell 1962: 35). There is some evidence that the Danes under Ivar established puppet kings in the kingdom: the names of Æthelred and Oswald appear on coins apparently struck in the region in the period after Edmund's death (Grierson & Blackburn 1986: 294). In 869 the Danish forces took winter quarters at Thetford, and defeated and killed King Edmund. Ten years later events took a still more serious turn: 'The host went from Cirencester into East Anglia, and occupied that land, and shared it out' (Garmonsay 1953: 76).

The following decades saw a series of campaigns between the West Saxon kings (the only surviving indigenous dynasty) and the

Danish 'hosts' settled in the north and east of England. East Anglia remained under Scandinavian control until 917 when, to quote the *Chronicle* again, 'King Edward went with West Saxon levies to Colchester . . . many people, both from East Anglia and from Essex, who had previously been under Danish domination submitted to him, and the entire Danish host in East Anglia swore union with him' (Garmonsay 1953: 103).

Liberation did not lead to the restoration of an independent kingdom, however. East Anglia was absorbed into the growing West Saxon state. But it did not entirely lose its identity. Norfolk and Suffolk were ruled by the *ealdorman*, later earl, of East Anglia (Loyn 1984: 132). It was not until after the Norman Conquest that each of the two counties received its own earl. At the time of the Conquest, therefore, Norfolk had still not emerged as a distinct territorial unit, and although the two East Anglian counties were treated separately by Domesday, anomalies along their common boundary attest their former connection (Warner 1988: 11; Planche 1865). Diss gave its name to a Norfolk hundred, but lay in the Suffolk hundred of Hartismere; parts of the Suffolk vill of Mendham were to remain in Norfolk until the passing of the Divided Parishes and Poor Law Amendment Act of 1876.

Danish raiding resumed in the 980s, and in 1004 a fleet commanded by the Danish king Swein sacked Norwich. The Danes went on to Thetford, which was also burnt, but somewhere near here they were confronted by the local militia led by the East Anglian earl, Ulfketel Snelling: 'and there was a fierce encounter and great slaughter on each side. There were slain the chief men of East Anglia, but if they had been up to strength the army would never have got back to their ships: as they themselves admitted, they had never met with harder hand-play in England than Ulfketel gave them' (Garmonsway 1953: 136). The Danes returned in 1009, and in 1010 Thetford was sacked and the East Anglians defeated at the great battle of *Ringmer*, probably Ringmere in Wretham, north of Thetford (Garmonsway 1953: 140; Clarke 1937: 40). In 1013 all the people in the Danish-settled areas of England surrendered to Swein, and the English king Ethelred fled abroad. Swein died in 1013, but his son Cnut invaded. He first divided the country between himself and Ethelred's successor Edmund. Later he took the whole kingdom.

By that time he was already king of Denmark; from 1028 he was also king of Norway (Fisher 1973: 30–319).

Norfolk thus experienced two separate waves of Scandinavian conquest, the second of which placed it centrally within a political empire embracing both sides of the North Sea. Scandinavian influence was strong in the county during the tenth and eleventh centuries: this is clear from the large numbers of Scandinavian personal names which we find in Domesday, and from the Scandinavian words in Norfolk dialect. Like most of Late Saxon England, Norfolk was, in cultural terms, 'Anglo-Scandinavian'.

Whether there was a major influx of Scandinavian settlers is rather less certain. The *Chronicle*'s statement that the Danes 'shared out' the county in 879 need imply no more than its division among a small conquering elite (Davis 1955). The 'host' whose movements are described in tones of fascinated horror by the *Chronicle* was probably a fairly small band of fighting men, many of whom presumably returned to Denmark when the conquest was completed (Sawyer 1958). There is no documentary evidence to suggest a large-scale peasant immigration, and in Norfolk, as elsewhere in England, archaeological evidence for such a folk-movement is meagre. There are, it is true, many items of metalwork now known from the county which are of Scandinavian origin, or Scandinavian style: the gilded bronze mount from Bylaugh; the trefoil brooches from Bircham, Costessey, and Heacham (Margeson 1991a and b). But these need indicate nothing more than trade with Scandinavia, or the presence of a Danish elite and the consequent prevalence of Danish taste. A small conquering group, rather than a mass of land-hungry peasants, is suggested by the virtual absence of distinctive pagan Viking burials, with grave goods and under burial mounds, of the kind common in Denmark in this period. It is sometimes suggested that this absence reflects the rapid conversion of the Viking armies, following Guthrum's baptism in 878: but given the tenacity of paganism in the Viking homelands in the face of Christian evangelisation a century later, this in itself suggests that the Vikings formed a small minority of the county's population (Hodges 1989: 154).

There are a number of Danish place-names in the county (Mills 1991; Schram 1961). Forty Domesday vills are called *þorp*, a term meaning 'hamlet' or 'dependent settlement'; some twenty-

---

107

E

one feature the element *bý*, 'village' or 'settlement'; and a number incorporate other Scandinavian elements, most notably *kirkja*, 'church'; *lundr*, 'grove'; *skogr*, 'small wood'; and *pveite*, 'clearing'. Several, like Carleton, have names which appear to be English in origin, but show strong Scandinavian influence: many others have English suffixes (especially *tūn*), but prefixes formed by a Scandinavian personal name. All these names have traditionally been interpreted as evidence for large-scale Danish immigration (Stenton 1942).

Places with names containing Scandinavian elements tend to cluster in certain areas of the county. Ignoring for a moment *þorp* names, the most notable concentration is on the former island of Flegg (itself a Danish name) (Figure 5.1). Here the majority of place-names have the suffix *-bý*; Ashby, Billockby, Clippesby, Hemsby, Herringby, Mautby, Oby, Ormesby, Rollesby, Scratby, Stokesby, and Thrigby. Another, slightly more diffuse concentration can be found along the southern bank of the river Yare, and round along the northern bank of the Waveney: Kirby Bedon, Rockland St Mary (*lúndr*), Ashby St Mary, Carleton St Peter, Thorpe, Haddiscoe (*skógr*), Aldeby, Kirby Cane, and Thwaite. Another smaller cluster occurs around the headwaters of the main tributaries of the Bure, between North Walsham and Corpusty; and a fourth, which includes Ashby, Wilby, and the Rocklands (All Saints, St Mary, and St Peter), in Shropham hundred, around the headwaters of the river Thet (Figure 5.1). This pattern is not quite as haphazard as it first appears. All these clusters lie within the 'peripheral zone' of Roman-British and early Saxon settlement, that swathe of sparsely-settled country running along the central watershed and down the east coast (compare with Figures 2.5, 3.1, and 3.2). It is possible that Viking peasant immigrants were encouraged to settle in these remote spots (for these can hardly have been the homes of the Viking elite, who presumably resided at the major estate centres – all of which maintained their English names). But there is a simpler, and more likely explanation. The major concentrations of Danish place-names probably indicate not areas of immigrant settlement, but places first established or (more probably) first attaining tenurial independence in the period after the late ninth century, when many of the county's elite will have been Scandinavian speakers. Many of these places, and many

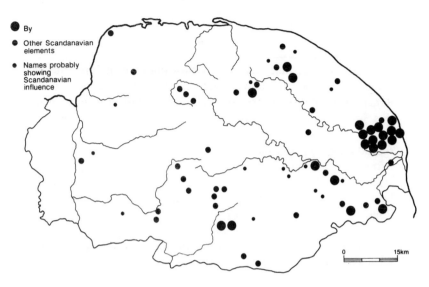

Fig. 5.1 The distribution of major place-names incorporating Scandinavian elements (excluding *þorp*, and personal names)

bearing English suffixes like *tūn*, have as their first element a Scandinavian personal name, but this again does not necessarily mean that they had any connection with Viking settlers. Scandinavian personal names were widely adopted in eastern England by the indigenous population, emulating the social elite in precisely the same way that local peasants, in the twelfth and thirteenth centuries, happily gave their children such Norman names as William, Henry, or Stephen.

Places with names containing the element *þorp* are widely and evenly spread across the centre of the county. They were clearly, for the most part, places of minor importance. Domesday refers to some of them simply as 'thorpe', and many are today distinguished by the name of an adjacent village (Honingham Thorpe, Gayton Thorpe, Burnham Thorpe, etc.). Thorpe appears to have passed into local dialect as the term for a minor settlement, and cannot indicate the location of ethnic Scandinavian communities, since new places with this name were being established in the county well after the Viking settlements, and indeed, after the

Norman Conquest: Thorpe Green in Weasenham St Peter, for example, did not exist as a settlement before the twelfth century (Wade-Martins 1980b: 69).

It should be stressed that many historians would strongly disagree with these arguments. They would contend that a major influx of Scandinavian settlers did occur, and would point to the Scandinavian words used in Norfolk's minor place-names, such a *gata*, 'street', or *bekkr* 'stream', arguing that the widespread adoption of such terms suggests something more than the cultural dominance of a landowning elite. More research is certainly needed into this complex topic. Whatever the scale of Scandinavain settlement in the county, however, there is no doubt that many other forces were moulding its character in the late Saxon period: in particular, economic growth, population increase, the expansion of cultivation and, above all, the progressive fission of the ancient estates.

Landscape and settlement

Norfolk was England's most populous county in 1066. Around 27,000 separate individuals are listed in Domesday, implying an actual population of some 150,000, a density of around 15 per square kilometre (Ellis 1883: 470). No less than 726 separate vills are recorded, the vast majority of which survive as modern ecclesiastical parishes, although a small proportion cannot now be identified (Dymond 1985: 97–100). These were mostly small places, little more than single farmsteads, like *Appethorpe* in Forehoe, or *Halas* in Depwade; most have probably survived as farms or small hamlets under different names. *Middeltūna* in Depwade, for example, can be identified with the hamlet of Bustard's Green in Forncett (Davenport 1906). The few medieval vills which Domesday fails to mention, like Worthing or Bilney, almost certainly existed as settlements at the time, but were included within the returns for a neighbouring estate, of which they still formed a part.

Population growth during later Saxon times did not, for the most part, lead to an increase in the number of individual settlements. Instead, existing hamlets and villages simply expanded *in situ*. Wade-Martin's Launditch Survey shows this tendency well. At Horningtoft, Longham, Tittleshall, Sutton, Weasenham,

Wellingham, and Beetley, the main focus of settlement remained where it had been in Middle Saxon times – that is, next to the site now occupied by the parish church – but expanded, sometimes as a kind of ribbon development along lanes which still survive today (Wade-Martins 1980b). In the absence of excavations on Saxon rural sites, we have little information about what such changes in the configurations of surface debris actually mean in terms of the layout of settlements: but at North Elmham, settlement certainly intensified within the excavated area from the end of the tenth century (Wade-Martins 1980a).

Continuity of settlement was usual, but not universal. At Mileham, the village appears to have shifted northwards from around the parish church, to a new site ranged along the east–west road which still forms the main thoroughfare through the village (Wade-Martins 1980b: 41–2). Nevertheless, even here, a single nucleus of Middle Saxon settlement was replaced by a single nucleus of Late Saxon settlement. Moreover, in those few areas of the county in which Middle Saxon settlement seems to have been comparatively dispersed, the Late Saxon period saw the development of a more nucleated pattern. In Marshland, there was 'a clear polarisation of settlement', with the abandonment or contraction of settlements on the less imposing roddons,* and the expansion of a few centres which became the principal medieval foci: places like West Walton, Walpole St Peter, or Tilney All Saints (Silvester 1988: 158).

The Late Saxon settlement pattern was, therefore, essentially one of nucleated settlements, small villages. Yet it was a pattern which, at the time of the Norman Conquest, was on the point of dissolving. Fieldwalking surveys suggest that farmsteads may already have begun to drift away to the edges of greens and commons. But the great diaspora of settlement was, at this time, still in its early stages, and the puzzles that it poses can be left for a later chapter.

Because the settlements listed by Domesday consisted of small nucleations beside parish churches, or (more rarely) at farms or hamlets which still bear their name, it is possible to map in some detail the density of population in 1066 (Figure 5.2). Earlier

---

* A raised bank of silt and gravel running through the peat, marking the line of a former watercourse.

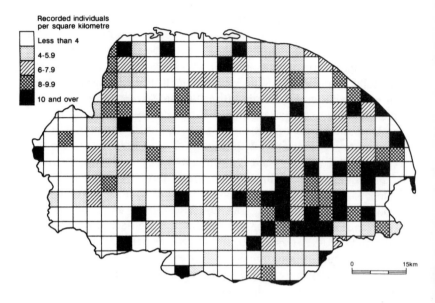

Recorded individuals
per square kilometre

Less than 4

4-5.9

6-7.9

8-9.9

10 and over

0   15km

Fig. 5.2   Norfolk: population density in 1066

attempts to do this, using the hundred as a unit of measurement
and mapping, emphasised the distinction between the heavily-
settled south and east of the county, and the more sparsely-
settled north-west (Darby 1952: 117). Figure 5.2 does not
challenge this distinction, but it does allow us to refine it slightly.
In part, the overall densities in the north–west were lowered by
the absolute absence of settlement from the high, dry interfluves
away from the principal valleys. Where major valleys occur, as
in the Burnhams or the Creakes, population densities were
comparable to those in the south and east of the county. Moreover, mapping by hundreds tends to obscure the fact that not
everywhere in the south and east was equally choked with people.
On the poorly-draining interfluves densities were markedly lower
than in the valleys themselves: settlements on the interfluves
were fewer in number, and less populous, than those located in,
or beside, the major valleys. In both the north-west of the
county, and south-east, we thus see once again the crucial contrast between valley and interfluve, river and watershed, which

was of such vital importance in moulding the character of the county.

And yet even the more remote parts of the interfluves were being opened up for cultivation. Everywhere in Late Saxon Norfolk, land was falling under the plough. Pollen diagrams show an increase in arable farming from Middle Saxon times onwards, and by 1066, to judge from the density of plough-teams recorded by Domesday, more land in the county lay under the plough than anywhere else in England (Bennett 1983; Godwin 1968; Simms 1972; Peglar et al. 1989). Plough-teams, like people, were particularly thick on the ground on the claylands of the south-east (Darby 1952: 113). Here, and elsewhere, many settlements which, in the Middle Saxon period, seem to have been specialised establishments for the exploitation of grazing or woodland, were now as intensively arable as everywhere else.

This emphasis on arable farming did not, of course, mean that animal husbandry was neglected: livestock were essential for traction, and for the maintenance of soil fertility. Not only cattle and oxen but, on the principal demesnes at least, large flocks of sheep were kept, their distribution strongly biased towards the north and west, prefiguring the 'sheep-corn' farming region of later times (Darby 1952: 144–6).

In spite of the extent of cultivation, large areas of woodland still existed in some districts. Norfolk is one of the counties for which Domesday mainly records woodland not in terms of its dimensions or area, but according to the number of swine it could support: the number of pigs that could be run in it during autumn to fatten on beech-mast and acorns (Rackham 1986a: 165, 1980: 119–23). This method of assessment appears to suggest that most woods were being used as woodpastures and swinepastures, rather than being managed as coppice-with-standards, the form of exploitation which became ubiquitous in the region in post-Conquest times. This is because pigs and other animals cause considerable damage to regenerating coppice stools, and the two forms of land use are, in effect, incompatible. In thirty-five places, Domesday tells us that there was more woodland in 1066 than in 1086, and Rackham has suggested that this change reflects not a real reduction in woodland, but an increase in the proportion being coppiced (Rackham 1986b: 120). If this is so, then on the same logic some areas of coppiced woodland may have been omitted entirely from the Survey.

As we shall see, some of the woodland recorded by Domesday belonged to, and therefore appears in the entry for, an estate which lay beyond the vill in which it was physically located. Nevertheless, such anomalies will probably not radically distort the pattern of distribution revealed by Domesday. Figure 5.3 shows, not surprisingly, that the greatest areas of woodland were concentrated along the central watershed, as in Early and Middle Saxon times. Yet Domesday, rather interestingly, does not show those other concentrations which, if we can trust the evidence of place-names, had formerly existed around the edges of the Broads, or in the area to the north of Lynn. Watersheds were now the main determinant of woodland distribution, almost regardless of soils or drift geology: and as in earlier centuries, this was true on a local, as well as regional level. Hempnall lies on the boundary between Depwade and Henstead hundreds: all along the hundred boundary a great swathe of medieval fields bore names indicating the clearance of woodland in early medieval times: much of this was probably the 'woodland for 208 swine' which Domesday records in the various entries for the vill, although some had doubtless disappeared before 1066.

Some areas were thus still well wooded: but on the whole, given the density of its population, Norfolk must have been growing short of wood and timber in the Late Saxon period. It is this, of course, which explains why extensive turbaries developed in the river valleys in the east of the county from the eleventh century onwards, excavations which later flooded, to form the strings of lakes now known as the 'Norfolk Broads'. Perhaps as much as 900 million cubic metres of peat were removed from these during the three or four centuries in which they were in operation (Lambert *et al.* 1960).

The break-up of the great estates

The great density of population was one striking feature of Late Saxon Norfolk. Another was its complex social and tenurial structure. Vills of 'classic' medieval form, containing and coterminous with a single manor, were rare here. A single vill usually embraced a number of estates, each held in 1086 by a different

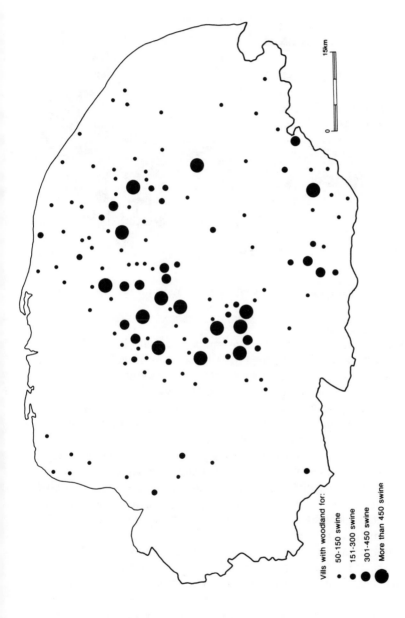

Vills with woodland for:

- · 50-150 swine
- • 151-300 swine
- ● 301-450 swine
- ⬤ More than 450 swine

Fig. 5.3 Norfolk: the distribution of woodland in 1066

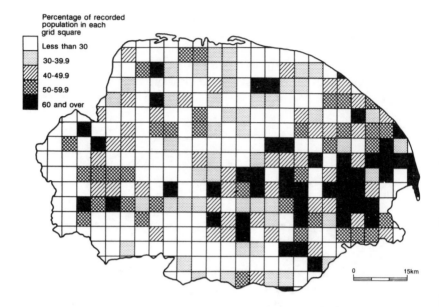

**Percentage of recorded
population in each
grid square**

☐ Less than 30

▨ 30-39.9

◪ 40-49.9

▩ 50-59.9

■ 60 and over

0   15km

Fig. 5.4 Norfolk: the combined distribution of sokemen and free men in 1066

tenant-in-chief, and the information about it is therefore scattered through two, three or more sections of the survey. Even when a vill appears as a single entry, the description of the main manor – its plough-teams, stock, bond population, etc. – is usually followed by an account of 'sokemen' – *sochemanni* – or free men – *liberi homines* – living there, who might themselves have under-tenants and plough-teams. Free men and sokemen were numerous in the county, as they were in neighbouring counties, although they were not evenly distributed (Figure 5.4). Their presence has often been associated with the Viking incursions: in Dodwell's words, 'It is . . . evident that the exceptionally large number of free peasants, *liberi homines* and sokemen . . . and the peculiarities of their distribution . . . are most easily understood when regarded as the result of Scandinavian influence' (Dodwell 1941; 154). The precise character of this influence has been debated. Some historians have argued that the upheavals of the Danish incursions retarded a decline in the status of a once free peasantry to bond status which, in areas further to the west, continued inexorably. Others have seen the free peasants as the direct lineal descendants of the demobbed Danish army (Dodwell 1941: Loyn 1962: 54).

We need to be a little wary of these arguments. As we have seen, the evidence for large-scale peasant immigration is, in fact, equivocal. Moreover, the only reason why Danes and free peasants have ever been associated is that the latter tend to be most numerous in the areas supposedly most intensively settled by the former (Davis 1955). And although historians in the past have tended to conflate them, important differences between *sochemanni* and *liberi homines* soon emerge from a careful reading of Domesday.

We have already discussed sokemen. They had no connection with Viking settlers. Instead, they were men whose ancestors had owed their obligations to no lords but the Wuffingas, or their retinues. The rights to their dues and labour – the 'customary dues' mentioned by the Survey – had now, in many cases, been permanently alienated from the Crown, passing with the land on which they dwelt into other hands. In Domesday we usually find sokemen attached to particular estates, listed after the main chattels and resources as a kind of appendix. Here their land is said to be 'at' so many acres or carucates, or they themselves are said to 'dwell in' or 'on' so many carucates of the estate concerned. Almost certainly, this means that sokemen usually paid their taxes through the estate to which they were attached, rather than directly, on their own account. Yet sokemen had not been depressed to the status of villein: they were probably equivalent to the *geneat* described by the Late Saxon treatise on estate management, the *Rectitudines Singularum Personarum*. They were not listed among the chattels of an estate, and were not tied to the soil. They could go elsewhere, alienating their land and passing on to a new possessor the ancient renders due from it (Dodwell 1948: 297).

Liberi homines were in a rather different position. Many are accorded an entry in their own right, rather than appearing as a manorial appendix. They are frequently described as 'holding' their land, the term also used by Domesday to describe the tenurial position of major landowners. Unlike sokemen, *liberi homines* seem to have had a *direct* relationship with public authority, paying their own taxes, and by implication, usually attended the hundred courts (although their *soc* had, in many cases, been usurped by some local landowner). Moreover, while the status and obligations of the sokeman were, in most cases, obvious to contemporaries, and needed no elaboration (they were ancient and passed with the land on which he dwelt), those of the free man could be very varied. Free men had usually entered into a variety of *private* arrangements involving obligations to social superiors. We read that certain individuals were subject to superiors 'in commendation only'; 'at jurisdiction (*soc*) and in commendation only'; 'at fold-rights and in commendation only'. Such relationships were largely the result of free men having 'commended' themselves to a powerful individual – becoming his man, owing him services or payments in return for support and protection (Dodwell 1948). But obligations might also be owed because, while many free men held their own land, some held 'thegnland', land on a long or life lease, for which they rendered certain services (Dodwell 1948: 293–5; Miller 1951: 49–65). Such land could not be alienated, and thus it is that we often hear of free men who could not go with their land to another lord, who could not 'give or sell their lands'.

Discussion of these social groups can be hampered by the terms we use to describe them. The phrase 'free peasantry' is particulary problematic. Even if we restrict its use to the *liberi homines* it can be misleading, for it implies too clear a dividing line between the holders of large estates on the one hand, and small peasant proprietors on the other. There was no such line. Instead, there was a continuum, running without a break from the *liber homo* with three carucates, via men like Algar Trec, with half a carucate in Osmondiston, to the man with 10 acres, or less. Problematic, too, is the phrase 'middle-class society' sometimes employed for sokemen and free men. In the sense that most did, indeed, occupy a social position some way between the bond villein and the owner of a manorial estate, the term is reasonable enough. But it has its dangers. It makes such people sound like members of the modern bourgeoisie, living in nucleated families, in a society ruled by the force of law and policed by the local constabulary. But eleventh-century Norfolk was an uncertain place, and where the bonds of lordship are weak, other bonds, most notably those of kinship, have to be strong. Many of the groups of sokemen and free men recorded by the Survey

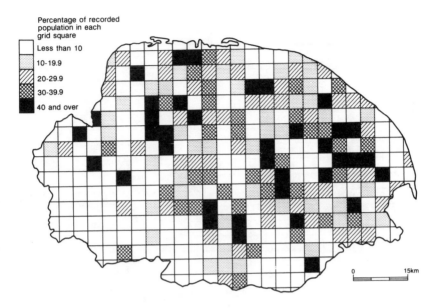

Percentage of recorded
population in each
grid square

Less than 10

10-19.9

20-29.9

30-39.9

40 and over

0   15km

Fig. 5.5   Norfolk: the distribution of sokemen in 1066

were probably related by blood, groups of patrilocal kinsmen
dwelling on ancestral acres. Domesday's phraseology sometimes
hints at the existence of a number of distinct groups of sokemen
or free men in a vill: in Mileham, for example, Archbishop Stigand
had held '3 sokemen, 1 carucate and 1 acre of land. . . . Also four
sokemen, 30 acres of land. . . . Also 1 sokeman, 1 carucate of
land; 1 sokeman, 8 acres. . . . Also 7 sokemen, 40 acres of land.'
As in early medieval Wales, it is possible that some lineages had
holdings scattered across several vills: we are told that twelve
liberi homines dwell 'in Weybourne, in Salthouse, in Kelling, and
in Bodham and hold 3 carucates and 15 acres'.

Earlier attempts to map the distribution of sokemen and
freemen have tended to treat both together as an undifferentiated
class of 'free peasants' (Darby 1952: 361; Dodwell 1941). This
is unfortunate, for the distribution of each separately is rather
different from that of both combined. Sokemen were widely, and
fairly evenly, scattered throughout the county: they were characteristic of the old estate heartlands (Figure 5.5). *Liberi homines*,
in contrast, were concentrated in particular areas, especially in

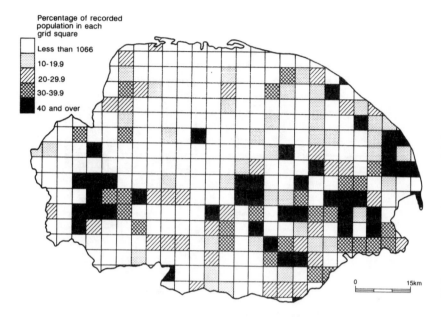

Fig. 5.6 Norfolk: the distribution of free men in 1066

the north-east of the county, the south-east, and the south-west (Figure 5.6). This distribution becomes less curious when we examine the topography of these areas. The south-western concentration corresponds to the silt fens of Marshland, and the higher ground immediately to the east; the north-eastern concentration with the islands of Flegg, and with areas surrounding the marshes in the former Broadland estuary. Both these districts were, as we have seen, probably occupied by specialised grazing estates in the Middle Saxon period, and a connection with cattle-rearing is also suggested in the south of the county, on the claylands, for most of the vills in which free men were numerous lay on, or beside, the moist soils of the interfluve plateau, good grass country. The plateau clays had, as we have seen, been falling to the plough for several centuries, and in Marshland too Domesday shows that much land was now under the plough. On the eastern side of the country, the low-lying grazing marshes were not, and could not, be cultivated. But the surrounding islands and peninsulas were, by the time of Domesday, densely settled. These areas appear – on the available evidence – to have been fairly sparsely settled in Early Saxon times: but Domesday reveals them as districts of intense arable activity.

The *liberi homines* in all these areas were probably not the descendants of Danish settlers, but of Middle Saxon farmers whose main activity had been the production of cattle and dairy produce, men who – because they dwelt in remote marshes, islands, and moors, far from the main arable lands of the archaic estates – had owed few other obligations. As cultivation in these areas expanded during later Saxon times, as population levels increased, these privileged groups had often succeeded in usurping full proprietorial rights over their land. Where smaller concentrations of free men occur elsewhere in the county, the same explanation probably applies.

In some cases, settlements dominated by free men may have begun as single farmsteads: population expansion might soon, through partible inheritance, produce a small community of free men. Domesday perhaps shows the early stages in such a process at places like Buxton, where in 1086 'Five free men, brothers' held seven carucates of land; or at Alby, where in 1066 'Asford, 1 free man' had held a carucate of land, but where in 1086 'now his four sons hold'. We are surely seeing here the emergence of new patrilocal kin groups as the frontiers of cultivation expanded.

All this suggests that the break-up of the great estates occurred in at least two ways. On the one hand, there was 'fission from above', as the East Anglian kings and their West Saxon and Anglo-Danish successors granted away estates or portions of estates, and the obligations due from their inhabitants, to aristocratic families. They in turn sold or granted away further fragments, or divided them through inheritance: but great landowners possessed many estates, so that division between coheirs was less likely to lead to the division of individual territorial units. On the other hand, there was 'fission from below', as peripheral areas of estates passed into the ownership of local cultivators: division between heirs would, in this case, be more likely to divide the individual unit, giving rise to groups of free men. These different processes of fission are, to some extent, also reflected in place-names. The core areas of the ancient estates are represented by those groups of parishes which share the same name, distinguished now by some additional term like 'Great' or 'Little', or by the dedication of their parish church. The peripheral, outlying farms, in contrast, those fragments which were granted to or usurped by smaller individuals, in whole or part, tend to have only one parish bearing the name: they had originally been single settlements, rather than extensive areas. Not all peripheral, outlying areas of the county came to be characterised by *liberi homines*. They were, in particular, strangely absent from the central watershed running down through the middle of the county. This district had not seen the kind of economic expansion witnessed by Flegg or Marshland, or the southern claylands. Domesday shows it as an area of low population density. Marshland, and the north-east, were areas with fertile, easily worked soils; the claylands of the south-east were characterised by less easily worked soils, but they had been cleared of most of their woodland in remote prehistory. On the remote central watershed, in contrast, the soils were often heavy or acid, and extensive tracts of woodland still survived at the time of Domesday, militating against easy conversion to arable. Yet while for the peasant such woodland might appear as an obstacle or a challenge, to the larger landowner it was something else: an economic asset in a county in which reserves of wood and timber were dwindling fast. Domesday shows that the central watershed was dominated, for the most part, by small highly manorialised vills, or by berewicks attached to estates located in the neighbouring valleys. Aristocrats, royal administrators, and ecclesiastical houses had apparently fought hard to maintain or gain possession of vills here, and also to control the local population, preventing local farmers from usurping proprietorial rights, and from destroying woodland through overgrazing or conversion to arable.

Indeed, in the county as a whole there is a close correspondence between the tenurial structure of a vill, and the extent of its woodland resources. Those vills which contained the highest proportion of *liberi homines* usually had little or no woodland. Those with substantial reserves of woodland, in contrast – that is, with woodland sufficient for sixty or more swine – were characterised by stronger lordship. Out of 130 such vills, only twenty-two (17 per cent) contained two or more free men. Moreover, most of the largest totals of woodland were attached to places which had been ancient estate centres, especially those which had remained in royal hands, and/or were, by 1066, the centres of hundreds: places like Mileham (with woodland for 1,150 swine); Saham Tony (845); East Dereham (630); North Elmham (1,000); Kenninghall, (324); Buckenham (235); Aylsham (412). There can be little doubt that much of this woodland really lay in neighbouring vills. As portions of estates had been pilfered or alienated, rights to woodland had been retained. Thus, in the case of Earsham, the 'woodland for 340 swine' recorded in Domesday almost certainly includes much that was later found within the parish of Denton, and probably in other areas further to the west in Earsham hundred. It is only because its possession was under dispute that Domesday tells us that an area of woodland lying in Colkirk belonged to Fakenham, a vill lying several kilometres to the north with which, to judge from the layout of later parishes, it did not even share a common boundary.

The close interest in the dwindling reserves of woodland may not have been merely economic. Woodland provided the elite with hunting, as well as with grazing, wood, and timber. In Hempnall, Domesday records woodland sufficient for 200 swine, and goes on to describe how 'In part of this woodland St B(enedict) claims what (it) held before 1066, called *Schieteshaga*.' This sounds like a settlement, but no population, stock or teams are recorded. In the West Midlands, Hooke has shown how the term *haga* was used to denote some kind of enclosure associated with hunting (Hooke 1981: 233–47). These were not parks in the post-Conquest sense, although they may sometimes developed into them (*Schieteshaga* may have occupied the same site as the medieval Shelton Park in Hempnall). Rather, they were areas used to corral deer prior to the hunt, or – perhaps – to protect them during breeding. Once again, we only hear of this feature because of its disputed ownership, and other *hagas* may have existed elsewhere in the dwindling woodlands of Domesday Norfolk.

The break-up of the great estates must have posed many problems of resource allocation, especially as it was accompanied by a considerable increase in the county's population. The configuration of parish boundaries often suggests a desire to maintain contact with dwindling reserves of woodland or pasture. Thus for example in Henstead hundred the long tapering parishes of Saxlingham Thorpe, Saxlingham Nethergate, Shottesham

St Mary, and Shottesham All Saints reach out towards the watershed between the Tas and the Broom Beck, where they share a boundary with the significantly named parish of Woodton, in the adjacent hundred. Moreover, at some time during the early medieval period, complex arrangements were made for dividing up the great marshes which had developed in the former Broadland estuary, with the valuable grazing land parcelled out in such a way that some parishes lying at a distance from the marsh edge, such as Chedgrave or Stockton, had (and still have) detached portions in the marsh (Rackham 1986b: 381).

The chronology of estate fission is obscure. 'Fission from above' may have begun in Middle Saxon times (some of the personal names appearing as prefixes to *hām*s may represent early owners, rather than administrators) but there are signs that up to the end of the ninth century, the patrimony of the Wuffingas may, in fact, have survived largely intact. Wymondham may have been a unique survivor in 1066, but a century before large estates of 4,000 to 6,000 hectares may have been more common. Post-Conquest traditions asserted that as late as the 970s the estates of Dereham and Hingham were rated at $40\frac{1}{2}$ and 60 carucates respectively (Blomefield 1805, II: 431). More significantly, the way that Domesday treats the *hām*s, and other adjacent vills sharing the same name, is interesting in this context. It often omits their qualifiers ('North', 'Great', etc.), describing them each by the old estate name only, or describing one as 'the other', as in the case of Lopham. It is comparatively rare to find the present qualifier in Domesday, suggesting that individual portions of these estate heartlands had not been separated for long enough to have acquired their own names.

It is possible that 'fission from below', the hiving off of outlying portions of estates, especially former grazing farms, was accelerated by the upheavals of the Scandinavian conquest, and the West Saxon reconquest (Fellows-Jensen 1990: 18–19). A late date of fission is suggested by the fact that many of these places bear names which incorporate Scandinavian personal names, suggesting that their first true 'owners' lived in the period after the late ninth century. While it is likely that some of the people who gave their names to these settlements, like some of the free men we meet in the pages of Domesday, were of Danish descent, the real impact of the Viking incursions may have been to create conditions of disruption and discontinuity which favoured the usurpation of full proprietorial rights on the fringes of estate territories. Danish raiding and settlement may also have been responsible for the high proportion of sokemen in the population of the county in the late eleventh century, and it has been argued that the upheavals of conquest allowed peasant cultivators to maintain their ancestral status where, in areas further to the west, they were gradually depressed to the status of *gebur* or villein. But it is also possible that the distribution of these social groups has, at least in part, a more mundane explanation. For, if we look beyond Norfolk into the adjacent counties, it becomes apparent that the coincidence of free and soke populations, and the political boundaries of the Danelaw, is in reality not very close (Darby 1977). Thus, for example, there are comparatively few sokemen or freemen in central or southern Essex, or east Hertfordshire; conversely, in the Midlands they spill over the Danelaw boundary into Bedfordshire and Northamptonshire. Their distribution fits much more closely with aspects of regional climate than it does with ninth-century political boundaries. Free men and sokemen were most numerous where summer rainfall was lowest and, therefore, the harvest most dependable. These were also, for the same reason of course, the most populous areas of England. It seems likely that we are seeing here the long-term effects of climate on social structure. Where the harvest was most dependable men were less likely to fall into debt, less likely to fall into abject dependence on local lords with superior resources, and with the capacity for storing surplus produce.

Yet, as we have seen, within the county itself rather different factors determined the varying densities of the two distinct groups within the 'free peasantry'. The free men – the most socially and economically independent – were most numerous in those areas in which economic expansion, and in particular the conversion of pastures and wastes to arable, had been most marked during the later Saxon period. The silt fens of Marshland were one such area. But more significant were the islands in, and peripheries of, the Broadland marshes, and the level clay inter-fluves of the south: areas which together formed a broad band of poorly manorialised country running through the east of the county. By the time of Domesday, the basic social and tenurial division of Norfolk – between this zone, and the more highly manorialised areas in the west (the 'Good Sands', Breckland, and the Western Escarpment) – was thus already fixed. It was a division which was to be of immense significance in the later devolpment of the county.

The development of administrative organisation

Domesday shows that Norfolk was divided into thirty-three fiscal and judicial units called *hundreds* (Figure 5.7). We know from other, slightly later documents that each had its own court, which met for routine business once every three or four weeks, and for special session twice a year, at Michaelmas and Easter (Cam 1930: 10–11; Loyn 1984: 140–3). Norfolk's hundreds ranged in size from Clacklose, which covered around 34,000 hectares, to Henstead, which contained only 7,600 (Barringer 1979). In part, this variation was related to the fact that whereas medieval documents describe many simply as 'hundreds', some are termed half-hundreds (Diss and Earsham, and sometimes Shropham), while others are said to represent hundreds-and-a-half (Clacklose, Forehoe, Freebridge, Mitford). At the time of Domesday many hundreds were attached to particular manors (Cam 1944: 75–6). Clacklose was held with the manor of Wimbotsham, Diss and Earsham were attached to the manors of the same names. Guiltcross was attached to Kenninghall, Mitford to Dereham, Shropham to Old Buckenham, and North Greenhoe to Wighton. Domesday seems to suggest that East Flegg, West Flegg, and Happing were appendant to Yarmouth, while it strongly implies that Eynesford was attached to Foulsham manor, Forehoe to Hingham, and Wayland to Saham. Later tradition – as stated in the Hundred Rolls of 1274–75 – carried the association of Launditch and South Greenhoe hundreds with Mileham back to the time of William I, associations hinted at on a number of occasions by the Survey itself. Blomefield adds that the hundred of Humbleyard had been attached to the manor of Hethersett before the forfeiture of Earl Ralph, and although there are no obvious hints of this in the pages of the Survey and no other supporting evidence for the claim, the status of the manor as a probable centre of a great royal estate makes it plausible (Blomefield 1805 V: 23–4). At the time of Domesday, many of these manors were royal, but some – and the rights to profit from the hundred – had been alienated. Ramsey Abbey held Clacklose,

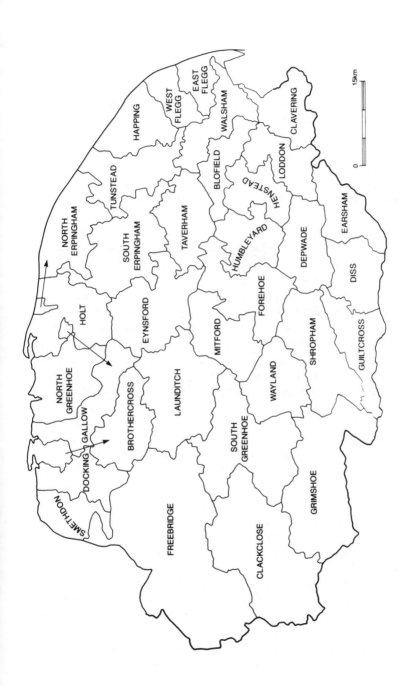

Fig. 5.7 Domesday Norfolk: hundreds

St Benets Tunstead, and Ely had Mitford (Cam 1926: 29). Stigand had Earsham, Forehoe, and Launditch, while Earl Ralph held Shropham.

In some parts of the country hundreds seem to have developed out of primitive tribal groupings, but most historians accept that in Norfolk earlier systems of territorial organisation were obliterated by the Danish settlement, and that hundreds were an entirely new system imposed by the West Saxons after the reconquest of the county from the Danes (Douglas 1932: clx). Several features of hundredal organisation in the county certainly suggest the arbitrary hand of the Late Saxon administrator, rather than slow evolution from tribal territory. Hundred boundaries sometimes run through the middle of groups of parishes bearing the same name: thus Burnham Overy and Burnham Thorpe lie in Gallow hundred, but the other Burnhams lie in Brothercross; the Barninghams and the Beckhams are sundered by the boundary between North and South Erpingham. In other ways their boundaries appear arbitrary and artificial: Brothercross hundred is divided into two distinct sections, separated by a broad swathe of Docking hundred, while the vill of Saxlingham formed a detached portion of Gallow, its nearest point some 7 kilometres from the main body of the hundred, with North Greenhoe in between. Moreover, the names of some hundreds seem to suggest a comparatively recent origin: Brothercross, Grimshoe, North Greenhoe, South Greenhoe, Guiltcross, Wayland, West and East Flegg, Forehoe, all contain Scandinavian words or personal names, and can hardly have been coined before the late ninth century (Anderson 1934) (interestingly, the term 'hundred' is always used in Norfolk, rather than the Scandinavian term *wapentake*, encountered in the northern Danelaw).

Yet at the same time, hundreds also display some more archaic features. Their boundaries, especially in the south and east, frequently correspond with important features of the natural topography: with the lower reaches of major rivers, and with watersheds. Moreover, some hundred names seem to be ancient. Three – Clavering, Loddon, and Happing – preserve the names of primitive folk-groups; and only six bear the names of the manors to which, at the time of Domesday, they were attached. If hundreds had simply originated as administrative units attached to important royal manors, then it is strange that this is not reflected in their nomenclature. Indeed, only eleven bore the names of any Domesday vill. The rest seem to have been named after their 'mootstow', their meeting-place, usually isolated from any centre of royal or seigniorial authority. Some hundreds met at fords, or so we may surmise from the names of Depwade, 'the deep ford'; Mitford, probably 'the middle ford'; and Eynesford (Anderson 1934). Smethdon, 'the smooth down', and Henstead, 'the high place', both sound like ancient assembly places. Several met at early earthworks. Launditch Hundred, as its name suggests, assembled at the point where this prominent linear earthwork was crossed by the Roman road (Rye 1920). The names of South and North Greenhoe, and Grimshoe, indicate that they met at barrows, while Forehoe met at the 'four howes', the linear barrow cemetery in Carleton Forehoe. According to Blomefield, the court of Freebridge was held at a barrow in Flitcham Burgh, while Ingmote Hill near Holt, suggested by Rye as the meeting-place for the Holt hundred, and 'Tunstead Hundred Hill', the meeting-place of Tunstead hundred, were also probably ancient burial mounds (Rye 1920: 27). Taverham hundred met on Frettenham Hill, and a mound called 'Court Hill' was excavated here in the nineteenth century (Rye 1920: 21). No burials or cremations were found, and while this may reflect the poor nature of contemporary excavation practices, or earlier robbing of the site, it is also possible that the mound was purpose-built as a meeting-place. Other specially constructed 'moot hills' are known, or suspected, elsewhere in the country (Adkins & Petchey 1984).

Hundreds themselves may have been created by the West Saxon conquerors, perhaps – as in the case of Forehoe – by throwing together two, three, or more ancient estates, or their residual patterns of jurisdiction. But their meeting-places may often have been older, originally serving different and perhaps larger territories. One indication of this is the way in which mootstows were sometimes located, not in the centre, but on the edge of hundreds. Thus Henstead Hundred probably took its name from the 'hean stede', the 'high place', identified by Schram with the Medberge, 'gemot-berg', the 'hill of assembly', mentioned in a document of 1219 (Anderson 1934: 79). This lay at Upper Stoke, close to the boundary with Humbleyard, suggesting that this might have originated as the meeting-place for a territory embracing both hundreds. Strangely located, too, is Tunstead Hundred Hill (Rye 1920: 27). This was in the extreme north of the hundred, almost in North Erpingham hundred and no more than 4 kilometres from the boundary with South Erpingham, suggesting that the three hundreds may once have formed a single territory. It is possible that the existence of such early subdivisions of the kingdom, larger than the Domesday hundred, can be discerned in the tendency, later in the medieval period, for two or more hundreds to be repeatedly grouped together for certain purposes, perhaps reflecting archaic arrangements 'older than the hundred itself' (Cam 1944: 91). The Ramsey chronicles record a command from William II to hold a joint session of $3\frac{1}{2}$ hundreds (probably the hundred and a half of Freebridge, Smethdon, and Docking, which was incorporated in Smethdon some time after the Domesday Survey). Freebridge and Smethdon shared a bailiff throughout the thirteenth century (Cam 1930: 94). Brothercross hundred met at the ford near Burnham Overy church, almost on the boundary with Gallow. The boundary between the two hundreds was changed in the century of so after Domesday, so that Raynham, Burnham Thorpe, and both the Creakes passed from Gallow to Brothercross. Yet their combined external boundary remained the same, and in 1373 they were treated as one hundred, *Galowebrothycross* (Cam 1930: 149; Anderson 1934: 66). Domesday refers to the 'three hundreds of Yarmouth', probably East and West Flegg, and Happing, which shared a single bailiff down to the end of the Middle Ages (Cam 1944: 100). Later documentary references suggest a measure of confusion in this area. In 1294 we have a reference to 'Eccles in Flec', although Eccles lies well inside Happing hundred. Flegg may once have been the name for a larger territory embracing all three hundreds: a document of 1014 refers to the 'regione qui dicitur Flegg' (Anderson 1934: 70).

Issues of similar complexity surround the lower levels of administrative organisation in the county. The main tax in Late Saxon England was the geld, and in East Anglia this was collected in a distinctive way. In other parts of England, vills contributed a sum related to their assessed hidage or carucatge, a kind of 'rateable value'. In Norfolk and Suffolk, Domesday records the carucatage of each vill but indicates that the geld was collected on a quite independent basis: each vill (sometimes two) paid a stated number of pence when £1 was paid by the hundred as a whole (Loyn 1984: 119; Warner 1988: 26–30; Johnson 1906: 5–6; Davis 1954: 60–1). Curiously, there seems to be no discernible relationship between the stated sums and the carucatage of the vill in question. A more interesting peculiarity of the region was that vills were grouped, for purposes of geld collection, into units called leets. Domesday alludes to these on two occasions: its description of the royal lands in South Greenhoe begins with the statement: 'Of 14 leets', while the first entry concerning the holdings of Ely Abbey states: 'Hundred of Clacklose of 10 leets'. But it is only later documents, relating to medieval Suffolk rather than Norfolk, that reveal that leets were units of roughly equal assessment, usually containing two or three vills which were not contiguous but scattered across the hundred (Loyn 1984: 19; Warner 1988: 27; Douglas 1932: clxi). Medieval references reveal hundreds composed of six, nine, ten, twelve, fourteen, fifteen, or even twenty-four leets (Douglas 1932: clxi). There have been several attempts to reconstruct the grouping of vills into leets from the individual vill assessments given to us by Domesday: most are little more than guesswork, but plausible reconstructions can sometimes be attempted. Thus, for example, the hundred of North Greenhoe contains eighteen vills. Of these, three lack any stated assessment, while those of Walsingham and 'the other Walsingham' were combined, paying 2s. The same sum was paid by Field Dalling, Hindringham, Holkham, Stiffkey, Thursford, and Warham. Barney, Egmere and Quarles paid 6d each, and Wighton contributed 7d, suggesting that they combined to form another leet. Only the 4d paid by Houghton spoils an otherwise regular pattern of assessment, of eight leets contributing around 2s each.

Leets were unknown to the West Saxons, and must have been a feature of the county before the reconquest, and administrative reorganisation, of the tenth century. Some historians have suggested that they were a Danish institution; others that they date back to the pre-Viking kingdom (Davis 1954: clxi; Warner 1988). Yet however old the *concept* of the leet, the pattern which existed at the time of Domesday cannot have been of any great antiquity. The leet was a subdivision of the hundred, and the hundredal system seems to have been a recent introduction.

Moreover, leets were units of comparatively equitable assessment: yet, as we have seen, the two centuries before the Conquest seem to have seen a phenomenal increase in population, and expansion of cultivation, which would have destroyed the equitable nature of assessment, surely encouraging some reorganisation. The West Saxon conquerors may, however, have taken over, and adapted, a more ancient system of fiscal assessment.

One indication of this is that leets are not the only unit below the level of the hundred which we encounter in early medieval Norfolk. In 1928, Douglas drew attention to a survey of lands in Norfolk and Suffolk belonging to Bury St Edmunds, drawn up some time between 1045 and 1065 (Douglas 1928). This refers to 'hundreds' which are very different from those encountered in Domesday. They were fairly small units, responsible for contributing food-rents to the abbey: those in Norfolk are called Elsington (Islington) Hundred, Spelhoge Hundred, Clencware hundred, and Lynware hundred. Douglas plausibly argued that these were simply the leet under a different name. Each was divided into varying numbers of smaller units, called *manlots* – 'man-shares'. This is a Scandinavian term, and Douglas suggested that these 'hundreds' were 'folk-divisions which probably took their origin from the Scandinavian invasions' (Douglas 1928: 377). But their names imply an older, or at least indigenous, origin. Clencware and Lynware are familiar forms of Old English territorial name: Spelhoge ('speech hill'), Fuwelege ('wild bird clearing'), and Aenehogo ('the eagle's hill') are also Old English names, and apparently refer to meeting-places rather than settlements (Anderson 1934: 63–4).

Early medieval documents in East Anglia also make sporadic references to yet another archaic unit, the 'ferding'. A list of Roger Bigot's encroachments on the lands of the Abbey of St Benets of Holme, dating to the years 1101–07, describes Potter Heigham and a lost place called *Scharstede* as lying 'in Ludham Ferding' (Stenton 1922: 226; West 1932: 169–70). The term may also occur in the place-name Winfarthing, the 'ferding of Winna' (Mills 1991). The term means simply 'fourth part', and sometimes it was simply a quarter of a hundred: thus Ludham contributed almost precisely a quarter of the geld assessed on the hundred of Happing. Sometimes, however, the term seems to have a different, more archaic significance. The entry for Babergh in

Suffolk in the *Kalender* of Abbot Sampson informs us that 'here are the ferdings . . . which in other hundreds are called leets and they are 15 in number' (Douglas 1932: clxii). Babergh was a double hundred, and ought therefore to have had eight ferdings: so it is just possible that the ferding was originally a quarter, not of a hundred, but of some smaller unit of assesment, around half the size of the hundred, or fifty carucates. It is, indeed, an interesting coincidence that the notional area of the 'small hundred' of the Bury assesment was twelve carucates, in other words, a quarter, or ferding, of such a unit. If such an 'archaic hundred' (to coin a phrase) had been the basis for fiscal assessments in the pre-Viking kingdom, then it was perhaps originally imposed, not on a pattern of petty vills and splintered lordships, but on large, discrete estates. Some traces of such a system, and of its fourfold subdivision, should therefore be sought in places where such estates survived reasonably intact into the Late Saxon period. We have already suggested that the 'hundred and a half' of Forehoe originally comprised three Middle Saxon estates, based on Costessey, Hingham, and Wymondham: and that the last of these places was both a half-hundred, and an archaic estate which had not undergone any significant degree of fission. Domesday gives taxation assesments for eighteen places in the hundred. These varied widely, from 8*s* 5*d* down to 4*d*. The best 'fit' of possible combinations suggests that the hundred was originally divided into leets each paying 1*s* 8*d* (Douglas 1927: 86). Wymondham's contribution was 6*s* 8*d*: that is, it must have been composed of four leets. It is noteworthy that the organisational structure of the town was based, throughout medieval times, on an archaic fourfold division into the 'shifts' of Norton, Suton, Wattisfield and Silfield.

We can pursue this enquiry no further: some readers will, perhaps, already have tired of this attempt to heap inference upon untestable inference. What does seem clear, however, is that the administrative structure of the county as revealed in Domesday, while in itself a fairly recent innovation, incorporated elements of considerable antiquity, some perhaps introduced by Scandinavian lords, others dating back to the kingdom of the Wuffingas. Neither the Scandinavian invasions, nor the West Saxon conquest, entirely destroyed indigenous forms of administrative organisation (Campbell 1986: 171–89).

The development of urban life

Not everything in Domesday Norfolk was rural. The survey explicitly acknowledges the existence of three towns, by recording burgesses in Thetford, Norwich, and Yarmouth. The name Norwich first appears on a coin of King Athelstan, minted some time after 930. Excavations mounted in the city in 1985 strongly suggest, as we have seen, that the town grew up in the eighth and ninth centuries on the north bank of the river Wensum, in the area now known as Fishergate. This area was, some time in the tenth or early eleventh centuries, defended by a substantial bank and ditch, although it remains unclear whether this was in 917, when the town was reconquered by the English; or following the Danish raids of 993, 1004, or 1016 (Ayres, forthcoming, Atkin 1985).

Norwich was sacked by the Vikings in 1004, but thereafter it expanded dramatically. An undefended extension to the town was established in the area of Needham, to the south of the river Wensum, just above the 6-metre contour. It appears to have been a planned settlement, a kind of Late Saxon 'new town', with a rough grid of streets. This area included pottery kilns, and a market-place, the present Tombland. Some of the city's present churches probably originated at this time, most notably St Martin (at Palace) and St Michael Tombland. By the middle decades of the century, in addition, it is likely that small areas of suburbs had begun to develop along the approach roads to the town. By 1066 Norwich had 1,320 burgesses, implying a population of over 5,000 and suggesting that the city was comparable in size to London.

The importance of Norwich by the time of the Norman Conquest, and its phenomenal growth in the subsequent centuries, should not be allowed to obscure the significance of the county's other main town. It is possible that Thetford was as big as, or even bigger than, Norwich in the tenth century: even in 1086 its recorded population, 948 burgesses, ran it close. Like Norwich, Thetford lay some way from the sea but was on a navigable waterway – in this case, the River Ouse. Its origins as a town are usually associated with its use as a Danish military base during the campaigns of 869–70, but it may well have existed as a settlement of some importance before: why else did the Vikings occupy it in the campaign of 869? Accumulating finds of Ipswich

Ware, coins and metalwork immediately to the west of the Late Saxon town on the southern banks of the river suggest the existence of a sizeable, probably proto-urban settlement here before the late ninth century. By the tenth century, certainly, the town was substantial (Dunmore & Carr 1976; Rogerson & Dallas 1984; Atkin 1985). Excavations have revealed fenced plots, wooden houses, and gravelled roads, and considerable evidence for industrial activity, including leather working, iron smelting and, above all, pottery production: the town was the main centre for the manufacture of a distinctive wheel-thrown class of pottery now called, not surprisingly, Thetford Ware (although this was also produced in Norwich, and at rural locations like Kirstead, in the south of the county: Atkin, Ayres, & Jennings 1983; Wade 1976). In one part of the excavated area a large number of kilns were found grouped together, possibly representing a single commercial enterprise. Adjoining areas were apparently used for storing fuel, and for weathering clay prior to use. Textiles were also produced in the town on a substantial scale, as indicated by numerous finds of spindlewhorls, needles, pins, woolcombs, and linen smoothers. The town was defended by a substantial bank and ditch in the early tenth century, and possessed a mint (Carson 1949; Rogerson & Dallas 1984). By the eleventh century, it had twelve churches, and had broken through its earlier defences to the south of the River Thet: the town ditch was levelled and built over.

Norwich and Thetford were not the only places with urban functions in Late Saxon Norfolk. Yarmouth was also a borough by 1066, although Domesday tells us very little about it, except that its seventy burgesses paid the king £18 for their freedoms. On the other side of the river, in Suffolk, the inhabitants of Gorleston included twenty-four fishermen: we can surmise that Yarmouth's prosperity was also, in part, based on fishing, to judge from finds made during excavations on Fullers Hill in 1974 which included traces of dwellings and/or workplaces associated with quantities of fishbones and fish-hooks (Rogerson 1976). Domesday also mentions markets at Litcham, Cawston, and perhaps Dunham. It mentions no others, but there must have been one at Downham Market, for it is referred to in a document of 1050: and, as we shall see, other places may well have been developing urban functions by the time of Domesday. Nevertheless. only Norwich and Thetford had mints, a pattern shared by Suffolk (which had only one, at Bury), and in sharp contrast to Wessex, where major urban centres like Winchester were supported by middle-ranking and lower-order market centres of sufficient importance to warrant their own mints.

As the excavations at Thetford demonstrate, urban growth was not solely the result of an expansion in marketing – although this was important, as the great increase in the volume of coinage in circulation from the end of the ninth century shows. It was also associated with a phenomenal increase in the output of craft industries. As in other aspects of the county's life, the contrast with the Middle Saxon period is clear. In place of monopolistic markets, controlled production and long-distance exchange, a more market-based economy had emerged.

Other areas of England were experiencing economic expansion in the Late Saxon period, but seldom on the scale of Norfolk. Not only was Norwich the largest city in England after London; the rural hinterland was thriving, with a greater density of population and plough-teams than any other county. The reasons for all this are complex, and not fully understood. The county's location on the eastern seaboard may have been a factor, given that the Viking expansion had created a trading network based on the North Sea basin. But neither Norwich nor Thetford seem to have been heavily involved in long-distance trade, and much of the county's prosperity was probably due to a range of more local factors, each stimulating, and being stimulated by, the others, in a complex pattern of mutual support and feedback. Climatic conditions and fertile soils encouraged population growth, and also created a substantial degree of personal freedom for a large section of the population: this in turn created broad-based wealth, which fuelled economic development in the non-agricultural sphere, and stimulated the growth of towns and markets. The growth of these in turn encouraged further expansion in the rural economy: for while Thetford and Norwich may not seem vast concentrations of population by modern standards, the impact of even small urban centres on predominantly rural populations is usually profound. In one sense towns were parasitic, in that they depended on the surrounding hinterland for material sustenance. But they were also economic dynamos, engines for growth, which in their turn invigorated the surrounding rural economy.

6

Pagans, saints, and churches

Paganism and conversion

We do not know the extent to which the inhabitants of the *Civitas Icenorum* had, by the end of the fourth century, come to embrace Christianity. The archaeological evidence is certainly meagre: we have, as yet, no Christian religious structures in the county like that excavated at Icklingham, just over the county boundary in Suffolk (West & Plonviez 1976). There are only a few stray finds which may attest the presence of the cult. These include, in particular, a hand-shaped lead plaque from Scole, similar to examples found in Colchester and St Albans, decorated with punched designs probably derived from the Christian symbol of the chi-rho; and lead tanks discovered near Oxborough in the last century, and more recently near Stoke Ferry, decorated with incised cross-like motifs, which may be baptismal fonts from Romano-British churches. There is certainly little evidence that Christianity long survived the demise of the *Civitas*. The cemeteries of the fifth century, dominated by the rite of cremation, seem resoundingly non-Christian. It is possible that the county's two Eccles place-names, as we have seen, derive from the British *egles*, and indicate the survival into the migration period of Romano-British Christian communities. But other derivations for these names are also possible. Christianity was adopted by the population of towns and by wealthy villa-owners, but had probably made little impact on the religious experience of countryfolk. The pagan beliefs of the incoming Angles may have had much in common with those of the indigenous population, and assimilation would have been an easy matter. Christianity probably disappeared from the county soon after the imperial system which sustained it.

The conversion of the East Angles two centuries later, as described by the historian Bede, followed a pattern shared with other English kingdoms. The ruling dynasty was first converted, adopting the new faith for a range of reasons which were probably more to do with *realpolitik* than with abstract notions of philosophy or morality. The rest of the population adopted the new faith only gradually. We have already seen how King Raedwald was converted to Christianity while in Kent, and how he earned Bede's enmity by erecting in his temple, on his return to East Anglia, two altars, one heathen and one Christian (HE, II: 15). His son Eorpwald at first adhered to paganism, but was eventually persuaded by Edwin of Northumbria to accept Christianity (HE, II: 15). Murdered in about 628, the kingdom again relapsed into paganism until the return from exile of Eorpwald's half-brother Sigeberht. The conversion now began in earnest. In 630 the monk Fursa came from Ireland and was given an old *castrum*, or Roman fortification, in which to establish a community. The place was called *Cnobheresburg*: 'that is, Urbs Cnobheri' (HE, III: 19). It was 'pleasantly situated' close to woods and the sea. Cnobheresburg is normally identified with the Saxon shore fort of Burgh Castle, and the excavations carried out here from 1958 to 1961 discovered evidence of Middle Saxon occupation on some scale, although not of an unequivocally ecclesiastical nature (Johnson 1980, 1983). The Roman fort at Caister-on-Sea is another possible candidate: a substantial Middle Saxon cemetery has been discovered outside its walls. Either way, the choice of a Roman fort was not unusual. Early missionaries often settled within ruined Roman towns or military installations, partly because these provided suitably sheltered and enclosed places for monastic communities, but also, perhaps, because they represented a link with the imperial, and therefore the Christian, past.

After a few years, Fursa departed, first becoming a hermit with his brother Ultan, and then engaging in further missionary work in Gaul. He left his half-brother Foillan in charge of the community, together with the priests Goban and Dicuill (HE, III: 19). According to Bede, Fursa left because he foresaw that the area would soon be disturbed by the invasion of heathens, and an account of Foillan's life, probably first set down in the seventh century, tells how the monastery was indeed despoiled by pagans, presumably the invading army of Penda. The monks were redeemed from captivity, and the altar and books restored, but the community departed by ship to the kingdom of the Franks, never to return (Whitelock 1972: 6).

Sigeberht also supported the activities of the Burgundian monk Felix, 'Apostle of the East Angles', the kingdom's first bishop. His see was established at a place called *Dommoc*, probably modern Dunwich in Suffolk. A few years after this Sigeberht, after associating his kinsman Ecgric with him as joint king, retired into a monastery, probably at *Beaduricesworth* – the modern Bury St Edmunds (Whitelock 1972: 8). He was not there for long. Soon afterwards he joined the East Anglian army in repelling the invasion of Penda of Mercia in 635. Unarmed, except for a wand, he was killed by the forces of the pagan king, and thus became a martyr (HE, III: 18).

He was not the only member of the Wuffingas to be recognised as a saint. His successor, Anna, was also accepted as a martyr after he fell in battle against Penda in 654. He was, moreover, the father of no less than five saints: Jurmin, his son who died in the same battle; Etheldreda, who founded the nunnery at Ely; Ethelburga, who established the nunnery at Faremoutier in France; and Sexburga, who became a queen of Kent (Farmer 1984: 74). Later, post-Conquest sources also make St Withburga, founder of the nunnery at *Derham*, his daughter (Libermann 1889: 5). A later king, Æthelberht, was recognised as a martyr after his assassination by Offa of Mercia in 794 (Farmer 1984: 39; James 1917); but the kingdom's most famous royal saint was its last, King Edmund. According to the post-Conquest *Life* written by Abbo of Fleury, Edmund fought against the army of the Danes at Thetford and afterwards returned to a royal vill, *Heagelisdun* (Winterbottom 1972: 67–87). He was here attacked by Danish forces, but refused to surrender. Taking refuge in the church, he was shot full of arrows, his head removed, and his body dumped in *Haegelisdun* wood 'among the thick briars'. Local Christians buried it, and when peace returned went in search of the head: they found it calling out 'here, here, here' to them, held between the paws of a magical wolf: they removed it to Hoxne in Suffolk and later to Bury St Edmunds. The location of *Haegelisdun* is disputed. The fact that the subsequent resting-places of the saint's body were in Suffolk strongly suggests that this place, too, lay somewhere in that county, perhaps at Bradfield St Clare (Scarfe 1986: 57). But Hellesdon near Norwich, *Hailesduna* in Domesday Book, remains an outside possibility (although the story was only written down a century after the events, and all its details, not just the magical ones, should be treated with caution (Gransden 1985)). The large number of saints in the East Anglian royal family clearly indicates the close association of the dynasty with the faith, and the extent to which the one bolstered the fortunes of the other and vice versa.

We should not, however, confuse the conversion of the Wuffingas with that of their kingdom. 'The time scale of conversion was long. England in the eighth century was arguably more Christian than pagan, but in many respects rural populations were still possessed of pagan inclinations a thousand years later' (Morris 1989: 91). Although the most important tribal shrines of paganism would have been destroyed or Christianised by the beginning of the eighth century, if not before, those serving smaller social groups in more marginal locations may have survived into the tenth or eleventh centuries (Morris 1989: 92). Indeed, if we are to understand the development of Norfolk's religious topography it is important to remember that the pagan East Angles would have known a variety of shrines. Some, distinguished by the term *friðgeard*, were small private sanctuaries attached to particular individuals of lineages (Morris 1989: 63). Those described by the terms *hearg*, or *wih* or *wēoh*, in contrast, were places where larger social groups gathered. They were often on prominent hilltops, and sometimes occupied fairly central places within tribal territories: but, like the religious sites of earlier centuries, they could also be found close to the boundaries between social groups (Wilson 1985). Medieval references to a field called Harrow, almost certainly derived from *hearg*, in Hempnall parish, close to the watershed boundary between Depwade and Henstead hundreds, could well be an example. Pagan shrines were associated with groves, and especially with clearings in groves; with stones, probably including earlier megaliths; with springs or wells; and with trees, especially the oak and the ash (Morris 1989: 76–90).

There are, in Norfolk, no major place-names which incorporate the classic terms for pagan shrines, *hearg* or *wih*. But some may refer less directly to places of pagan sanctity. Just as the name Colkirk refers to the *kirkja* or church of a man called Cola, it is possible that Bintree refers to a sacred tree within the *friðgeard* of a man called Bina. Matlaske, 'the ash tree of the assembly', could be another example (Mills 1991). The name of Wayland hundred incorporates the Scandinavian element *lúndr*, 'a grove', perhaps a reference to Wayland Wood itself, in the parish of Watton (Anderson 1934: 77). The fact that the hundred takes its name from a grove suggests that this was the place where it met, and that this was, perhaps, originally a place of pagan worship (Rackham 1986b: 79). Other place-names hint at the religious significance of groves and clearings. It would be interesting to know why crosses were erected in the *þveits*, clearings, of Crostwight and Crostwick.

Some of the fourteen settlement names in the county which incorporate the element *wylla*, 'a spring or well', could have some religious significance, indicating the sites of pagan *wæterwyllas*, water shrines. The name of Bawdeswell, for example, may refer to a spring associated with *Balder*, the dying and reviving god of Scandinavian and old English mythology; while Ashwell (now Ashwellthorpe) is the 'spring by the ash tree', a combination of sacred features in one name which must surely be of some significance (Mills 1991). A local ballad collected in the early eighteenth century recalled the magical growth of a huge tree here (Blomefield 1805, V: 155–6). In this context, it is noteworthy that some parish churches in the county (although none in a parish with a name containing the element *wylla*) are associated with wells and springs. At Fersfield, processions were made from the parish church to 'A well of spring about 60 yards from the north gate of the churchyard, at the foot of the hill, which is still called *Tann*'s Well, being a corruption of Anne's Well' (Blomefield, 1805, I: 105). At East Dereham there were two springs. One, dedicated to St Withburga, who reputedly founded the nunnery here in the seventh century, can still be found in the west end of the churchyard. It was in Blomefield's time 'a spring of clear water, formerly said to have had many medicinal and healing qualities' (Blomefield 1805, X: 216). But there was also 'At some distance from the churchyard another spring called St Withburga's well'. There were wells associated with churches at Wereham, and at Bawburgh, the latter dedicated to St Walstan, who supposedly died in 1016 (Farmer 1984: 42–3). Another well dedicated to this saint lay in the adjacent parish of Costessey, isolated from any church, and other unassociated wells are recorded at Gressenhall, Burnham Norton, Taverham, and East Rudham. Shadwell, in the south–west of the county, takes its name from 'St Chad's Well', which still survives, some 200 metres south of the boundary between the hundreds of Guiltcross and Shropham and in origin, probably, the *scead wylla*, the 'boundary well'.

It is not impossible that some of these holy wells, and some of the *wylla* names, were the sites of pagan *wæterwyllas*. Several of the isolated holy wells are dedicated to saints who only became popular in the eleventh or twelfth centuries, like Anne or Walstan, possibly supporting Morris's suggestion that '*wæterwyllas* comprised the last class of pagan site to be Christianised', and that the 'springs so converted were among the least important places in the heathen hierarchy' (Morris 1989: 91).

We should not press any of this rather flimsy evidence too far. Nevertheless, the late survival of heathen shrines, and their development into church sites, is hinted at elsewhere. The ruined church of Caldecote sits on top of a striking mound, possibly but not certainly artificial, and fieldwalking in the immediate vicinity has revealed evidence of pagan Saxon occupation, and perhaps burial: an unusual association, given that parish churches in the county are usually located beside Middle Saxon settlements and quite unrelated to areas of Early Saxon activity. Here we may see signs of a pattern noted elsewhere in the country, of the pagan re-use of prehistoric monuments (or natural features which appeared to be such) as burial places, and perhaps as ceremonial foci. At Holkham, similarly, the church sits on an unusual mound, in reality natural but perhaps mistaken for a substantial barrow by the local pagan population, who seem to have buried their dead on its summit. At Cranwich the same error is apparent; the church sits within a slightly raised, almost circular church-yard, apparently a natural promontory but again associated with a pagan burial site. Bodney church sits on a large mound which may be natural, or artificial, or both.

Early monasteries

We do not know very much about the church in seventh- and eighth-century Norfolk. Bede tells us little about the activities of Felix, other than that he aided Sigeberht in the establishment of schools where boys could be taught letters. He tells us nothing at all about Felix's successors in East Anglia, beyond recording that the East Anglian see was divided, some time around 680, as a consequence of the infirmity of Bishop Bisi. It is other, later sources (like William of Malmesbury) which inform us that the new see was established at a place called Elmham, almost certainly North Elmham in Norfolk, rather than South Elmham in Suffolk (Howlett 1914: 128; Rigold 1962: 67–72; Wade-Martins 1980a: 3–11). Various documents provide a few other scraps of information about the early church in the kingdom. The episcopal lists of the two East Anglian sees have survived, inserted into a late eighth-century Mercian compilation; there are three episcopal confessions made to the Archbishop of Canterbury; and the 'F' version of the *Anglo-Saxon Chronicle* records the death of Ælfhun, bishop of *Dommoc,* in 798. The East Anglian bishops regularly appear as witnesses of Mercian charters up until the 820s, and appear in the lists of those attending synods at *Clofeshoh* in 747, 803, 824, and 825, and at Chelsea in 816 (Whitelock 1972: 16). Meagre though these references are, they do suggest that the church of the East Angles was no less well organised or influential than that of the other English kingdoms (Whitelock 1972: 15–18).

A letter written by King Ælfwald in the 740s to the missionary St Boniface in Germany assures him that masses and prayers were being said for him in the kingdoms' seven monasteries (Whitelock 1972: 16). One of these was almost certainly at Iken in Suffolk, for the *Anglo-Saxon Chronicle* records how St Botolph (a saint whom Bede does not even mention) founded a monastery at *Icanho* in 653/4 (West, Scarfe, & Cramp 1984). But we can only really guess at the locations of the others, relying on the information provided by later chronicles and traditions, occasionally supported by scraps of archaeological evidence.

Local tradition has long associated Felix with the tiny parish of Babingley, in the far west of the county, north of Kings Lynn (Moralee 1982). Here the ruined church, the earliest fabric of which appears to be of fourteenth-century date (Batcock 1991: 88), is – uniquely for Norfolk – dedicated to the saint. In the area to the south of the church, fieldwalking has revealed a particularly substantial Middle Saxon settlement. Two other early ecclesiastical sites are suggested by William of Malmesbury's *De Gestis Pontificum Anglorum*, a thirteenth-century work which may well incorporate lost early East Anglian material. William describes how, after Felix's death at Dommoc, his body was taken to a place called *Seham* (Hamilton 1890: 147). This, according to William, was the site of a monastery which had been founded by the saint himself. The *Liber Eliensis* also gives *Seham* as Felix's resting-place, but suggests that the monastery here had been founded by nobleman called Lutting, under the direction of one Abbot Wereferd (Blake 1962: 17). Both the *Liber*, and William, relate that the church at *Seham* was destroyed by the Danes, round about the time that they sacked the monastery of Ely in Cambridgeshire (that is, immediately after the martyrdom of King Edmund). Whitelock has suggested that this description shows 'that both William of Malmesbury and the *Liber Eliensis* meant the Cambridgeshire Soham', but this is by no means certain (Whitelock 1972: 4). Saham Tony in west Norfolk is also a possible candidate.

William of Malmesbury also relates how Felix founded a church at *Redham*, Reedham, a tradition which also appears in the *Liber Eliensis*, and in the *Liber Albus* of Bury St Edmunds. The latter also mentions the churches at Babingley, together with those at Loddon, and at Mendham in north Suffolk, where there was later an important minster with lands lying north of the Waveney, in Norfolk. The relevant passage is worth quoting in full.

In the wall of Loddon church a certain inscription was found. Felix bishop and Werned Abbot and Luthing Aetheling. He maden the kirke at Lodne [Loddon] and the Kirke at Redeham [Reedham] and the halige Kirke at Babingeley. At Mendam a bishop was found in a wooden coffin and in a leaden tablet was contained – Hier lieth biscop Eadmund Kinges thean. He sette Lodne and he sette Redham and he sette Mendham and there hise bones restan. (BM Add. Mss. 14847)

It is interesting that this account, unlike that of William of Malmesbury, refers to Lutting and Werned – presumably the same individuals who, according to the *Liber Eliensis*, founded the monastery at *Seham*. Loddon church has no fabric which is obviously earlier than the fifteenth century, but Reedham is more interesting. This church, dedicated to St John the Baptist, stands on a low hill a kilometre north-east of the village. In March 1981 the building was gutted by fire. Examination by the Norfolk Archaeological Unit revealed – among other aspects of a complex history – that the builders responsible for the earliest phase of the structure, dating to the eleventh or early twelfth centuries, made extensive use of high-quality Roman tiles. Moreover, those involved in subsequent building programmes, from 1300 through to 1500, had access to substantial quantities of Cretaceous limestone, probably originating in Lincolnshire. This too was apparently looted from an important Roman building somewhere in the vicinity, almost certainly of a military nature, given that the only other place in the county where similar stone was been found is the Saxon shore fort at Brancaster. The foundations of a circular Roman building, interpreted as the base of a lighthouse, were indeed apparently discovered somewhere close by in the nineteenth century, although the details are obscure. Once again, perhaps, we may have evidence for the establishment of an early church site in close proximity to an abandoned Roman military installation (Rose, forthcoming).

Burgh Castle, Babingley, North Elmham, Reedham, perhaps Loddon, and just possibly Saham: a seventh place can be added to this tentative list of early ecclesiastical sites. According to the post-Conquest text called the *Resting Places of the English Saints*, Withburga, daughter of King Anna, founded a nunnery at *Derham*, and died there in 654 (Liebermann 1889: 5–6). A holy well dedicated to her, as we have seen, still stands in the churchyard of East Dereham. The modern inscription, however, records that her body no longer lies there, for it was translated to Ely, to lie with her sister Ethelburga, in the tenth century. The account of this event provided by the *Liber Eliensis* is dramatic (Blake 1962: 120–3). In 974 Abbot Brihtnoth visited *Derham* with a group of armed men, and gave a great feast to the town's inhabitants. While the latter slept off the after-effects, Brihtnoth and his men seized the saint's body and fled. They reached Brandon, on the edge of the Fens, unmolested, but by this time the townsfolk were in hot pursuit, and lining the banks of the river rained a variety of projectiles down on the fleeing party. In vain: the abbot urged on the oarsmen, and made good his escape. It is, needless to say, quite impossible to assess whether any of this really happened. Even if it did, doubt has recently been expressed over whether Withburga is today associated with the right Dereham (Bond, Penn, & Rogerson 1990: 33). For both the *Liber Eliensis* and the *Resting Places* refer simply to *Derham*: and there is another Dereham in the county, West Dereham, much closer to Ely, on the edge of the Fens some 5 kilometres east of Downham Market. Fieldwalking here has, in fact, located the site of a substantial Middle Saxon settlement, to the south of the church: one or two of the finds, including fragments of carved stonework, may hint at some early ecclesiastical significance. Nevertheless, the *Liber Eliensis* clearly has East, rather than West Dereham, in mind, for it describes how Brihtnoth's party fled 20 miles overland to Brandon. East Dereham is, indeed some 20 miles from Brandon, but West Dereham only half this distance. *Both* Derehams are, therefore, possible early ecclesiastical sites: and it is curious that the confusion between the two should mirror so closely that between North and South Elmham.

Before the end of the seventh century, monasticism in Britain displayed 'topographical preferences for boundaries (of one sort or another) and extremes' (Morris 1989: 128). Monastic communities were, for the most part, founded by restless ascetics like Fursa, men who sought seclusion from the everyday world, as well as the spiritual challenges which isolation might bring. Remote and marginal locations also fitted in well with the needs of Dark Age kings, for it was easier to donate the land necessary for a new community in areas of woodland, marsh, and waste, away from the main cores of long-settled tribal land. The possible early ecclesiastical sites discussed above would all fit in well with such a pattern. All lie within the 'peripheral' zones of Early Saxon settlement, in areas of sparsely-settled woodland, waste and marsh on the margins of the kingdom. This becomes very clear when Figure 6.1 is compared with Figure 3.2. Reedham and Loddon lay within the once well-wooded land on the fringes of the Broadland marshes; Reedham overlooked the marshes themselves, as did Fursa's Cnobheresburg, whether this was at Burgh Castle or Caister-on-Sea. On the other side of the county,

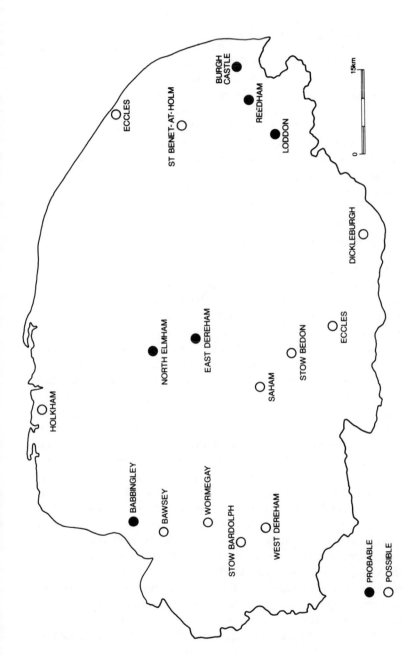

Fig. 6.1 Possible Middle Saxon monastic sites

Babingley stood on the very edge of the kingdom, close to the Wash, and within a tract of woodland which, to judge from the place-name evidence, occupied the area to the north of Lynn. West Dereham was located beside the peat fen, an area not drained until the post-medieval period. The peripheral nature of the remaining sites – East Dereham, Saham, and Elmham – is less immediately obvious. All lie in the upper reaches of major river valleys in the heart of the county. But all lie close to the sparsely-settled corridor of the central watershed, and in all cases the names of neighbouring parishes attest the presence of woodland in Early Saxon times. They thus occupy marginal locations, but in the *interior* of the county. In the case of Elmham, the choice of such a liminal position was no doubt also determined by a desire to serve the needs of communities based on both the east and the west of the county, sundered by the watershed.

With these characteristics in mind, it is possible to point to a number of other places where early Christian communities may have been established. St Benet's Abbey at Holme was refounded in 1019, after its destruction by the Vikings: its original foundation date is unknown, but could well have been as early as the late eighth century (Dymond 1985: 129). Stow Bedon and Stow Bardolph are the only places in the county with names incorporating the element *stōw*. This often means no more than 'place', but can have the sense 'religious place'. The church at Stow Bedon has no obviously early fabric, but is dedicated to St Botolph, the founder of *Icanho*. While in general this dedication is usually a late one, in East Anglia it may sometimes indicate an early site. Stow Bedon lies near the central watershed, and the names of neighbouring parishes suggest a well-wooded landscape. Stow Bardolph church has no early fabric (it was largely rebuilt in the nineteenth century) and an unremarkable dedication: but it stands, like West Dereham, beside the Fens, on the very edges of the Middle Saxon kingdom. The two Norfolk Eccles also occupy peripheral locations, the one within the central watershed, the other on the coast (its church has long since tumbled into the sea). It is just possible that these names may indicate, not the survival of sub-Roman Christianity, but the presence of religious communities established during the seventh century. Attention might also be drawn to the parish church of Holkham, isolated in the north-west of Holkham park on its unusual mound, a kilometre from a Roman road, less than a kilometre from the sea, and – uniquely in Norfolk – dedicated to St Withburga, the founder of the monastery at *Derham*. Lastly, metal-detectors working near the churches at Wormegay and Bawsey – both former islands on the edge of the Fens – have discovered Middle Saxon *styli*, writing implements, indicating the presence of literate and therefore, perhaps, ecclesiastical communities.

Readers will have noticed that this list of possible early monasteries in Norfolk includes considerably more than the seven mentioned in King Ælfwald's letter of the 740s for the *whole* kingdom. The list, of course, is highly speculative – little hard evidence supports any of these suggestions, and most may simply be wrong. Others, however, may represent short-lived communities, like Cnobheresburg: for early monasticism was, in Morris's words, 'locationally unstable' (Morris 1989: 138). Others still may have been established after the 740s. But it could well be that Aelfwald was only including royal foundations, and excluding those which – if events in Middle Saxon East Anglia followed the pattern attested from elsewhere in England – were now being established in some numbers by members of the aristocracy. Bede, in a well-known letter, argued that these foundations were corrupt. He says that landowners were simply declaring themselves abbots, and their families monastic communities, in order to ensure the permanent alienation of estates which would normally have returned to the hands of the king (Douglas 1968: 735). A more charitable interpretation would be that noble families were now founding monasteries in precisely the same way that royal lineages had done in earlier decades. Either way, as monasteries increased in numbers, they seem to have become more stable institutions, and were often established in more congenial, less marginal locations, close to the centres of royal and comital estates. By this time, the church in England had passed the pioneer stage.

Minsters

By the tenth century, the term which Bede used for a monastery – *mynster* – had taken on a rather different meaning. It was now used to designate long-established churches, superior in the ecclesiastical hierarchy to the local foundations more recently created by smaller landowners (Morris 1989: 128–39; Blair 1985: 1988). It was with the proliferation of such local churches, in the last centuries of Saxon England, that the parish system developed. Before this, ecclesiastical organisation had been based on territories much larger than the medieval parish. Each minster served, and was supported by, a *parochia* as extensive, in some cases, as an entire hundred. Minsters were staffed not by single priests, but by small communities, comparable in some senses to the 'team ministeries' of the modern church.

Some historians describe the minster system as if it was a coherent, standardised structure, purpose-built to ensure the evangelisation of the early kingdoms (Blair 1988). Others, however, have argued that the system lacked any such unity or purpose: and that any it *appeared* to have was the result of late Saxon administrators' attempts to put order into a system characterised by complexity and chaos (Morris 1989: 130–4). Certainly, the available evidence makes it clear that minsters varied widely in the extent of their endowments, in the level of their staffing, and in the size of their *parochiae*. This variety reflected complex origins. Some minsters developed from monasteries established during the seventh and eighth centuries by royal and noble households, where these had failed to develop – later in the Saxon period – into true monasteries, following a regular Benedictine rule. Most, however, were probably established, from the start, as small teams of priests, on royal or comital estates. Their main purpose was, initially at least, presumably to serve the spiritual needs of their founders, rather than to evangelise the surrounding countryside.

In Norfolk it is extremely difficult to discover the sites of early minsters, or to reconstruct the pattern of their territories. This is partly, once again, because of the marked absence of early charters. But it is also because the establishment of local churches went further here, and earlier, than almost anywhere else in England. Domesday mentions no less than 250 rural churches in Norfolk, more than in any other county except Suffolk: and, as we shall see, its coverage is unquestionably very incomplete. The sheer scale of this precocious explosion of church-building ensured that, to all intents and purposes, the minster system had ceased to exist by the time of Domesday, and few traces of it can be discerned in post-Conquest documents. Nor can the evidence of archaeology be of much assistance in our region. In particular, because of the absence of good local freestone, Norfolk lacks the kinds of pre-Conquest sculpture which, elsewhere, has been used to identify important early churches (Morris 1989: 135–8).

There are, however a few scraps of documentary evidence. There is one pre-Conquest charter which explicitly refers to a minster: that for Dickleburgh, dating from between 1044 and 1052. By this document Osulf and Leofrun left land at Dickleburgh and Semer (now Semere Green) to Bury St Edmunds Abbey, on condition that

Four priests should sing, two after Osulf's day, and two after Leofrun's day, and each week [they are] to sing twelve masses. And we desire that whosoever is abbot of St Edmunds Bury should be the guardian of the minsters, and their priests must never transfer or surrender them to themselves or their kin. (Hart 1966: 86–9)

At the time of Domesday the manor of Dickleburgh was still held by two priests, and as late as 1454 the church was divided into four separate portions, each served by a different rector who took the services in turn: the Portion in the Marsh, the Portion in the Field, Long Moor Portion, and Sea Mere Portion (Blomefield 1805, I: 191–3). It is just possible that the Dickleburgh charter relates in some way to the refounding of a much earlier community. The name of the parish has as its second element either *berg*, 'hill', or *burh*, 'fort'; the first element, according to Mills, is a personal name, *Dicel* (Mills 1991). There is no recorded Old English name which sounds anything like this, but there is an early *Irish* name: *Dicuill* or *Dicul*. The only person with this name recorded in Early Saxon Norfolk was none other than the Dicuill who was Fursa's companion at Cnobheresburgh: a surprising coincidence, if that is what it is.

There are a couple of other entries in Domesday which seem to refer to minsters. In Thetford, we learn of 'one church of St Mary which Archbishop Stigand held: now the four sons of bishop Erfast hold it. Always attached to this church have been the four churches of St Peter, St John, St Martin and St Margaret, six carucates of land less half a bovate.' This certainly sounds like an urban minster, which had retained control over daughter churches in its *parochia*, although the situation here is complicated by the fact that St Mary's was, at this time, the cathedral church of the East Anglian diocese. At Langley, Domesday records the presence of '1 whole priest and 2 halves. They hold 100 acres of free land and appertain in the church of St Andrew'. This was presumably the church in Langley itself although this has, since the Middle Ages, been dedicated to St Michael.

It is possible that other minster churches should be sought amongst those to which Domesday attributes particularly large endowments of land. Of the twenty-five churches with 40 acres or more, five are places we have met with already as potential early ecclesiastical sites: Thetford St Mary, Reedham, Loddon, Elmham, and Stow Bardolph. Most of the others, however, are in minor, peripheral vills, places which are unlikely to have served as important religious central centres. Moreover, Domesday itself makes it clear that large endowments are no necessary guide to ancient status: the church at Swanton had 60 acres of land, but these were 'the alms of very many men'.

In the absence of other 'hard' evidence we are forced – not for the first time in this book – to fall back on more speculative lines of enquiry. One approach is to examine the layout of parish boundaries. As these became fixed in the course of the eleventh and twelfth centuries, they came to form a complex web imposed on the natural topography of the county. Parishes varied greatly in their size, but they also display another interesting pattern of variation. Some shared boundaries with only two or three other parishes, but others were contiguous with eight, nine, ten, or even more. In cases like North Walsham (Figure 6.2), the resulting pattern – of a parochial 'core' and a ring of attached parishes – is visually striking. To some extent, of course, variations in the number of 'contacts' is simply a function of size: and numerous complex factors of relief and topography will have been instrumental in moulding the parochial mesh. In some cases, however, it is likely that patterns like that around North Walsham developed through the breaking away of parishes at the edges of an ancient minsterland.

There are fifty-six parishes in the county which have 'contact scores' of eight or more. Of these, two – West Dereham and Stow Bedon – have already been mentioned as possibly sites of early monasteries, while no less than nineteen are places which

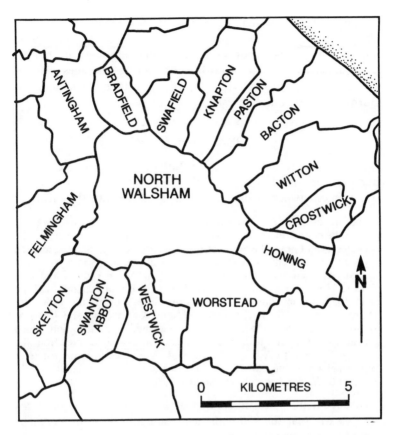

Fig. 6.2 The layout of parish boundaries in the area around North Walsham

were probably the centres of archaic estates: East Dereham, North Elmham, Cawston, Aylsham, Wymondham, Tunstead, North Walsham, Holt, South Creake, Wighton, Docking, Saham, Great Massingham, Mileham, Hingham, Fakenham, Blofield, Loddon, and Diss. Most of these places were, indeed, hundredal manors, or had given their names to hundreds. To these places we may add Swaffham (nine contacts), a large manor though deficient in sokemen, which Domesday informs us 'belonged to the realm and King Edward gave it to Earl R[alph]'. Such a coincidence of early estate centres, and minster sites, would not be surprising, given that kings and *comites* tended to establish churches close to their principal residences. On this basis, attention might also be drawn to large churches of cruciform plan (a characteristic of the 'after-life' of minster churches (Morris 1989)) in two places which were important royal manors: Burnham Overy and Snettisham.

Parish churches

By the middle decades of the eleventh century, there were large numbers of churches in Norfolk. The will of Eadwine, made some time between 1030 and the Conquest, reveals this clearly:

I grant the estate at Algarsthorpe to St Edmund except ten acres which I give to the church there. And Leofric is to have the three acres which he occupies. And I grant the estate at Little Melton to St Benedicts, and ten acres to the church.... And ten acres south of the street to Bergh church. And ten acres north of the street to Apton church, and four acres to Holverstone church, and four acres to Blyford church, and ten acres to Sparham church.... And after Ketel's death the estate [at Thorpe] is to go to St Edmund's without controversy; and [that] at Melton to the church which Thurward owned; and the land which Edwin, Ecgferth's son had, free to the church; and eight acres from the estate at Thorpe, to Ashwell church; and eight acres from the estate at Wrenningham to the old church, and two acres to Fundenhall church, and two to Nayland church. (Whitelock 1930: no. 33)

This document is worth quoting at length because it indicates very clearly that the 250 churches (excluding those in Norwich) recorded by Domesday must represent a serious underestimate of the true number in existence in the county. While the survey mentions the churches at Sparham, Wrenningham, Hapton, and Fundenhall, those at Little Melton, Ashwell(thorpe), Nayland, Bergh, and Holverston are passed over in silence. Comparison of Domesday's record with other contemporary or near-contemporary sources suggest omissions on a similar scale. No less than thirty-five of the churches mentioned in pre-Conquest charters – many of which were confirmed to St Benet's Abbot by Edward the Confessor as late as 1047 – are ignored (Cotton 1980). The *Inquisitio Eliensis*, a document probably based on the original returns for the Survey, similarly mentions several churches which it omits: at East Dereham, Bridgham, Northwold, West Walton, and Pulham (two) (Cotton 1980).

Internal evidence also suggests substantial omissions. There are a number of places – nine in all – where Domesday mentions a priest, but no church. While some of these may have been non-resident landowners, this was not always the case: the priest at Hevingham sang three masses a week. Most telling of all, however, is the evidence for systematic omissions. Only one church is recorded in the whole of Earsham hundred, and one in Forehoe, yet in the hundred of Depwade which lay between them no less than thirteen are listed. It is, to say the least, unlikely that such differences reflect real variations in the density of local churches. They suggest, instead, that certain hundred courts, or commissioners, were unsure about whether churches should be included in the returns of the survey or not.

It is one thing to demonstrate the incompleteness of Domesday's record, quite another to estimate the likely scale of omissions. Cotton has suggested that almost every parish in the county had a church by the time of Domesday (Cotton 1980). His conclusion was based, in part, on architectural evidence. Of forty-six churches which, at the time he was writing, appeared to have good evidence of pre-Conquest fabric, only eighteen appear in Domesday. Assuming that the overall pattern of omissions was in the same ratio, this would suggest that the 250 rural churches mentioned in Domesday represented a real total of over 650. Unfortunately for this elegant argument, art historians and archaeologists are today rather less confident that they once were of their ability to distinguish between churches built before, and after, the Conquest. Even the ruins of the possible Late Saxon cathedral at North Elmham have been assigned to the post-Conquest period by Stephen Heywood, who suggests that they really represent a private chapel built by Bishop Losinga, after the removal of the see to Thetford in 1071 (Heywood 1982). Eric Fernie has drawn attention to a

school of minor churches, inhabiting the hundred years from the second quarter of the eleventh century to the second quarter of the twelfth, which is neither simply 'Saxon' or simply 'Norman'. . . . Indeed it is probably true to say that half, if not the majority, of surviving buildings commonly grouped under the label 'Anglo-Saxon' fall into this category. (Fernie 1983: 171)

Nevertheless, it seems likely that Cotton's conclusions are not far wrong, given that Domesday mentions churches in some of the smallest, poorest, most remote vills in the county. Even a place like Pudding Norton, with a recorded population of only eight, could have a church. There were, no doubt, vills without churches in Domesday Norfolk, but they must have been unusual.

As we have seen, this proliferation of churches seems to have resulted from the activities of local landowners, and some of the parish churches in Late Saxon Norfolk were apparently the private property of local lords, a source of profit and prestige. But probably not all. A will drawn up in the first two decades of the eleventh century by one Siflaed refers to the church at Marlingford as 'my church' (Whitelock 1930: 37). But it goes on to declare that this is henceforward 'to be free and Wulfmaer my priest is to sing at it, he and his issue, so long as they are in holy orders', suggesting that the church was passing out of the hands of the estate owner and into those of a hereditary priestly kindred. Eadwine's will, which bequeaths numerous portions of land to a large number of churches, implies that these were not simply the private property of some other landowner. Nor were all churches necessarily founded by single individuals. It is quite possible that some were established by groups of related freemen, or even by unrelated neighbours: Domesday explicitly refers to one such case in Suffolk, but not, unfortunately, in Norfolk (Warner 1986: 42).

The proliferation of local churches probably occurred after the Viking incursions, rather than before. There is, it is true, little hard evidence: excavations at Barton Bendish and Guestwick revealed only tantalising traces of possible Late Saxon wooden churches beneath the present stone structures (Rogerson & Ashley 1987: 63; Rogerson & Williams 1987: 79). But the use of the Scandinavian term *kirkja*, 'church', in the names of Kirby Cane, Kirby Bedon, and Colkirk suggests that possession of a church was still unusual enough to be a distinguishing feature of a place, worth commenting on when these names were coined some time after 870 (Gelling 1981: 8). The Viking incursions may, in the medium term, have actually encouraged local church-building. Although the scale and longevity of the disruption caused to ecclesiastical organisation at this time may, in the past, have been exaggerated by historians (Whitelock 1945), disruption there certainly was. Monasteries were presumably sacked and expropriated (Bond, Penn, & Rogerson 1990: 56), and the region lacked its own bishop for several decades. All this may have encouraged the fission of ecclesiastical territories in the same way that it may have encouraged the disintegration of secular ones. Local landowners may have been in a better position to assert their rights, to erect new churches within the territories of old minsters, and thus threaten the latter's revenues.

Nevertheless, we should not necessarily envisage a rash of church-building in the late ninth and early tenth centuries. There are some signs that many of the churches recorded by Domesday were fairly recent additions to the landscape. It is noteworthy that while the holdings of the free men described in the survey show a fairly random scatter of values, from a few acres up to several carucates, the endowments of churches display a more structured pattern, with a marked clustering at particular values. Thus, of the 220 churches for which figures of landed endowment are given, a majority – 149 – have clear subdivisions of a carucate: 10 have 60 acres, 24 have 30, 10 have 24 (i.e., a fifth of a hide); 24 have 20 acres (a sixth of a hide), and so on. This may suggest a pattern of original endowments which had not yet been obscured by random gifts of odd acres, of the kind suggested by the will of Eadwine.

All this leads to a more important, but also more difficult question. Why were there so many churches in the county in the eleventh century? It might be argued that a high density of churches simply reflects a high density of population, combined with the county's considerable wealth in the Late Saxon period. But there is almost certainly more to it than that. Almost every Late Saxon settlement in Norfolk seems to have had its church: twenty-six Domesday vills had two or even more churches recorded by Domesday Book. Some of these entries relate to what were later to be contiguous but administratively distinct vills, bearing the same basic name but distinguished by some prefix like 'Great' or 'South'. But many were places which always remained as unitary vills, like East Carleton, Tattersett, Hempnall, or Shouldham. Churches continued to proliferate in some places even after Domesday: indeed, by the thirteenth century Shottesham had no less than four (Batcock 1991: 10). But in general, the post-Conquest period seems to have witnessed some reduction in numbers. Thus the church at Algarsthorpe, mentioned in the will of Eadwine, quoted earlier, disappeared;

while at Itteringham aerial photographs have revealed the site of a lost apsidal church, almost certainly of eleventh- or twelfth-century date, in the south–east of the parish. In some cases, as probably at Hempnall, a church continued to exist but as some kind of non-parochial chapel. Yet in spite of such disappearances, some very small parishes survived into the Middle Ages – like Frenze, covering only 200 hectares, or Thorpe Parva, extending over less than 160. Indeed, there were at least 928 separate parishes in the county by the thirteenth century, with an average size of around 5.75 square kilometres: the lowest of any county in England.

Late Saxon Norfolk thus experienced church-building on a ferocious scale, almost certainly well beyond the needs of an admittedly very dense population. Competitive church-building is indicated, and this must surely be a manifestation of Norfolk's curious social structure. In a county in which vills of 'classic' form, containing and coterminous with a manor whose population consisted largely or entirely of dependent tenants, were rare, we should perhaps not expect to find a straightforward pattern of ecclesiastical provision. Moreover, in a region in which there was no sharp and simple division between 'lords' and 'peasants', but a complex and subtle gradation of freeholders, questions of status must have been acute: and a church was an important index and symbol of status. Ownership of a church was one of the attributes, according to a law of Cnut, of thegnly rank (Morris 1989: 253); and while most of Norfolk's church-builders could never have aspired to the other requirements laid down by the law, the possession of a fortified gatehouse and five hides of land, ownership of a church may well have been important in the negotiation of local status. It may, indeed, have helped to confirm the rights to ownership usurped by families over outlying portions of ancient estates.

There may have been another factor at work. Later in the Middle Ages, there were at least twelve villages in the county in which two parish churches stood in the same churchyard: East Carleton, Antingham, Barnham Broom, Rockland St Mary, South Walsham, Great Melton, Reepham, Bedingham, Blo Norton, West Dereham, Stiffkey, and Wicklewood (Batcock 1991: 10). In a number of other places churches did not share the same churchyard, but were built so close together that their churchyards practically joined: these included Barton Bendish, Marsham, Gillingham, Shottesham, and Kirby Bedon (there may have been other examples of both categories: different authorities argue about particular examples: Cotton 1980; Batcock 1991; Warner 1988). The most intriguing case of all is that of Reepham. Here there were not only three churches within one churchyard (until the destruction of one by fire in 1543), but each belonged to a separate parish, each of which was a separate vill at the time of Domesday: Whitwell, Hackford, and Reepham. The three parishes meet at this point, although Whitwell church stands on a little parochial peninsula within the parish of Hackford, connected to its own parish by a narrow strip of land, 200 metres long and only 3 metres wide (Batcock 1991: 10).

We do not know how many of these places already possessed their extra churches at the time of Domesday: the survey only notes two churches in the case of Shottesham and Carleton. Shared and adjacent churchyards are known from other counties of eastern England, but nowhere in these numbers. They have been attributed to the activities of free peasants, responding to a shortage of ecclesiastical accommodation, brought about by local population pressure and the failure of manorial lords to improve provision (Warner 1986): a problem that, in later centuries, would have been solved by additions to an existing stone building (Morris 1989: 232). This explanation is possible, but not entirely convincing in cases like Reepham. The erection of a second church in one yard seems to express both a desire for separation, and the need to maintain a link with some location of communal importance: shared churchyards thus seem to articulate the emergence of a new social entity and yet its desire to preserve continuity with a place of ancestral significance. It is possible, therefore, that shared churchyards are a manifestation of the growth and division of free kindreds, with the erection of the second church marking, perhaps, the point at which one branch of a family became spatially and socially distinct, through migration to a new settlement. In the case of Reepham, an early seventeenth-century map shows that the tithable land of the three parishes lay intermixed in an area of open field lying to the south–west of their churches. This may represent the original arable land of a kindred which had migrated to settlements – Hackford, Whitwell – strung along its periphery. Reepham lies

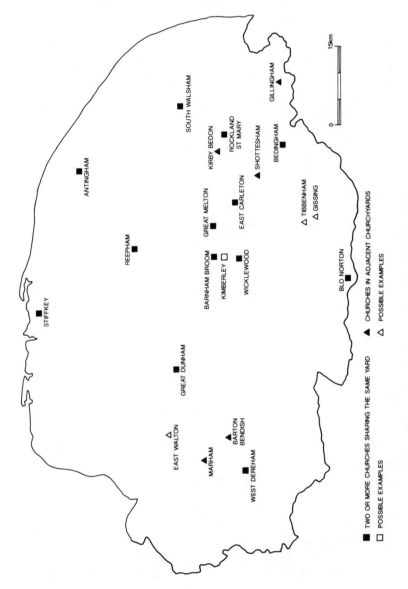

Fig. 6.3 The distribution of shared and adjacent churchyards in Norfolk

STIFFKEY

ANTINGHAM

REEPHAM

GREAT DUNHAM

EAST WALTON

MARHAM

BARTON
BENDISH

WEST DEREHAM

BARNHAM BROOM
KIMBERLEY
WICKLEWOOD

GREAT MELTON

EAST CARLETON

SOUTH WALSHAM

KIRBY BEDON

ROCKLAND
ST MARY

SHOTTESHAM

BEDINGHAM

GILLINGHAM

TIBENHAM

GISSING

BLO NORTON

0   15km

■   TWO OR MORE CHURCHES SHARING THE SAME YARD
□   POSSIBLE EXAMPLES

▲   CHURCHES IN ADJACENT CHURCHYARDS
△   POSSIBLE EXAMPLES

on the fringes of the cental watershed, and neighbouring villages bear names with woodland associations: it may be that there were particular opportunities here for the expansion, fission and migration of a kin group in Late Saxon times. Elsewhere, the daughter settlements perhaps took the form of the common-edge farms and hamlets which, as we shall see, were now beginning to appear all over the county. Such speculation perhaps receives a measure of support from the general coincidence between the distribution of churches with shared and adjacent churchyards, and the areas of the county in which free men were particularly thick on the ground (compare Figures 5.4 and 6.3): areas in which the expansion, and fission, of free kindreds was perhaps proceeding apace in the last century of the Saxon period.

This is no more than one final speculation, to end a chapter brimming with speculations. The development of ecclesiastical organisation in the county remains truly mysterious. The evidence of documents will probably contribute little to our understanding in the future: the challenge is one for archaeology to answer.

7

The Norman Conquest
and beyond

The distinctive character of Norfolk did not disappear in the centuries after the Norman Conquest. The county continued to enjoy a thriving economy, continued to support a dense population; continued, above all, to be distinguished by particularly complex patterns of social and tenurial organisation (Schofield 1965; Darby *et al.* 1979). Continuity is evident in other ways. The principal patterns of regional variation within the county were perpetuated into the Middle Ages, and indeed beyond – the contrast between the east and the west, and between valley and interfluve. There was considerable stability also in the location of central places, both administrative and economic.

In part, all this was simply due to the fact that the same factors of location, topography, climate, and soils continued to mould the county's character after, as before, the Norman Conquest. But to some extent it was also because of the lasting influence of tenurial patterns, patterns of ownership and authority, which were established during the Saxon period. These long outlasted the particular circumstances which had engendered them, surviving into – and modifying the development of – much later structures of social and economic organisation. For Norfolk's tenurial complexity was not so much eradiacted as fossilised by the impact of the Norman Conquest. Vills on the familiar textbook pattern, in which all tenants were villeins or bordars holding of a single manor, continued to be rare: and manors frequently extended into two or even more parishes. In the early seventeenth century, for example, it was noted of the king's manor of Aylsham that its 'Limmits Butts and Bounds cannot be sett Foerth but by plott by reason other lords land lye intermixed wth his Hignes lands their and doeth extend into other out townes neere adioyninge' (Campbell 1981: 14). Such complexity was to have a profound effect on the development of settlement, field systems, and much else.

The impact of the Norman Conquest

The new Norman elite cared little for the complex, and confusing, range of social and tenurial relationships which had been familiar to the county's pre-Conquest inhabitants. Commendation, sokeland, thegnland, and the rest were now subsumed within a much simpler system. Here, as elsewhere in William's kingdom, all land was held, ultimately, of the king, in return for services: all social relationships were embedded in land tenure, and vice versa. There was no place in such a system for groups of un-attached free peasants. Their land must now be held directly from the king or, more usually, from some tenant-in-chief. And yet the nature of the transition to the new system ensured, in a variety of ways, that older patterns of complexity were per-petuated. Where ancient estate centres (like Aylsham) had retained fragments of outlying soke land, and dependent sokemen, in neighbouring vills, these now became detached portions of the main manor, or parts which, while continuous with its principal lands, extended over a parish boundary. Complexity also arose from the way in which the free population came to be fitted in to the new framework. Free men might be incorporated within manors by the aggressive policies of in-dividual magnates – 'added' to manors, 'delivered to make up' manors, in the words of Domesday. But often their relationship with feudal superiors was determined by pre-Conquest ties. If a free man had been commended to or otherwise dependent on a Saxon lord, the latter's successor would generally claim his land as a part of his fee. In places where a number of *liberi homines* had been commended to a number of different Saxon lords, each of whom had a different successor, the result was a complex, multi-manorial vill.

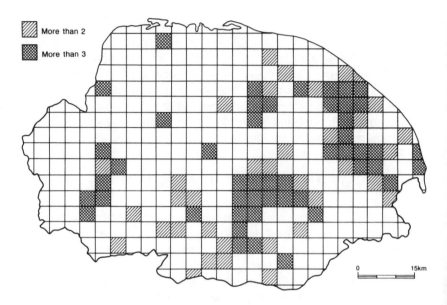

Fig. 7.1 Tenurial organisation in medieval Norfolk: the number of manors per vill recorded in the *Nomina Villarum* of 1316

It is difficult to exaggerate the extent of manorial complexity in the county during the Middle Ages. The *Nomina Villarum* of 1316 shows that only 163 of the vills in the county – less than a quarter – were held by single lords (Blake 1952: 56). Some, like Thompson, had as many as nine. This document suggests that the areas of greatest manorial complexity in 1316 were, in general terms, the same as those in which Domesday records a high density of free tenures, although there are important differences, especially in the extreme south-east of the county (compare Figures 5.6 and 7.1). Here the *Nomina Villarum* records many single-manor vills in an area which, at the time of Domesday, had contained large numbers of *liberi homines* – partly, perhaps, because the small size of vills in this densely settled region tended to preclude the presence of more than one lordship in each. Yet the *Nomina Villarum* is only a very rough guide to the strength of local lordship. To begin with, it unquestionably underemphasises the extent of manorial complexity. Unfortunately, Norfolk lacks a comprehensive series of Hundred Rolls which, in neighbouring

164

counties, have been used to provide a more detailed picture of tenurial arrangements. Of the copies and drafts that have survived the most interesting is that for Hevingham, dated to 1279, which has been examined – in association with a number of contemporary manorial documents – by Bruce Campbell (1986). The *Nomina Villarum* groups Hevingham with the adjacent vill of Stratton, and lists six lords: the Hevingham document lists seven head tenants in the vill. Three of these – the Prior of Gislingham, the Master of the Knights Hospitaller's Preceptory at Carbrooke, and the Prior of the Cluniac Abbey of Broomholme – had only small acreages, occupied by single free tenants. The holdings of the other four, however – the Bishop of Norwich, the Earl of Gloucester, the King, and the Lord John le Mareschal – were more substantial, although only those of the Bishop, and of Lord John, had all the features required of a true manor – demesne, free tenants, and bond tenants. The King's lands, in contrast (which formed an outlying portion of the ancient royal estates of Aylsham and Cawston) were entirely held by free tenants, some of whom themselves had under-tenants; while the Earl of Gloucester's holding was divided into two sub-manors. One of these was sublet in its entirety. To add to this confusion, the four main manors – as Campbell has demonstrated from a range of other documents – all extended into neighbouring townships. Moreover, the largest single holding in the vill was actually a subtenancy: one William le Cat held land as a direct tenant both of the Bishop and of John le Mareschal; as both a direct and a sub-tenant of the Earl; and as a sub-tenant of the Prior of Gislingham. Yet Cat's holding was accounted a manor in its own right, and had its own court.

Even where there was only one manor in a vill, this often contained large numbers of free tenants, owing no more (in many cases) than suit to the manorial court. For tenurial distinctions established before the Conquest did not suddenly disappear: even sokemen were not necessarily depressed to the status of villeins. Twelfth- and thirteenth-century documents often show their descendants as 'molmen' or 'censuarii' (Douglas 1927). These were dependent tenants, but they held their land on comparatively easy terms, for limited services or a money rent. Even the villeins and bordars of medieval Norfolk had a fairly privileged position: they generally owed services which, compared with those in other parts of the country, were light, and often commuted to a money payment at an early date. *Inquisitions Post Mortem* reveal that the value of labour services was often negligible. In 1309 Robert Tosny's great manor of Saham was worth 90 per annum: but out of this the works of his customary tenants were worth only 70s (Dodwell 1948: 290). By the thirteenth century an active market in peasant land had developed in the county (Williamson 1984). On many manors, even villein land changed hands with bewildering rapidity, the manorial court acting merely as a kind of solicitor's office, ratifying a mass of transactions. To some extent, lordship was weak in all parts of the county: but in general the central and southern claylands, the north-east, and to some extent the silt fens in Marshland, continued to be more poorly manorialised, and more tenurially complex than the light soil areas of the North and west. The broad east/west division in the tenurial and social character of the county was thus maintained into the Middle Ages.

All this does not mean that the landscape of medieval Norfolk was entirely lacking in expressions of lordly power. The great baronial families established by the Conquest built their castles: the Warennes at Castle Acre, the d'Albinis at Old Buckenham and Castle Rising. They endowed abbeys and priories like those at Castle Acre, Wymondham, and Binham (indeed, by the early fourteenth century there were around seventy abbeys, priories and friaries in the county). But the most ubiquitous expressions of early medieval lordship were, unquestionably, parish churches. The two centuries following the Conquest saw the replacement of wooden with stone structures on a massive scale. This transformation may reflect the ability of new, more powerful lords to direct the wealth of the county to construction projects. But it also expresses a keen willingness to do so, as if building in stone expressed confidence in proprietorship, and a superiority over tenurial predecessors. By 1250, at the latest, there can have been few, if any, parishes in the county which lacked a stone-built church. A few of the county's Norman churches are particularly impressive – like South Lopham – but many are more lowly edifices, largely because in prosperous communities such structures were largely or entirely rebuilt later in the Middle Ages.

Eleventh- and twelfth-century churches manifest, in a subtle way, patterns which had long been important in the evolution of the county. The central watershed still had an influence. To its south and east, the quoins and openings in these predominantly flint-built structures were constructed with limestone imported from Caen in France; to the north and west, Barnack-type limestone, imported via the Wash from the Midlands, was used (Harris 1989). The most distinctive feature of the county's early churches is their round towers: there are over 120 of these in the county, compared with forty-one in Suffolk and small numbers in other eastern counties (Heywood 1988). Stephen Heywood has convincingly argued that round towers were a fashion adopted from northern Germany, particularly from Schleswig-Holstein: although it may well be that the absence of local freestone, and the difficulties of constructing corners in buildings composed entirely of flint, encouraged the imitation of north German example. In spite of the Norman Conquest and the consequent strengthening of cultural contacts with northern France, Norfolk's ancient links with places on the far littoral of the North Sea were maintained.

The development of settlement

Lordship might manifest its presence in individual buildings, but the overall structure of the landscape proclaimed its weakness: and nowhere more so than in the pattern of settlement. The county lacks the kinds of planned, regulated medieval villages encountered in parts of the North and the Midlands: indeed, by the thirteenth century villages of any kind were rare in many districts. For the nucleated settlements around parish churches began to dissolve around the time of the Norman Conquest. Farms drifted off to the edges of commons, forming girdles of settlement around the moors, fens, heaths, or greens from which the resultant hamlets often took their names. Expansion of settlement through the subsequent centuries brought further additions to these common-edge agglomerations. The vast majority of medieval farms looked out over commons. Only the post-medieval removal of such areas, largely through late eighteenth- and early nineteenth-century Enclosure Acts, has obscured this essential feature of the county's settlement pattern. Fieldwalking surveys have shown that settlement in the Middle Ages was much more densely packed around common margins than was the case by the time the earliest maps of the county were made. Faden's map of 1797, surveyed before most of the county's commons were enclosed, nevertheless gives something of the flavour of the medieval situation (Plate 8). In many places, the migration to the commons was so complete that the parish church was left entirely isolated in the midst of the ploughed fields.

The commons which formed the new foci for settlement took a variety of forms. It is useful to distinguish – although the distinction can in places be an arbitrary one – between 'low' and 'high' commons. The former were the 'fens' and 'moors' which occupied damp, low-lying areas: extensive grazing marshes in the valleys of the major rivers, smaller pockets in their tributaries. The 'high' commons occurred on the interfluves above: on patches of acid sand and gravels in the north and west, and in areas of poorly-draining land – often in slight depressions in the plateau – on the claylands. The latter were often the source of streams feeding into the main rivers. These were bounded by ribbons of common-land, which connected (and thus obscured the neat distinction between) 'high' commons and 'low'. Often, commons were linked to other commons, sometimes forming long inter-connected chains. Thus, for example, it was still possible in the late eighteenth century to travel from Shipdham to East Harling – a distance of more than 20 kilometres – without ever leaving a common. As a result, commons were often shared by two or more adjacent vills. Agreements for intercommoning the moors and greens around East Dereham had been established by 1251, but manorial records are full of disputes over neighbouring communities' rights to pasture (BM *Cottonian ms Claudius* G 11 ff. 221–33).

Commons were usually areas which were difficult, or im-possible, to cultivate. They were pockets of residual waste which had, in most cases, probably never been cultivated. To judge from names like Stubbs Green, Wood Green, or White (*þveit*) Green, many had once been woodpastures, especially those on the principal watersheds. Continued grazing prevented the regeneration of felled or fallen trees, and thus ensured the gradual emergence of open pasture. The characteristic curvilinear, concave/convex outlines of commons sometimes followed the contours, below which waterlogging prevented arable use, or above which changes in the nature of the soil (especially the presence of acid sands and gravels) militated against crop husbandry. Sometimes their boundaries seem to have been more arbitrarily fixed, however, enclosing a range of different soil types, or cutting in an apparently random manner across areas with perfectly homogeneous soil and drainage characteristics. Either way, the precise layout of boundaries was the result, not of the dictates of topography, but of human decisions and agreements.

Common-edge settlement was already taking place by the time of Domesday. Scatters of Thetford ware are located by field-walking surveys on the edges of commons, and a number of Domesday vills (such as Honingham Thorpe) can probably be identified with later common-edge hamlets. Moreover, some small, remote Domesday vills, located on clay interfluves in the south of the county, have churches which stand (or stood) on common edges, suggesting that they originated as common-edge hamlets within larger vills: examples include Mulbarton, Shelton, and Hardwick. As the process of migration intensified in the post-Conquest period few common-edge settlements became separate parishes, although many were the sites of minor manors created by the process of subinfeudation in the twelfth and thirteenth centuries.

Common-edge settlements can be found in many areas of England, but nowhere, except perhaps in the northern parts of Suffolk, were they so prominent a feature of the medieval landscape. The reasons for their ubiquity here remain obscure. One possibility is that the drift to the commons was a response to a shortage of grazing which, many historians have suggested, became acute in the more densely settled regions of England in the early Middle Ages (e.g., Fox 1980: 96–9). Peasants may have established their homes on common edges in order to stake a clear and visible claim to a dwindling resource (Williamson & Bellamy 1987: 84). Unfortunately, this theory cannot explain why common-edge drift was equally prominent in areas of the county in which there was no shortage of grazing in the early Middle Ages. Thus, for example, long lines of farms developed around the fringes of the great grazing marshes in the Yare valley, or in Marshland (Silvester 1988: 160–4). In reality, the reasons for common-edge settlement are probably complex, and may indeed have changed over time. Fieldwalking surveys show that some of the first settlements to migrate from the older nucleations actually stand, not on the common edges themselves, but a little way back from them. It is possible that some occupy, not so much the edges of residual areas of waste, but sites on the periphery of the established arable land *between* the commons. Perhaps, as in early medieval Wales, splitting of settlements (possibly, as again in Wales, associated with the division of family land between co-heirs) led to the development of girdles of settlement around the edges of fertile, long-manured arable, because heirs were understandably reluctant to take on the clearance and cultivation of entirely new areas of land. As population pressure built up, remaining areas of grazing and waste were more highly prized, and their boundaries became fixed. Farms congregated around their margins simply because, in a landscape in which (as we shall see) communal farming was poorly developed, this was a sensible place to live, allowing as it did easy access to grazing, and to the other resources offered by the common. It is the strongly nucleated villages of the Midlands, constricted and constrained by their encircling open fields, which are, perhaps, the oddity. In Norfolk, the lack of developed open field agriculture, combined with the active market in peasant land, allowed farms to drift up to common edges and offered little incentive for them not to do so.

The extent to which common-edge drift occurred in the county varied, however. In the west it mainly took the form of overflow from settlements which remained, essentially, nucleated. Thus in Breckland linear settlements often built up along the margins of 'low' commons, strung along terraces above the flood-plain (Davison 1980, 1983). It was in the east of the county that wholesale migration from earlier sites most often occurred, leaving churches isolated (Figure 7.2). This pattern is open to a number of interpretations. It probably owed something to environmental differences between the two areas. In the east, there were greater opportunities for settlement migration, because supplies of water were more freely available on the common edges: either because commons occupied damp areas on the clay plateau, with water-retentive soils, or low-lying areas on the floors of the principal river valleys. In the north and west, in contrast, many commons were located on the dry interfluves, where it was difficult to establish permanent settlements. But the

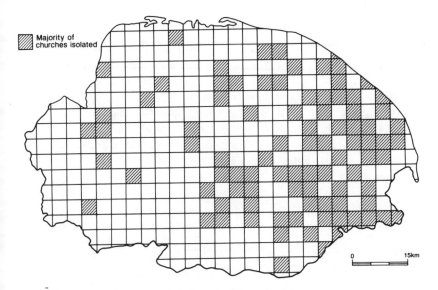

Fig. 7.2 Isolated churches in Norfolk (*source*: Faden's map of Norfolk (1797); various early estate maps. A church is here defined as 'isolated' if it lies more than 200 metres from a settlement containing more than two dwellings)

broad east/west division also corresponds, rather closely, to variations in patterns of tenurial organisation, and these were probably also a factor, although precisely how remains unclear. It is possible that weak lordship directly encouraged the migration to commons in some way. The initial stages of this process, as suggested above, may have been associated with the division of land between members of free lineages. Where vills were held by powerful nobles, in contrast, their inhabitants may have consisted largely of bond tenants who occupied dwellings close to the manorial centre to which they owed dues and services: such people had less opportunity, or incentive, to move away from the principal settlement site. Perhaps more important, however, were the indirect effects of weak and confused lordship on the development of settlement, through the kinds of agrarian arrangements which it engendered. For variations in settlement within the county were intimately connected with those in the nature of field systems.

171

Medieval field systems

A considerable proportion of Norfolk was already being farmed as arable land by the time of Domesday. But cultivation continued to expand in the following centuries, and as late as 1290 an extent for Cawston recorded nearly 109 acres of assart land (Campbell 1981: 20). By this time, open-field agriculture was established in all parts of the county. Some authorities have suggested that on the claylands, open fields had always been of limited extent, with much land being enclosed direct from the 'natural forest' (Smith 1974: 5). There is no evidence to support such a view. Even in the sixteenth and seventeenth centuries, open fields were extensive here, to judge from maps of Langley, Raveningham, Brooke, Scole, and Morley (maps in the Norfolk and East Suffolk Record Offices). Even where early maps show most of the land in hedged closes, the layout of their boundaries usually suggests that open fields had once extended over most of the parish, excluding areas of commonland and, in some cases, consolidated manorial demesne. Glebe terriers, field books, medieval extents and surveys all tell the same story (Skipper 1989). Elsewhere in Norfolk, in the light soil areas of the north and west, open fields were unquestionably ubiquitous, often surviving far into the post-medieval period.

But Norfolk's open fields differed from those of the 'Shires'. Vills in the Midlands and the north-east of England usually had two or three great fields, one lying fallow each year, which were in turn divided into a multiplicity of furlongs of roughly equal size, which formed the basic unit for crop rotation (Hall 1980, 1982). In Norfolk, in contrast, medieval documents refer to units called *precincts*, *stadia* or *quarentena*, and *pecia*. The last was the Midland *selion* or strip under a different name: but the others were not just local terms for the larger Midland units. The precinct was simply an arbitrary division of a township's cultivated land, for the purposes of description or survey, and lacked any agrarian significance. The *stadia* was an area which could be arable, or pasture, or meadow. The term 'field' was also employed in the county, but rarely in the Midland sense. Norfolk's 'fields' were sometimes as small as a Midland furlong, and while on occasions the term was used for a much larger area of arable, seldom do we find only two or three, of equal area, within a vill (Allison 1957; Postgate 1973; Campbell 1980b).

All this went hand-in-hand with a more fundamental difference. Whereas in the classic Midland vill the strips of individual tenants – free or bond – were evenly scattered through the area of the vill in the two or three great fields, in Norfolk they were normally clustered in restricted areas of the arable (except in some parts of the Breckland (Bailey 1989: 51)). This, in turn, was probably related to another significant difference between the two regions. The normal unit of tenure in Norfolk was not the virgate (although these are sporadically mentioned) but something variously called a *tenementum*, *plena terra*, or *eriung*. These units usually contained between 10 and 15 acres, and were used to assess rents and services, and also to allocate the burdens of manorial office – for electing, in particular, the *messors* responsible for collecting manorial dues. They were probably established by manorial authorities, or by communities in response to seignorial impositions, in the period after the Norman Conquest (Campbell 1980a: 178). By the thirteenth century, *tenementa* normally bore a family name, yet they contained the holdings of a number of unrelated individuals. It has been suggested that, originally, these units had formed compact holdings, held by the families from which they derived their name (Campbell 1980a: 178). Their division between different proprietors, through partible inheritance and alienation, was presumably accompanied by their disintegration into strips, and the emergence of an open-field landscape. For as reserves of potential arable dried up, the population of the county continued to grow, and holdings inevitably became subdivided (Campbell 1980a: 178–82).

Differences in the structure and layout of open fields between Norfolk, and Midland England, betray differences in origins. In parts, at least, of the Midlands, regular open-field systems came into existence as a result of conscious planning, probably directed by local lords, in the Middle or Late Saxon period (Hall 1982). They were originally laid out in the form of a number of very long furlongs, which entirely obliterated the pattern of boundaries in the earlier landscape. In Norfolk, in contrast, open fields seem to have emerged organically, through the disintegration of formerly compact, and presumably enclosed, fields. Medieval strip and furlong boundaries thus often perpetuated those of pre-existing fields: a sixteenth-century map of Scole makes it clear that the early coaxial field systems in the central Waveney valley survived into the medieval period not as hedged closes, but as unhedged furlongs. There are, moreover, clear indications that Norfolk's open fields developed rather later than those in the Midlands. The *tenementa* which, as we have seen, were probably in origin compact blocks of land, are frequently associated with farms located on the edges of the commons. Their establishment, and subsequent disintegration into strips, must therefore have occurred *after* common-edge drift had taken place in the eleventh and twelfth centuries.

The divergent development of Norfolk's field systems was probably due, at least in part, to the county's distinctive social and tenurial characteristics in the Late Saxon period; its confused manorial structure, and the weakness of local lords. Yet while lordship was comparatively weak everywhere in the county, in some districts, as we have seen, it was weaker than in others: and these differences seem to have had an important effect on the development of field systems during the early Middle Ages.

Those in the north and west of the county were, by the thirteenth century, the most highly regulated (Campbell 1980a, 1983; Allison 1957). Here flocks of sheep, grazed on the upland heaths, were systematically folded on the arable land, thus ensuring a continuous flow of nutrients from the one to the other and maintaining the fertility of soils which were, for the most part, easily exhausted. Under the 'fold course system', arrangements for folding were highly systematised. The sheep were organised in communal flocks, dominated by the stock of the manorial lord (or his lessee), and under the control of a manorial shepherd. These flocks ranged over both the heaths and the open-field strips of the tenants. Often there was more than one manor in a village, and so the fields and commons were divided into separate, continuous blocks called 'fold courses' which might, like the manors themselves, extend across parish boundaries. 'Within euery Towne and vyllage is most commonly ii or iii manors or more and to euery manor a Shepps Course or ffouldcourse belongyng' (Allison 1957: 16). The sheep grazed on the unsown arable land, when it lay fallow or before sowing in autumn or spring. The areas of fallow land, winter corn, and spring corn therefore had to be as compact as possible. They were, therefore, divided into 'shifts', similar in principle to but much less continuous than the two or three great open fields of a classic Midland vill. When a tenant's land lay within a sown shift, he sowed it accordingly. But when it lay within a fallow shift, he was prevented from doing so, and was compensated in some way by the manorial lord: either with permission to cultivate a temporary 'break' in the village heaths, or with some of the demesne arable, or by a reduction in rent or services (Allison 1957: 18). Such arrangements were necessary because, as we have seen, holdings tended to be concentrated in one restricted area of the arable, rather than being widely scattered, as in the Midlands. There was, therefore, a greater chance that a high proportion of a tenant's land would lie unsown in any given year.

The tenants benefited from the manure dropped by the sheep as they roamed across the arable land, but the systematic night-folding – the 'tathing' – was a manorial privilege, and tenants could usually only benefit from this in return for an annual payment based on the number of acres so treated. The lord was the dominant figure in the agrarian regime: it was he who was responsible for supervising the system, and in whom the rights of foldcourse were invested. The system was thus highly controlled, and organised, although it was considerably more flexible than the classic open-field systems of the Midlands.

Not all the light soil areas of the county were, however, organised in this way. In most parts of the north–east, things were very different. Here a broadly similar 'sheep-corn' husbandry was practised, but common-field arrangements were much less tightly structured, presumably because of the weakness of local lordship, and the high degree of manorial complexity (Campbell 1980a, 1980b, 1983, 1986). The foldcourse did not really exist as an institution, and there was no attempt to rationalise the disposition of fallow, winter-, and spring-sown strips into a pattern of 'shifts'. Instead, the tenants enjoyed almost complete freedom in how they organised their cropping patterns, and because it would have been impractical (to say the least) for communal access to be maintained to fallow strips scattered indiscriminately among sown ones, fallow grazing rights did not exist, although rights to graze over the land in the autumn and winter were maintained. Most land was sown in the spring, and it was therefore comparatively easy to fence off the limited areas of growing autumn-sown crops with hurdles and temporary fences. The result was a highly individualistic and innovative agricultural system. Fodder crops, principally peas and beans, were substituted for bare, year-long fallows; fertilisers – including the dung from sheep folded on individual strips – were assiduously applied. All this was labour-intensive, but then labour was not in short supply in this populous region in the twelfth and thirteenth centuries. High labour inputs also ensured thick sowings, and careful weeding and harvesting. High yields were produced, and a phenomenally dense population supported (B. Campbell 1983, 1986).

We must, of course, be a little careful about ascribing the success of medieval agriculture here entirely to to the weakness of lordship, and the resultant flexibility of agricultural arrangements. The area was, and is, one of the most fertile in England. How much stress we should lay on environmental conditions, and how much on institutional factors, is unclear. Equally unclear, in the absence of detailed study, is the nature of agrarian arrangements in those areas of equally weak lordship on the claylands in the centre and south-east of the county. Here, the heavy soils prevented such an emphasis on spring-sown crops, and may therefore have ensured that fallowing arrangements were more rigidly organised. Nevertheless, in many places fields seem only to have been thrown open after the harvest, rather than throughout the fallow season. Agriculture here may have been less sophisticated than in the north-east, but sufficient nevertheless to maintain phenomenally high population levels. In the silt fens of Marshland in the far south-west similar flexible arrangements existed, and here too high levels of population built up during the twelfth and thirteenth centuries. In all these districts, settlement was considerably more dispersed than in the 'foldcourse' areas of the north and west. It is likely that in the latter areas the need to maintain the pattern of shifts, and the integrity of foldcourses, was a factor in constricting the spread of settlement across the landscape, as was (in a more general sense) the more communal nature of agricultural organisation.

Norfolk, in common with many other areas of medieval England outside the Midlands and the North–East, was thus characterised by a fairly dispersed pattern of settlement, and by irregular open-field systems. Attempts to explain the divergent development of Midland and non-Midland landscapes have, in the past, often taken the form of simplistic, mono-causal explanations (e.g., Williamson 1989). In reality, as Dyer has argued, dispersed settlement patterns probably developed in different ways, for different reasons, in different regions (Dyer 1990). In Norfolk there seems little doubt that the irregular nature of fields and settlements owed much to the ways in which structures of social and territorial organisation had developed in the pre-Conquest period. It is likely that the county's divergence from the Midlands in these respects began long before the time of Domesday. Indeed, it is a curious fact that the distribution of at least one distinctive feature of the county's medieval landscape had, to the west, a sharp edge: and one which corresponded to the probable western boundary of the kingdom of the East Angles. It is not only the distribution of Ipswich Ware that stops sharply at the River Nene. On the silts of Marshland, green- and common-edge settlements were a dominant feature of the medieval landscape: on the identical soils on the far side of the river, they were totally absent (Silvester, forthcoming).

Marshland was something of an anomaly: for the most part, the landscape of west Norfolk was characterised by rather more structured field systems, and by a more nucleated pattern of settlement. The clearest, most significant contrast in landscape and social organisation was thus between the east of the county and the west. It was a contrast which was to influence the development of the county far into the medieval period, and indeed beyond. Yet that other ancient contrast – between valley and interfluve – also continued to be important. Thus medieval woods were mainly located on the watersheds; so too were most deer parks. The latter were particularly prominent on the central watershed, especially as this swung south beyond Dereham: Shipdham, Whinburgh, Southburgh, Attleborough, Silfield (Wymondham), Buckenham, and Tibenham all had large watershed parks. The association of parks with watersheds in general, and with the central watershed in particular, was mainly due to the fact that substantial areas of woodland and woodpasture had survived in these localities up until the time of the Conquest, areas which could now be enclosed and converted to specialised hunting use. But patterns of tenurial organisation were also probably important, especially on the central watershed. As we have seen, there were many strongly manorialised vills here, in which local lords could enclose areas of waste with relative ease, without the opposition of other landowners.

The growth of towns

Norwich was dramatically affected by the impact of Conquest. The main area of the town, south of the River Wensum, was partly obliterated by the construction of the castle in the early 1070s. No less than ninety-eight properties were destroyed: recent excavations in the area of the Castle bailey have discovered some of their remains. Four hundred metres away, beside the river Wensum, Bishop Losinga began in 1096 the construction of the magnificent new cathedral, to replace that at Thetford, to where the see had been moved from North Elmham in 1071. The new cathedral was accompanied by the conventual buildings for a community of Benedictine monks, and a bishop's palace. The construction of all this involved the removal of further houses and, probably, two parish churches. Yet the impact of the Conquest on the city was not entirely negative. Servicing the new military and ecclesiastical communities must have given the city's economy a boost: while the urban area was extended, probably from the 1070s, by the creation of the 'New' or French borough. This was established to the west of the castle around a roughly planned grid of streets, focusing on a new market (the city's present market-place). The New Borough contained at least 125 French burgesses by the time of Domesday. Norwich continued to flourish in the following centuries, maintaining its position as second city in the realm. Like other towns and cities of importance, it gained defences: earthen ramparts early in the twelfth century, a ditch with nine gates in the mid-thirteenth, and – built over a long period of time from the late thirteenth to the late fourteenth centuries – a substantial wall of flint rubble, 4 kilometres long and enclosing an area of more than 3 square kilometres (Green & Young 1981; Campbell 1975; Norwich Survey 1980).

Yarmouth also seems to have expanded in the two centuries following the Conquest, and Norfolk's other great urban centre – Kings Lynn – now appeared. This probably originated as a major centre for salt production on the edge of the Wash marshes, but it was extensively developed by Bishop Herbert Losinga in the late eleventh century, and a pattern of streets was laid out in a rough grid. A planned extension, Newland, was added to the north early in the following century (Parker 1971; Owen 1980). The development of Lynn was probably in part responsible for the decline of Thetford, which was less conveniently situated higher up the River Ouse. But other markets and urban centres in the county were flourishing in the early Middle Ages.

Indeed, no less than 140 medieval markets are known in Norfolk, one for every 4,000 hectares, although not all were in existence at the same time (Dymond 1985: 152–64). Many were short-lived affairs, the result of wildly optimistic seigniorial speculation, and did not lead to the development of urban communities. Those which were more successful, and did, usually survived as towns right up until the late seventeenth century. What is interesting is that these survivors were, for the most part, places which had been important from very early times. Their names will be familiar from earlier chapters: places like Hingham, Wymondham, Loddon, Aylsham, North Walsham, Foulsham, East Dereham, Cawston, Holt, Fakenham, Diss, Burnham, Swaffham; places which had been the centres of ancient estates, had often become hundredal manors, and had perhaps been the sites of minsters. They are, therefore, classic examples of what Everitt has called the 'primary towns' of England: settlements which were not planted towns on virgin sites, nor simply existing agricultural villages developed by the acquisition of market grants in the two centuries following the Conquest, but sites of ancient importance (Everitt 1979). It is possible that some had already gained trading functions during the later Saxon period, as a result of the presence of courts and assemblies to which numbers of people would be regularly drawn from the surrounding country-side. Most, it is true, did not receive market charters until the thirteenth century, but markets could come into existence without charters. Indeed, quite important examples were never formally recognised, including those at New Buckenham, East Dereham and even Kings Lynn (Dymond 1985: 156). Some of Norfolk's 'primary towns' may well have possessed prescriptive or customary markets for centuries before formal recognition.

Other early towns in the county do not quite, but very nearly, fall into Everitt's classification. Downham Market is an interesting case. A market here is mentioned in a charter of 1050, and was presumably established by the monks of Ramsey Abbey at the southern end of their manor of Wimbotsham. The latter was probably, in Middle Saxon times, the centre of a large estate; it was certainly a hundredal manor in the Late Saxon period. Downham was thus a kind of surrogate 'primary town', growing up on a navigable river (the original name of the town was Downham *hithe*) and close to the county's main east–west Roman road (which seems to have been diverted from its original course to run through the town).

Remarkably few of the county's urban centres were true planted towns, planned creations of the late eleventh or twelfth centuries. We have mentioned Lynn: the other examples were less successful. One is Castle Acre, set within a defended annex of the castle built by the Warennes, and occupying the ground between it and the great Cluniac Priory which they also founded. Another is Castle Rising. Here the original grid of streets was probably laid out when the castle was first built by the d'Albinis in the late eleventh century, and partly oblitered when it was extended in the thirteenth. The most visibly striking today, however, is New Buckenham, again created by the d'Albinis, and again associated with a castle. It was established in the 1140s on a virgin site where the wastes of the Banham, Carleton Rode, and Buckenham met. Like Castle Acre, it was defended, and covered an area of around 5,000 square metres, with streets laid out in a neat grid. Buckenham is not entirely unrelated to the pattern of 'primary towns', in that it may have taken over some of the functions of the ancient estate centre of Old Buckenham. Watton is the only other possible example of a true planted town in the county. The earliest property boundaries here seem to indicate a measure of planning, perhaps dating from 1204, when the de Vaux family established a Wednesday market. This was in spite of the opposition from the de Tosny family, who argued that it would be prejudicial to the fortunes of their own market at Saham, the adjacent parish. Robert de Tosny was still actively competing in 1299, when he received a grant of a Monday market: but it was Watton that flourished, so that today the ancient estate centre of Saham is no more than a village on its periphery (Dymond 1985: 157–9).

In addition to these planted towns, one or two other urban centres in the county appear to have developed as the result of medieval market grants. The most notable are Harleston, which seems to have grown up in the early thirteenth century as a fairstead and later market in a corner of Redenhall parish; and Worstead, which received its market charter in 1336. The pattern of urban development in the county was not, therefore, immutably fixed. Nevertheless, the basic structure of Norfolk's urban framework owed, and indeed still owes, a great deal to the early administrative and, probably, ecclesiastical role of key Saxon settlements. Continuity is evident in another way: the highly polarised nature of the Late Saxon urban hierarchy was maintained into the Middle Ages and beyond. The phenomenal size of Norwich tended to suppress the development of other significant urban centres across a broad swathe of the county.

Norfolk's experience of largely organic, rather than planned urban growth may be another reflection of the relative weakness of local lordship. It is certainly a pattern deeply etched in the county's urban topography. Most Norfolk towns have marketplaces which seem to have originated as areas of common land (Wymondham, for example, or Swaffham), although the characteristic concave–convex outline has usually been obscured, to some extent, by islands of encroachment, created as temporary stalls gradually became more and more permanent.

The modern landscape

In a host of ways, the patterns of the remote past continued to influence the development of the county into the late Middle Ages and beyond. The long period of population expansion came to an end around 1300; the subsequent downturn led to the shrinkage of many settlements, especially those on the interfluves. There was, initially, little outright desertion, but massive thinning of common-edge agglomerations (Davison 1990: 22, 68). Most true desertions – that is, those leading to the disappearance of a parish and vill as an independent entity, or its reduction to one or two houses and a church – occurred later, sometimes in the fifteenth century, more often in the sixteenth, seventeenth or eighteenth centuries (Allison 1955; Davison 1988; Cushion et al. 1982). Deserted sites are especially common in Breckland, but the main determinant of their location seems to have been not so much soils as topography. Almost all were on interfluves: Quarles, Waterden, Holkham, and Egemere between the Burn and the Stiffkey valleys; Houghton and Barwick between the Tat and the Heacham River. There are noticeable clusters along the central watershed: Testerton, Oxwick, Godwick, Little Bittering, and Pattesley; Croxton and Fulmondeston. Even in Breckland, desertion was most severe away from the major valleys. These places sometimes disappeared through the overstocking of commons and foldcourses by landlords or lessee graziers in the fifteenth and sixteenth centuries, which denied local farmers their rights to pasture and undermined their arable husbandry; sometimes through simple engrossment of holdings; sometimes through emparking; often through a combination of these processes. Whatever the precise cause or causes, it was in part the origin and early development of such places which sealed their fate. They were small; inconveniently situated in relation to markets and, often, water; and (especially on the central watershed) highly manorialised. For all these reasons they were particularly vulnerable to both enforced and voluntary out-migration.

The long-established contrast between the west and the east of the county was even more significant in the development of the late and post-medieval landscape, determining among other things when and how open fields disappeared. In the west of the county, planned, general enclosure was the norm. Where the power of lords was particularly strong, especially in the smaller interfluve parishes, this tended to occur through engrossment of holdings and general enclosure agreements in the seventeenth or early eighteenth centuries. Elsewhere, the process was often delayed until the late eighteenth or early nineteenth centuries, and carried out through Parliamentary Act. In the east of the county, in contrast, open fields disappeared far more gradually, at an earlier date: and through the progress of piecemeal enclosure. In most districts, this process began in the fifteenth or sixteenth centuries, and was usually well advanced by the end of the seventeenth. As a result, in the eastern half of the county Parliamentary enclosures were almost entirely restricted to areas of common grazing.

Piecemeal enclosure of open fields in the east was instigated, not so much by manorial lords, as by a class of yeoman farmers, who prospered here in the period after the Black Death. Conversion to pasture was a major reason for enclosure on the claylands: on the light arable loams of the north-east, motives were more complex. In both areas, however, it was the relative weakness of lordship, and in particular the absence of a developed fold-course system, which allowed and encouraged the process.

Many other aspects of the county's social and economic development, and landscape history, correspond to this basic east/west split, rather than to the distribution of soil types or farming regions. Thus, for example, the largest landed estates developed in the west of the county, especially on the 'Good Sands'; most of the farms and cottages constructed in the county before 1700 are to be found in the east, rather than in the west; while it was the former areas, rather than the latter, which were most affected by industrial development in the late medieval and early modern periods.

From the Middle Ages up to the present day, the administrative integrity of the county has been maintained: changes in 1974 merely moved 9,000 acres in Lothingland, south of Yarmouth, from Suffolk to Norfolk. And in ways too complex to be discussed here the county maintained a distinct cultural identity throughout the post-medieval period. In part, this identity rested on the structures of social and tenurial organisation established in the remote past; in part, it was a consequence of environment, terrain, and location. Thus, for example, the county continued to receive influences, and immigrants, from the lands on the far side of the North Sea: the refugee Protestant 'Strangers' in the sixteenth century, new crops in the seventeenth. The characteristic 'pantiles' which replaced thatch as the principal roofing material in the county during the eighteenth century were originally developed in the Low Countries; the distinctive shaped gables of many of its seventeenth-century buildings may owe something to Flemish influence.

The industrial downturn of the eighteenth and nineteenth centuries – when the county's textile production declined in the face of competition from the north of England – made Norfolk for the first time a rural backwater. Today, as the construction of the Channel Tunnel strengthens the links between the south-east of England and France, the county may continue to be on the periphery of economic activity, although road and rail improvements ever threaten its isolation. For the moment, it remains a land apart, distinct in the appearance of its landscape, and in the speech of most of its inhabitants, from London and the South-East.

References

Adkins, R. & Petchey, M. (1984) 'Secklow Hundred Mound and other meeting mounds in England', *Archaeological Journal*, **141**, 243–51.

Allen, D. (1970) 'The coins of the Iceni', *Britannia*, **1**, 1–33.

Allison, K. (1955) 'The lost villages of Norfolk', *Norfolk Archaeology*, **31**, 116–62.

Allison, K. (1957) 'The sheep-corn husbandry of Norfolk in the sixteenth and seventeenth centuries', *Agricultural History Review*, **5**, 12–30.

Anderson, O. (1934) *The English Hundred Names*, Lund.

Arnold, C. (1988) *An Archaeology of the Early Anglo-Saxon Kingdoms*, London.

Arnold, C. (1983) 'The Sancton-Bason potter', *Scottish Archaeological Review*, **2**, 17–30.

Arnold, C. (1981) 'Early Anglo-Saxon pottery: production and distribution', in *Production and Distribution: a Ceramic Viewpoint*, ed. H. Howard & E. L. Morris, Oxford.

Arnold, H. (ed.) (1879) *Henrici Archidiaconi Huntendunensis Anglorum*, London.

Atkins, M. (1985) 'The Anglo-Saxon urban landscape in East Anglia', *Landscape History*, **7**, 27–40.

Atkin, M., Ayres, B., & Jennings, S. (1983) 'Thetford-Type Ware production in Norwich', *East Anglian Archaeology*, **17**, 61–104.

Ayres, B. (forthcoming) 'The urbanisation of East Anglia: the Norwich perspective', in *Flatlands and Wetlands*, ed. J. Gardiner, *East Anglian Archaeology*,

Bailey, M. (1989) *A Marginal Economy? East Anglian Breckland in the Later Middle Ages*, Cambridge.

Barringer, C. (1979) 'Some remarks on the early administrative geography of Norfolk', *Bulletin of the Norfolk Research Committee*, **22**, 2–5.

185

References

Barringer, C. (forthcoming) *Wymondham in the Seventeenth Century*,

Bassett, S. (1989) 'In search of the origins of Anglo-Saxon kingdoms', in *The Origins of Anglo-Saxon Kingdoms*, ed. S. J. Bassett, London.

Batcock, N. (1991) 'The ruined and disused churches of Norfolk', *East Anglian Archaeology*, **51**.

Bell, M. (1989) 'Environmental archaeology as an index to continuity and change in the medieval landscape', in *The Rural Settlements of Medieval England*, ed. M. Aston, D. Austin, & C. Dyer, Oxford.

Bennett, K. (1983) 'Devensian late-glacial and Flandrian vegetational history at Hockham Mere, Norfolk, England'. *New Phytologist*, **95**, 457–87.

Blair, J. (1985) 'Secular minster churches in Domesday Book', in *Domesday Book: a Reassessment*, ed. P. Sawyer, London.

Blair, J. (1988) 'Minsters in the landscape', in *Anglo-Saxon Settlements*, ed. D. Hooke, Oxford.

Blake, E. (1962) *Liber Eliensis*, London.

Blake, W. (1952) 'Norfolk manorial lords in 1316', *Norfolk Archaeology*, **30**, 235–86.

Blomefield, F. (1805) *An Essay Towards a Topographical History of the County of Norfolk*, London.

Bohme, H. W. (1986) 'Das ende der Romerherrschaft in Britannien und die Angelsachsische Besiedlung Englands im 5 Jahrhundert', *Jahrbuch des Romisch-Germanischen Zentral Museum*, **33**, 466–574.

Bond, R., Penn, K., & Rogerson, A. (1990) *The North Folk: Angles, Saxons, and Danes*, North Walsham.

Bradley, R. (forthcoming) 'Where is East Anglia? Themes in regional prehistory', in *Flatlands and Wetlands*, ed. J. Gardiner, *East Anglian Archaeology*,

Bruce-Mitford, R. (1984) 'The Sutton Hoo ship burial: some continental connections', *Angli e Sassoni al di qua e al di la del mare*, vol. 1, Spoleto.

Cam, H. (1926) 'The King's government, as administered by the greater abbots of East Anglia', *Proceedings of the Cambridge Antiquarian Society*, **29**, 25–49.

Cam, H. (1930) *The Hundred and Hundred Rolls*, London.

Cam, H. (1944) *Liberties and Communities in Medieval England*, Cambridge.

Campbell, A. (ed.) (1962) *The Chronicle of Aethelweard*, London.

Campbell, B. (1980a) 'Population change and the genesis of commonfields on a Norfolk Manor', *Economic History Review*, **33**, 174–92.

Campbell, B. (1980b) 'Commonfield origins: the regional dimension', in *The Origins of Open-Field Agriculture*, ed. T. Rowley, London.

Campbell, B. (1981) 'The extent and layout of commonfields in east Norfolk', *Norfolk Archaeology*, **28**, 5–32.

Campbell, B. (1983) 'Agricultural progress in medieval England': some evidence from east Norfolk', *Economic History Review*, 2nd ser., **36**, 26–46.

References

Campbell, B. (1986) 'The complexity of manorial structure in medieval Norfolk: a case study', *Norfolk Archaeology*, **39**, 215–62.

Campbell, J. (1975) 'Norwich', in *Atlas of Historic Towns* fasicule, ed. M. D. Lobel, London.

Carson, R. (1949) 'The mint at Thetford', *Numismatic Chronicle*, **9**, 189–223.

Carver, M. (1984) 'Sutton Hoo in context', *Angli e Sassoni al di qua e al di la del mare*, vol. 1, Spoleto.

Carver, M. (1989) 'Kingship and material culture in early Anglo-Saxon East Anglia', in *The Origins of Anglo-Saxon Kingdoms*, ed. S. Bassett, London.

Chatwin, C. (1961) *British Regional Geology: East Anglia and Adjoining Areas*, 4th edn, London.

Clark, J. (1936) 'The timber monument at Arminghall and its affinities', *Proceedings of the Prehistoric Society*, **2**, 1–51.

Clarke, R. (1935–37) 'The Roman villages at Brettenham and Needham and the contemporary road system', Norfolk Archaeology **26**, 123–63.

Clarke, R. (1957) 'The Fossditch – a linear earthwork in south–west Norfolk', *Norfolk Archaeology*, **31**, 178–96.

Clarke, W. (1894) 'Neolithic man in the Thetford district', *Transactions of the Norfolk and Norwich Naturalists Society*, **6**, 23–36.

Clarke, W. (1914) 'The Icknield Way in Norfolk', *Proceedings of the Prehistoric Society*, **2**, 539–48.

Clarke, W. (1937) *In Breckland Wilds*, 2nd edn, Cambridge.

Colgrave, B. (1940) *Felix's Life of Guthlac*, Cambridge.

Cotton, S. (1980) 'Domesday revisited: where were the 11th century churches?', *NARG News*, **21**, 11–17.

Courtenay, P. (1981) 'The early Saxon Fenland: a reconsideration', in *Anglo-Saxon Studies in Art and History*, ed. D. Brown, J. Campbell, & S. C. Hawkes, Oxford.

Cox, B. (1972) 'The significance of the distribution of English place names in *ham*, in the Midlands and East Anglia', *Journal of the English Place Name Society*, **5**, 15–73.

Cox, B. (1975) 'The place names of the earliest English records', *Journal of the English Place Name Society*, **8**, 12–66.

Coxe, H. (1841–44) *Rogeri de Wendover Chronica, sive Flores Historiarum*, London.

Cunliffe, B. (1977) 'The Saxon Shore: some problems and misconceptions', in *The Saxon Shore*, ed. D. Johnson, London.

Cunliffe, B. (1978) *Iron Age Communities in Britain*, London.

Cushion, B., Davison, A., Fenner, G., Goldsmith, R., Knight, J., Virgoe, N., Wade, K., & Wade-Martins, P. (1982) 'Some deserted village sites in Norfolk', *East Anglian Archaeology*, **14**, 40–107.

Darby, H. (1934) 'The Fenland frontier in Anglo-Saxon England', *Antiquity*, **7**, 185–97.

Darby, H. (1952) *The Domesday Geography of Eastern England*, Cambridge.

Darby, H. (1977) *Domesday England*, Cambridge.

References

Darby, H., Glasscock, R., Sheiall, J., & Verney, G. (1979) 'The changing geographical distribution of wealth in England 1086–1334–1525', *Journal of Historical Geography*, **5**, 3, 247–62.

Darvill, T. (1987) *Prehistoric Britain*, London.

Davenport, F. (1906) *The Economic Development of a Norfolk Manor*, Cambridge.

Davies, J. & Gregory, T. (1991) 'Coinage from a *civitas*: a survey of the Roman coins found in Norfolk and their contribution to the archaeology of the *Civitas Icenorum*', *Britannia*, **22**, 65–101.

Davies, J., Gregory, T., Lawson, A., Rickett, R., & Rogerson, R. (1991) 'The Iron Age forts of Norfolk', *East Anglian Archaeology*, **54**.

Davies, W. (1977) 'Annals and the origin of Mercia', in *Mercian Studies*, ed. A. Dornier, Leicester.

Davies, W. & Vierck, H. (1974) 'The contexts of the tribal hidage: social aggregates and settlement patterns', *Fruhmittelalterliche Studia*, **8**, 223–93.

Davis, R. (ed.) (1954) *The Kalendar of the Abbots of Bury St Edmunds and Related Documents*, London.

Davis, R. (1955) 'East Anglia and the Danelaw', *Transactions of the Royal Historical Society*, 5th ser., **5**, 23–39.

Davison, A. (1980) 'West Harling: a village and its disappearance', *Norfolk Archaeology*, **37**, 295–306.

Davison, A. (1983) 'The distribution of medieval settlement in West Harling', *Norfolk Archaeology*, **38**, 329–36.

Davison, A. (1988) 'Six deserted villages in Norfolk', *East Anglian Archaeology*, **44**.

Davison, A. (1990) 'The evolution of settlement in three parishes in south–east Norfolk', *East Anglian Archaeology*, **49**.

Dodgshon, J. McN. (1973) 'Place Names from *ham*, distinguished from *hamm* names in relation to the settlements of Kent, Surrey and Sussex', *Anglo-Saxon England*, **2**, 1–50.

Dodwell, B. (1941) 'The free peasantry of East Anglia in Domesday', *Norfolk Archaeology*, **27**, 145–57.

Dodwell, B. (1948) 'East Anglian commendation', *English Historical Review*, **63**, 289–306.

Douglas, D. (1927) *The Social Structure of Medieval East Anglia*, Oxford.

Douglas, D. (1928) 'Fragments from an Anglo-Saxon survey from Bury St. Edmunds', *English Historical Review*, **43**, 376–83.

Douglas, D. (ed.) (1968) *English Historical Documents, vol. 1, 550–1042*, London.

Douglas, D. (ed.) (1932) *Feudal Documents from the Abbey of Bury St Edmunds*, Oxford.

Drury, P. (1980) 'The early and middle phases of the Iron Age in Essex', in *Archaeology in Essex to AD 1500*, ed. D. Buckley, London.

Dumville, D. (1976) 'The Anglian collection of royal genealogies and regnal lists', *Anglo-Saxon England*, **5**, 25–50.

Dumville, D. (1977) 'Kingship, genealogies and regnal lists', in *Early Medieval Kingship*, ed. P. Sawyer & I. Wood, Leeds.

Dumville, D. (1989) 'Essex, Middle Anglia, and the expansion of Mercia in the south–east Midlands', in *The Origins of Anglo-Saxon Kingdoms*, ed. S. Bassett, London.

Dunmore, S. & Carr, R. (1976) 'The late Saxon town at Thetford: an archaeological and historical survey', *East Anglian Archaeology*, **4**.

Dunnett, R. (1975) *The Trinovantes*, London.

Dyer, C. (1990) 'Dispersed settlements in Medieval England: a case study of Pendock, Worcestershire', *Medieval Archaeology*, **34**, 97–121.

Dymond, D. (1985) *The Norfolk Landscape*, London.

Edlin, H. (1972) *East Anglian Forests*, London.

Edwards, D. & Green, C. (1977) 'The Saxon Shore fort and settlement at Brancaster, Norfolk', in *The Saxon Shore*, ed. D. Johnston, London.

Ekwall, E. (1928) *English River-Names*, Oxford.

Ekwall, E. (1960) *The Concise Oxford Dictionary of English Place-names*, Oxford.

Ellis, H. (1883) *A General Introduction to Domesday Book*, London.

Ellison, J. (1969) 'Excavations at Caister-on-Sea 1962–3', *Norfolk Archaeology*, **34**, 45–73.

Everitt, A. (1977) 'River and wold: reflections on the historical origin of regions and *pays*', *Journal of Historical Geography*, **3**, 1–19.

Everitt, A. (1979) 'Country, county and town: patterns of regional evolution in England', *Transactions of the Royal Historical Society*, 5th ser., 29, 79–108.

Farmer, D. (1984) 'Some saints of East Anglia', in *East Anglian and Other Studies Presented to Barbara Dodwell*, ed. M. Barber, Reading.

Fellows-Jensen, G. (1990) 'Place-names as a reflection of cultural interaction', *Anglo-Saxon England*, **19**, 13–22.

Fernie, E. (1983) *The Architecture of the Anglo-Saxons*, London.

Fisher, D. (1973) *The Anglo-Saxon Age c. 400–1042*, London.

Fleming, A. (1984) 'The prehistoric landscape of Dartmoor: wider implications', *Landscape History*, **6**, 5–19.

Fleming, A. (1987) 'Coaxial field systems: some questions of time and space', *Antiquity*, **61**, 188–202.

Fox, H. (1980) 'Approaches to the adoption of the Midland System', in *The Origins of Open-Field Agriculture*, ed. T. Rowley, London.

Frere, S. (1971) 'The forum and baths at Caister-by-Norwich', *Britannia*, **2**, 1–26.

Fulford, M. (1990) 'The landscape of Roman Britain: a review', *Landscape History*, **12**, 25–32.

Garmonsway, G. (ed.) (1953) *The Anglo-Saxon Chronicle*, London.

Gelling, M. (1978) *Signposts to the Past*, London.

Gelling, M. (1981) 'The word "church" in English place-names', *Bulletin of the CBA Churches Committee*, **15**, 4–9.

Gelling, M. (1984) *Place-Names in the Landscape*, London.

Godwin, H. (1968) 'Studies in the post-glacial history of British vegetation 15. Organic deposits of Old Buckenham Mere, Norfolk', *New*

Phytologist, **67**, 95–107.

Godwin, H. & Tallantire, P. (1951) 'Studies in the post-glacial history of British vegetation 12. Hockham Mere, Norfolk', *Journal of Ecology*, **39**, 285–307.

Gransden, A. (1985) 'The legends and traditions concerning the origin of the Abbey of Bury St. Edmunds', *English Historical Review*, **100**, 1–24.

Green, B. & Rogerson, A. (1977) 'The Anglo-Saxon cemetery at Bergh Apton, Norfolk', *East Anglian Archaeology*, **7**.

Green, B., Rogerson, R., & White, S. (1987) 'The Anglo-Saxon cemetery at Morning Thorpe, Norfolk', *East Anglian Archaeology*, **36**.

Green, B. & Young, R. (1981) *Norwich, the Growth of a City*, Norwich.

Green, C. (1977) 'Excavations in the Roman kiln field at Brampton, 1973–4', *East Anglian Archaeology*, **5**, 31–96.

Gregory, T. (1982) 'Romano-British settlement in West Norfolk and on the Norfolk fen edge', in *The Romano-British Countryside*, ed. D. Miles, Oxford.

Gregory, T. (1986a) 'Enclosures of "Thornham" type in Norfolk', *East Anglian Archaeology*, **30**, 32–7.

Gregory, T. (1986b) 'Warham Camp', *East Anglian Archaeology*, **30**, 22–7.

Gregory, T. (1991a) 'Excavations in Thetford, 1980–82, Fisons Way', *East Anglian Archaeology*, **53**.

Gregory, T. (1991b) 'Excavations at Thetford Castle 1962', *East Anglian Archaeology*, **54**, 3–17.

Grierson P. & Blackburn, M. (1986) *Medieval European Coinage*, Cambridge.

Grove, A. (1961) 'Climate', in *Norwich and its Region*, ed. F. Briers, Norwich.

Gurney, D. (1986) 'Settlement, religion and industry on the Fen-edge: three Romano-British sites in Norfolk', *East Anglian Archaeology*, **31**.

Gurney, D. (1990) 'Caister-on-Sea', *NARGH News*, **59**, 3–11.

Hall, D. (1980) 'The origins of open-field agriculture; the archaeological fieldwork evidence', in *The Origins of Open-Field Agriculture*, ed. T. Rowley, London.

Hall, D. (1982) *Medieval Fields*, Aylesbury.

Hamilton, N. (ed.) (1890) *William of Malmesbury's De Gestis Pontificorum Anglorum*, London.

Harke, H. (1990) '"Warrior graves?" The background to the Anglo-Saxon weapons burial rite', *Past and Present*, **126**, 22–43.

Harris, A. (1989) 'Late eleventh and twelfth century church architecture of the lower Yare valley, Norfolk', unpublished Ph.D. thesis, University of East Anglia, Norwich.

Harrod, H. (1874) 'On the site of the bishopric of Elmham', *Proceedings of the Suffolk Institute of Archaeology*, **4**, 7–13.

Hart, C. (1966) *The Early Charters of Eastern England*, Leicester.

Hart, C. (1971) 'The tribal hidage', *Transactions of the Royal Historical Society*, **21**, 133–57.

References

Haselgrove, G. (1982) 'Wealth, prestige and power: the dynamics of Late Iron Age political centralisation in England', in *Ranking, Resource, and Exchange*, ed. C. Renfrew & S. Shennan, Cambridge.

Hawkes, C. (1949) 'Caister-by-Norwich, the Roman town of Venta Icenorum', *Archaeological Journal*, **106**, 62–5.

Healy, F. (1988) 'The Anglo-Saxon cemetery at Spong Hill, North Elmham, Part VI. Occupation during the seventh to second millennia BC', *East Anglian Archaeology*, **39**.

Heywood, S. (1982) 'The ruined church at North Elmham', *Journal of the British Archaeological Association*, **135**, 1–11.

Heywood, S. (1988) 'The round towers of East Anglia', in *Minsters and Parish Churches: the Local Church in Transition*, ed. J. Blair, Oxford.

Hills, C. (1977) 'A chamber grave from Spong Hill, North Elmham, *Medieval Archaeology*, **21**, 167–76.

Hills, C. (1980) 'Anglo-Saxon cremation cemeteries with particular reference to Spong Hill, Norfolk', in *Anglo-Saxon Cemeteries 1979*, ed. P. Rahtz, T. Dickinson, & L. Watts, Oxford.

Hills, C. (1989) 'Spong Hill Anglo-Saxon cemetery', in *Burial Archaeology: Current Research, Methods and Developments*, ed. C. A. Roberts, F. Lee, & J. Bintliff, Oxford.

Hills, C. (forthcoming) 'Who were the East Anglians?', in 'Flatlands and Wetlands', ed. J. Gardiner, *East Anglian Archaeology*,

Hills, C. & Penn, K. (1981) 'Spong Hill Part II'. *East Anglian Archaeology*, **11**.

Hills, C., Penn, K., & Rickett, R. (1987) 'The Anglo-Saxon cemetery at Spong Hill, North Elmham, Part 4: catalogue of cremations', *East Anglian Archaeology*, **34**.

Hines, J. (1984) *The Scandinavian Character of Anglian England in the Pre-Viking Period*, Oxford.

Hinton, D. (1990) *Archaeology, Economy and Society: England from the Fifth to the Fifteenth Century*, London.

Hoare, C. (1918) *The History of an East Anglian Soke*, Bedford.

Hodder, I. (1979) 'Pre-Roman and Romano-British tribal economies', in *Invasion and Response: the Case of Roman Britain*, ed. B. Burnham & H. Johnson, London.

Hodge, C. & Hellyer, C. (1984) *Soils and their Uses in Eastern England*, Harpenden.

Hodges, R. (1982) *Dark Age Economics*, London.

Hodges, R. (1989) *The Anglo-Saxon Achievement: Archaeology and the Beginnings of English Society*, London.

Hood, C. (1938) *The Chorography of Norfolk*, Norwich.

Hooke, D. (1981) *Anglo-Saxon Landscapes of the West Midlands*, Oxford.

Howlett, R. (1914) 'The ancient see of Elmham', *Norfolk Archaeology*, **18**, 105–28.

Jacobson, G. & Bradshaw, R. (1981) 'The selection of sites for palaeovegetational studies', *Quaternary Research*, **16**, 1, 80–96.

James, M. (1917) 'Two lifes of St. Ethelberht, king and martyr', *English*

Historical Review, **32**, 214–44.

Johnson, C. (1906) 'Introduction to the Norfolk Domesday', in *The Victoria History of the County of Norfolk*, ed. W. Page, London.

Johnson, S. (1980) 'Excavations by Charles Green at Burgh Castle, 1958–1961', in *Roman Frontier Studies*, ed. W. Hanson & L. Keppie, Oxford.

Johnson, S. (1983) 'Burgh Castle: excavations by Charles Green, 1958–1961', *East Anglian Archaeology*, **20**.

Jones, G. (1971) 'The multiple estate as a model framework for tracing early stages in the evolution of rural settlement', in *L'Habitat et les Paysages Ruraux d'Europe'*, ed. F. Dussart, Liège.

Jones, G. (1979) 'Multiple estates and early settlement', in *English Medieval Settlement*, ed. P. Sawyer, London.

Kirby, D. (1991) *The Earliest English Kings*, London.

Knowles, A. (1977) 'The Roman settlement at Brampton, Norfolk; interim report', *Britannia*, **8**, 209–21.

Lambert, J., Jennings, J., Smith, C., Green, C., & Hutchinson, J. (1960) *The Making of the Broads*, London.

Larwood, G. & Funnell, B. (1961) 'Geology', in *Norwich and its Region*, ed. F. Briers, Norwich.

Larwood, G. & Funnell, B. (1970) *The Geology of Norfolk*, Norwich.

Lawson, A. (1976) 'Excavations at Whey Curd Farm, Wighton', *East Anglian Archaeology*, **2**, 65–100.

Lawson, A. (1983) 'The archaeology of Witton, near North Walsham, Norfolk', *East Anglian Archaeology*, **18**.

Lawson, A. (1984) 'The Bronze Age in East Anglia, with particular reference to Norfolk', in *Aspects of East Anglian Prehistory*, ed. C. Barringer, Norwich.

Lawson, A. (1986) 'Barrow excavations in Norfolk, 1950–82', *East Anglian Archaeology*, **29**.

Lawson, A., Martin, E., & Priddy, D. (1981) 'The barrows of East Anglia', *Anglian Archaeology*, **12**.

Liebermann, F. (ed.) (1889) *Die Heiligen Englands*, Hanover.

Loyn, H. (1962) *Anglo-Saxon England and the Norman Conquest*, London.

Loyn, H. (1984) *The Governance of Anglo-Saxon England 500–1087*, London.

Luard, H. (1890) *Flores Historiarum*, London.

McKinley, J. (1989) 'Spong Hill: the cremations', in *Burial Archaeology: Current Research, Methods and Developments*, ed. C. Roberts, F. Lee, & J. Bintliff, Oxford.

Margary, I. (1973) *Roman Roads in Britain*, 3rd edn, London.

Margeson, S. (1991a) 'A Viking mount from Bylaugh', *The Quarterly*, **3**, 16–17.

Margeson, S. (1991b) 'An Introduction to the Vikings in East Anglia', *The Quarterly*, **1**, 18–25.

Marshall, W. (1787) *The Rural Economy of Norfolk*, London.

References

Martin, E. (1976) 'The Icklingas', *East Anglian Archaeology*, **3**, 132–4.
Martin, E. (1988) 'Burgh: the Iron Age and Roman enclosure', *East Anglian Archaeology*, **40**.
Mathew, F. (1656) *To His Highness Oliver, Lord Protector . . . is humbly presented a Mediterranean Passage by Water between Lynn and Yarmouth*, London.
Mercer, R. (1976) 'Grimes Graves Norfolk – an interim statement on conclusions drawn from the total excavation of a flint mine shaft and a substantial surface area in 1971–1', in *Settlement and Economy in the Second and Third Millenium BC*, ed. C. Burgess & R. Miket, Oxford.
Mercer, R. (1981) *Grimes Graves, Norfolk. Excavations 1971–2*, Vol. 1, London.
Metcalf, D. (1984) 'Monetary circulation in southern England', in *Sceattas in England and on the Continent*, ed. D. Hill & D. Metcalf, Oxford.
Miller, E. (1951) *The Abbey and Bishopric of Ely*, Cambridge.
Mills, A. (1991) *A Dictionary of English Place Names*, Oxford.
Moralee, J. (1982) 'Babingley and the birth of Christianity in East Anglia', *NARGH News*, **31**, 7–11
Morris, J. (1973) *The Age of Arthur: A History of the British Isles from 350 to 650*, London.
Morris, R. (1989) *Churches in the Landscape*, London.
Murphy, P. (1984a) 'Environmental archaeology in East Anglia', in *Environmental Archaeology: a Regional Review*, ed. H. Keeley, London.
Murphy, P. (1984b) 'Prehistoric environments and economies', in *Aspects of East Anglian Prehistory*, ed. C. Barringer, Norwich.
Murphy, P. (forthcoming) 'Early farming in Norfolk', in *An Historical Atlas of Norfolk*, ed. P. Wade-Martins, Norwich.
Myres, J. (1969) *Anglo-Saxon Pottery and the Settlement of England*, Oxford.
Myres, J. (1970) 'The Angles, the Saxons, and the Jutes', *Proceedings of the British Academy*, **56**, 145–74.
Myres, J. & Green, B. (1973) *The Anglo-Saxon Cemeteries of Caistor-by-Norwich and Markshall*, London.
Newton, S. (1990) 'On the making of Beowulf, with special attention to the pre-Viking kingdom of East Anglia', unpublished Ph.D. thesis, University of East Anglia, Norwich.
Norwich Survey (1980) *The Work of the Norwich Survey*, Norwich.
Owen, D. (1980) 'Bishop's Lynn: the first century of a new town?', in *Proceedings of the Battle Conference 1979*, ed. R. Allen Brown, London.
Parker, V. (1971) *The Making of Kings Lynn*, London.
Peglar, S., Fritz, S., & Birks, H. (1989) 'Vegetation and land use history at Diss, Norfolk', *Journal of Ecology*, **77**, 203–22.
Planche, J. R. (1865) 'The earls of East Anglia', *Journal of the British*

Archaeological Association, **21**, 91–163.

Polanyi, K., Arensberg, C., & Pearson, H. (1957) *Trade and Markets in Early Empires*, New York.

Postgate, M. (1973) 'Field systems of East Anglia', in *Studies of Field Systems in the British Isles*, ed. A. Baker & R. Butlin, Cambridge.

Rackham, O. (1976) *Trees and Woodlands in the British Landscape*, London.

Rackham, O. (1980) *Ancient Woodland*, London.

Rackham, O. (1986a) 'The ancient woods of Norfolk', *Transactions of the Norfolk and Norwich Naturalists' Society*, **27**, 161–77.

Rackham, O. (1986b) *The History of the Countryside*, London.

Reid, A. & Wade-Martins, P. (1980) 'A re-examination of Panworth Ditch, Ashill', *Norfolk Archaeology*, **32**, 307–12.

Rigold, S. (1962) 'The Anglian cathedral of North Elmham, Norfolk', *Medieval Archaeology*, **6–7**, 67–108.

Robinson, B. & Gregory, T. (1987) *Celtic Fire and Roman Rule*, North Walsham.

Rogerson, A. (1976) 'Excavations on Fuller's Hill, Great Yarmouth', *East Anglian Archaeology*, **2**, 131–246.

Rogerson, A. (1977) 'Excavations at Scole 1973', *East Anglian Archaeology*, **5**, 97–224.

Rogerson, A. & Ashley, J. (1987) 'The parish churches of Barton Bendish', *East Anglian Archaeology*, **32**, 1–66.

Rogerson, A. & Dallas, C. (1984) 'Excavations at Thetford 1948–59 and 1973–80', *East Anglian Archaeology*, **22**.

Rogerson, A. & Gregory, T. (1991) 'General conclusions', in 'The Iron Age forts of Norfolk', ed. J. Davies *et al.*, *East Anglian Archaeology*, **54**, 69–72.

Rogerson, A. & Lawson, A. (1991) 'The earthwork enclosure at Tasburgh', *East Anglian Archaeology*, **54**, 31–58.

Rogerson, A. & Silvester, R. (1986) 'Middle Saxon occupation at Hay Green, Terrington St. Clement', *Norfolk Archaeology*, **39**, 320–3.

Rogerson, A. & Williams, P. (1987) 'The late eleventh century church of St. Peter, Guestwick', *East Anglian Archaeology*, **32**, 67–80.

Rose, E. (forthcoming) 'The church of Saint John the Baptist, Reedham; the reuse of Roman materials in a secondary context'.

Rye, W. (1883) *Some Rough Materials for the History of the Hundred of North Erpingham*, Norwich.

Rye, W. (1920) 'Hundred courts and mote hills in Norfolk', in W. Rye, *Norfolk Handlists*, 1st ser., Norwich.

Salway, P. (1970) 'The Roman Fenland', in *The Fenland in Roman Times*, ed. C. W. Phillips, London.

Sawyer, P. (1958) 'The density of the Danish settlement in England', *University of Birmingham Historical Journal*, **6**, 1–17.

Sawyer, P. (1971) *The Age of the Vikings*, London.

Sawyer, P. (1979) 'Medieval English settlement; new interpretations', in *English Medieval Settlement*, ed. P. Sawyer, London.

Scammell, J. (1974) 'Freedom and marriage in medieval England', *Economic History Review*, **27**, 523–37.

Scarfe, N. (1986) *Suffolk in the Middle Ages*, Ipswich.

Schofield, R. (1965) 'The geographical distribution of wealth in England 1334–1649', *Economic History Review*, 2nd ser., **17**, 483–510.

Schram, O. (1961) 'Place names', in *Norwich and its Region*, ed. F. Briers, Norwich.

Silvester, R. (1988) 'The Fenland Project number 3: Marshland and the Nar Valley, Norfolk', *East Anglian Archaeology*, **45**.

Silvester, R. (forthcoming) ' "The addition of more-or-less undifferentiated dots to a distribution map"? The Fenland Project in retrospect', in *Flatlands and Wetlands*, ed. J. Gardiner, *East Anglian Archaeology*.

Sims, R. (1972) 'The anthropogenic factor in East Anglian vegetational history: an approach using A[bsolute] P[ollen] F[requency] techniques', in *Quaternary Plant Ecology*, ed. H. Birks & R. West, Oxford.

Simm, R. (1978) 'Man and vegetation in Norfolk', in *The Effect of Man on the Landscape; the Lowland Zone*, ed. S. Limbrey & S. Evans, London.

Simms-Williams, P. (1983) 'The settlement of England in Bede and the Chronicle', *Anglo-Saxon England*, **12**, 1–41.

Skipper, K. (1989) 'Wood-Pasture: the landscape of the Norfolk claylands in the Early Modern Period', unpublished M.A. dissertation, University of East Anglia, Norwich.

Smith, A. (1974) *County and Court*, Oxford.

Smith, J. (1978) 'Villas as a key to social structure', in *Studies in the Romano-British Villa*, ed. M. Todd, Leicester.

Smith, J. T. (1982) 'Villa plans and social structure in Britain and Gaul', *Bulletin de l'Institut Latine et de Centre de Recherches A. Piganiol*, **17**, 321–6.

Smith, R. (1987) *Roadside Settlements in Lowland Roman Britain*, Oxford.

Stafford, P. (1985) *The East Midlands in the Early Middle Ages*, Leicester.

Stenton, F. (1922) 'St Benet of Holme and the Norman Conquest', *English Historical Review*, **37**, 225–35.

Stenton, F. (1942) 'The historical bearing of place-name studies; the Danish settlement of eastern England', *Transactions of the Royal Historical Society*, 4th ser., **24**, 1–24.

Stenton, F. (1959) 'The East Anglian kings in the seventh century', in *The Anglo-Saxons: Studies Presented to Bruce Dickens*, ed. P. Clemoes, London.

Stevens, C. (1947) 'A possible conflict of laws in Roman Britain', *Journal of Roman Studies*, **37**, 132–4.

Stevens, C. (1966) 'The social and economic aspects of rural settlement', in *Rural Roman Settlement in Britain*, ed. C. Thomas, London.

References

Swift, G. (1983) *Waterland*, London.

Taylor, C. (1983) *Village and Farmstead*, London.

Wade, K. (1976) 'Excavations at Langhale, Kirstead', *East Anglian Archaeology*, **2**, 10–29.

Wade, K. (1983a) 'Exploitation patterns', in 'The archaeology of Witton, near North Walsham, Norfolk', *East Anglian Archaeology*, **18**, 74–76.

Wade, K. (1983b) 'The early Anglo-Saxon period', in 'The Archaeology of Witton, near North Walsham, Norfolk', *East Anglian Archaeology*, **18**, 50–69.

Wade, K. (1988) 'Ipswich', in *The Rebirth of the Town in the West*, ed. R. Hodges & B. Hobley, London.

Wade-Martins, P. (1974) 'The linear earthworks of West Norfolk', *Norfolk Archaeology*, **36**, 23–38.

Wade-Martins, P. (1977) 'A Roman road between Billingford and Toftrees', *East Anglian Archaeology*, **5**, 1–3.

Wade-Martins, P. (1980a) 'Excavations in North Elmham Park 1967–72', *East Anglian Archaeology*, **9**.

Wade-Martins, P. (1980b) 'Village sites in the Launditch Hundred', *East Anglian Archaeology*, **10**.

Warner, P. (1986) 'Shared churchyards, freemen church builders and the development of parishes in eleventh-century East Anglia', *Landscape History*, **8**, 39–52.

Warner, P. (1988) 'Pre-conquest territorial and administrative organisation in East Suffolk', in *Anglo-Saxon Settlements*, ed. D. Hooke, Oxford.

Webster, G. (1978) *Boudicca – The British Revolt Against Rome AD 60*, London.

Welch, M. (1985) 'Rural settlement patterns in the Early and Middle Anglo-Saxon periods', *Landscape History*, **7**, 13–26

West, J. (1932) *St Benet of Holme 1020–1210. The Eleventh and Twelfth Century Sections of the Cott. Ms. Galba Eii. The Register of the Abbey of St. Benet of Holme*, Norwich.

West, S. & Plonviez, J. (1976) 'The Romano-British site at Icklingham', *East Anglian Archaeology*, **3**, 63–125.

West, S., Scarfe, N., & Cramp, R. (1984) 'Iken, St. Botolph and the coming of East Anglian Christianity', *Proceedings of the Suffolk Institute of Archaeology*, **35**, 279–301.

Whitelock, D. (ed.) (1930) *Anglo-Saxon Wills*, Cambridge.

Whitelock, D. (1945) 'The conversion of the eastern Danelaw', *Saga-Book of the Viking Society*, **12**, 159–76.

Whitelock, D. (1972) 'The pre-Viking church in East Anglia', *Anglo-Saxon England*, **1**, 1–22.

Whittock, M. (1986) *The Origins of England 410–600*, London.

Williamson, J. (1984) 'Norfolk: the thirteenth century', in *The Peasant Land Market in Medieval England*, ed. P. Harvey, Cambridge.

References

Williamson, T. (1986) 'Parish boundaries and early fields: continuity and discontinuity', *Journal of Historical Geography*, **12**, 241–8.

Williamson, T. (1987) 'Early co-axial field systems on the East Anglian boulder clays', *Proceedings of the Prehistoric Society*, **53**, 419–31.

Williamson, T. (1988) 'Settlement chronology and regional landscapes: the evidence from the claylands of East Anglia and Essex', in *Anglo-Saxon Settlements*, ed. D. Hooke, Oxford.

Williamson, T. (1989) 'Explaining regional landscapes: woodland and champion in southern and eastern England', *Landscape History*, **11**, 5–13.

Williamson, T. & Bellamy, L. (1987) *Property and Landscape*, London.

Wilson, D. (1983) 'Sweden-England', in *Vendel Period Studies*, ed. J. Lamm & H. Nordstrom, Stockholm.

Wilson, D. (1985) 'A note on OE *hearg* and *weoh* as place-name elements representing different types of pagan Saxon worship sites', *Anglo-Saxon Studies in Archaeology and History*, **4**, 20–9.

Winterbottom, M. (ed.) (1972) *Three Lives of English Saints*, Toronto.

Woodward, B. (1864) 'The Old Minster, South Elmham', *Proceedings of the Suffolk Institute of Archaeology*, **4**, 1–7.

Young, A. (1809) *General View over the Agriculture of the County of Norfolk*, London.

Index

Abbo of Fleury, 139
Ælfwald, king of the East Angles, 74, 76, 143, 149
Aelle, king of Sussex, 74
aerial photography, 4, 40, 43, 158
Æthelbald, king of Mercia, 76
Æthelberht, king of the East Angles, 76, 139
Æthelberht, king of Kent, 74
Æthelfryth, king of the Northumbrians, 74
Æthelhere, king of the East Angles, 75–6, 78
Æthelred, king of the East Angles, 105
Æthelstan, king of the East Angles, 105
d'Albini family, 166, 180
Alby, 121
Aldburgh, 32
Aldeby, 108
Aldwulf, king of the East Angles, 76–8, 83
Algarsthorpe, 154, 157
Allemanni, 53
Ancilites, 34
Angles, 20, 49–70

Anglo-Saxon Chronicle, 49, 62–3, 74, 143
Anna, king of the East Angles, 75, 99, 139
Ant, river, 13
Antingham, 158
architecture, Anglo-Saxon, 155
Ardleigh series, Bronze Age cremation cemeteries of, 23
Arminghall, 22–3, 37
Arnold, C., 64
Ashby St Mary, 108
Ashill, 36
Ashwellthorpe, 141, 153
Aylsham, 87, 101, 103, 123, 153, 163, 165, 179

Babergh (Suffolk), 132
Babingley, 61, 143, 144, 145, 148
back-formation, in river names, 55
Banham, 100
Barford, 97
Barney, 131
Barnham Broom, 158
Barningham, 128
Barton Bendish, 156, 159

Barwick, 40, 182
Bassett, S., 62
Bastwick, 89, 91
Bawburgh, 96–7, 141
Bawsey, 21, 149
Beckham, East and West, 128
Bede, 3, 49, 53, 73–4, 77, 138–40
Bedingham, 158
Beetley, 65, 100
Beonna, king of the East Angles, 76, 79, 81
berewicks, 93
Bergh Apton, 68, 154
Bibracti, 34
Bicchamditch, 69–70
Bickerston, 85
Billingford, 40, 41, 102
Billockby, 108
Bilney, 65, 100, 110
Binham, 166
Bintree, 141
Bisi, bishop of the East Angles, 77
Bixley, 22
Blackwater, river, 36
Blickling, 101
Blofield Hundred, 100, 153
Blomefield, F., 65, 97, 101, 129, 141
Blo Norton, 85, 93, 158
Bodham, 119
Bodney, 142
Bohme, H., 50
Boniface, Saint, 143
Bordesholme, 53
Boructuari, 53
Botolph, Saint, 143, 148
Boudicca, 37
Boudiccan revolt, 37, 40
boulder clay, 7–8, 17
Bowthorpe, 97
Bradenham, 85
Bradfield St Clare (Suffolk), 140
Brampton, 32, 40, 41, 47, 103
Brancaster, 47, 55
Brandon (Suffolk), 145, 146
Brandon Parva, 97
Branodunum, 47, 55

Breccles, 101
Breckland, 11, 13, 21, 35, 125
medieval settlement in, 170
Roman settlement in, 45
Brettenham, 38, 41, 67
Bretwaeldas, 74
Breydon Water, 13
Bridgham, 154
Brihtnoth, Abbot of Ely, 145
Brisley, 65
Broads, Norfolk, 1, 13, 114, 124, 125
Bronze Age, 21–3
Brooke, 102
Brothercross Hundred, 128, 130
Bunwell, 96
Bure, river, 13
Burfield (in Wymondham), 99
burh, 30, 32
Burgh by Aylsham, 32
Burgh Castle, 47, 56, 67, 81, 138, 145, 146
Burn, river, 18, 40, 92, 182
Burnham (Deepdale, Norton, Overy, Sutton, Thorpe, Ulph, Westgate), Middle Saxon estate at, 92–3
Burnham Norton, 142
Burnham Overy, 128, 130, 153
Burnham Thorpe, 109, 128, 130
Bury St Edmunds Abbey, (Suffolk), 132, 140, 144
Bustards Green (in Forncett), 110
Buxton, 121
Bylaugh, 107

Caesar, Julius, 17, 32, 34
Caister on Sea, 47, 81, 138, 146
Caistor St Edmunds, 32, 67
Caldecote, 142
Campbell, B., 165
Camulodunum, 35
Carbrooke, 56
Carleton Forehoe, 97, 129
Carleton St Peter, 108
Carolingian Empire, 79
carstone, 7

Cassi, 33
Castle Acre, 88, 166, 180
Castle Rising, 61, 166, 180
castles, 166–7
Caston, 93
Catuvellauni, 33
Cawston, 101, 135, 153, 165, 179
Ceawalin, king of Wessex, 74
cemeteries
  Anglo-Saxon cremation, 49–54,
    64–9, 102–4
  Anglo-Saxon inhumation,
    49–54, 68–9, 103
  Bronze Age, 23
chalk, 7, 11
charters, absence of, 3, 92, 150
Chedgrave, 55, 124
Chet, river, 55
churches, parish, 2, 154–61, 166
  in Domesday, 154–6
  isolated, 170–1
  on pagan sites, 141–2
  round towered, 166–7
  in shared churchyards, 158–61
Clackclose Hundred, 101, 126
Clarke, W. G., 11
Clavering Hundred, 64, 72, 126,
  128
climate, 5, 125
Clippesby, 108
Cnava, Cnebba, Cnobhere,
  possible Dark Age leader in
  East Anglia, 64, 72
Cnobheresburg, 72, 138, 146
coastline, 5
Cockley Cley, 81
coinage
  Iron Age, 32–4, 41
  Middle Saxon, 81–2
  Roman, 41–2
coin hoards, 48
Colchester, 35, 37, 106
Colkirk, 141, 156
Colton, 97
commons, 167–70
  settlement beside, 167–71, 177
conversion, 74, 138–40

Costessey, 81, 107, 141
  Middle Saxon estate at, 96–8,
    133
Coston, 87
Cotton, S., 154–5
crag, 7
Cranwich, 142
Creoda, possible Dark Age leader
  in East Anglia, 72
Crostwick, 141
Crostwight, 141
Crownthorpe, 40–1, 96
Croxton, 182

Danish invasions, 3, 53, 105–10,
  156–7
Davies, W., 63
Davison, Alan, 21, 56, 89–90
Denton, 100
Denver, 40, 41
Deopham, 96–7, 100
Depwade Hundred, 129, 141,
  154
Dersingham, 84
deserted medieval settlements,
  181–2
Dickleburgh, 151
Dicuill, Irish priest, 139, 151
Diss, 103, 153, 179
Diss Hundred, 103, 106, 126
Diss Mere, 24, 58–9
Ditchingham, 22, 23, 42, 68, 103
Docking, 17, 40, 100, 153
Docking Hundred, 100, 128, 130
Dommoc, seat of the East Anglian
  bishops, 83, 139, 144
Doughton, 87
Downham (in Wymondham),
  98–9
Downham Market, 14, 126, 135,
  180
Drayton, 103
Dudwick (in Buxton), 89
Dunham, 135
Dunton, 102
Dunwich (Suffolk), 83, 139
Dyer, C., 177

ealdormen of East Anglia, 106
Earsham, 67, 87, 100
Earsham Hundred, 100, 126, 128, 154
East Angles, kingdom of, 6, 63, 76–83
East Carleton, 157, 158
East Dereham, 99, 101, 123, 124, 139, 141, 145–6, 153, 154, 168, 179
East Harling, 118, 168
Easton, 85, 96–7
East Rudham, 142
East Walton, 85, 103
Eccles, 55, 71, 130, 132, 148
Ecgric, king of the East Angles, 75, 82, 139
Edmund, last king of the East Angles, 105, 139–40
Edward, king, 106
Edwin, king of Northumbria, 74, 138
Egmere, 40, 131, 182
elm decline, 20
Ely
  abbey of, 99, 101, 128
  bishopric of, 77
enclosure
  Parliamentary, 10, 167, 182
  piecemeal, 182–3
Eni, king of the East Angles, 74
Eorpwald, king of the East Angles, 75, 138
Essex, 33, 34, 63, 82, 106
estates, Middle Saxon, 83–104
  break-up of, 114–26
Ethelburga, Saint, 139
Etheldreda, Saint, 139
Everitt, A., 64, 179
Eynesford Hundred, 100, 126, 129

Fakenham, 2, 93, 102, 103, 153, 179
Felix, Saint, 139, 143, 144
Feltwell, 101–2
Fenland, 6, 14, 33, 43, 63–4, 82, 91, 120

fens, 167–8
ferdings, 132–3
Fersfield, 141
Field Dalling, 131
field systems
  medieval, 172–7
  prehistoric, 25, 58
Fincham, 40
Fishergate, Norwich, Middle Saxon settlement at, 80, 134
Flegg, island and Hundreds of (East and West), 13, 45, 91, 126, 130
flint mines, 22
Flitcham, 129
Foillan, Irish priest, 138
fold course system, 174–5
Forehoe Hundred, 71, 126–9, 133, 154
Fossditch, 69–70
Foulden, 103
Foulsham, 87, 100, 126, 179
Franks, 53
Freebridge Hundred, 126, 129, 130
free men, 116–25, 163
'free peasantry', 116–125
Frenze, 158
Frettenham Hill, 129
Frisians, 53
Fritton, 96
Fulmodestone, 182
Fundenhall, 154
Fursa, Saint, 138–9, 146, 151

Gallow Hundred, 128, 130
Gallows Hill, Thetford, 36–7
Gariannonum, 47, 56
Gayton Thorpe, 109
  Roman villa at, 44
geld, 130–3
geology, 5, 7
gift exchange, 78, 84
Gillingham, 159
Gimingham, Middle Saxon estate at, 94–5, 103
Gipping, river (Suffolk), 7
glaciations, 8

Glandford, 56
Glaven, river, 18, 56
Goban, Irish priest, 139
Godwick, 89, 182
'Good Sands', 11, 17, 125
    Roman settlement in, 44
Great Massingham, 153
Great Melton, 158
Great Ouse, river, 43
Great Walsingham, 67, 102, 131
greens, 167–8, 177
Gregory, Tony, 3, 30
Gressenhall, 142
Grimes Graves, 21–2
Grimshoe Hundred, 128, 129
Grimston, 103
Griston, 101
Guestwick, 84, 156
Guiltcross Hundred, 100, 126, 128,
    142
Guist, 84
Guthlac, Saint, 56, 64
Gwyre, 63, 77

Hackford, 159
Hales, 25, 56, 89–91
ham, place-names in, significance
    of, 85–8, 102
Hamwih, 79
Happing Hundred, 45, 64, 68, 100,
    126, 128, 130, 132
Happisburgh, 68, 100
Hardwick, 89, 169
Harke, H., 54
Harpley, 22
Hartismere Hundred (Suffolk),
    106
Hatfield (Herts), ecclesistical
    council at, 77
Heacham, 102, 103, 107
Heacham river, 182
heaths, 11, 21, 167–8
Heckingham, 56, 89–91
Hellesdon, 140
Hempnall, 114, 123, 141, 157,
    158
Hempstead, 84

Hemsby, 108
henges, 22
Henstead Hundred, 123, 126, 129,
    141
Herringby, 108
Hertford (Herts), ecclesiastical
    council at, 77
Hethersett, 101, 126
Hevingham, 165
Heywood, S., 155
Hilgay, 7, 14
hillforts, 28–32
Hills, C., 53–4, 65–7
Hindringham, 131
Hingham, 87, 100, 124, 126, 153,
    179
    Middle Saxon estate at, 96–9,
    133
Hockham Mere, 24, 58
Hodges, R., 52
Hoe, 99
Holkham, 40, 131, 142, 148–9,
    182
    estate, 11
    hill fort at, 28–30, 36
Holme-next-Sea, 38
Holt, 13, 100, 129, 153, 179
Holt Hundred, 100, 129
Holverston, 154
Honingham, 96–7
Honingham Thorpe, 96–7, 109,
    169
Horningtoft, 110
Horsey, 84, 91
Horstead, 84
Houghton, 131, 182
Houghton estate, 11
Hoxne (Suffolk), 140
Humbleyard Hundred, 101, 126,
    129
Hun, king of the East Angles, 76
hundred rolls, 164–5
hundreds, 100–1, 126–33
    boundaries of 70–1, 128
Huns, 53
Hunstanton, 7, 13, 21
Huntingdon, Henry of, 63

Index

Icel, possible Dark Age leader in East Anglia, 71–2
Iceni, 7, 32–6
Icklingham (Suffolk), 71
Icknield Way, 38
Iclingas, 71
Idle, river, battle on, 74
Iken (Suffolk), 143
-*ingas* names, 62, 64, 88
Ipswich, 79–81
Ipswich Ware, 79–81
distribution of, 81–2, 177
Iron Age, 24–36, 41
Islington, 132
Itteringham, 158
Ivarr the Boneless, 105

Jurmin, Saint, 139

Kelling, 119
Kempstone, 40, 41
Kenninghall, 100, 103, 123, 126
Kent, 139
Keswick, 89
Kettlestone, 67
Kimberley, 97
Kings Lynn, 1, 55, 61, 178
Kirby Bedon, 108, 156, 159
Kirby Cane, 108, 156
Knapton, 94–5

Langham, 85
Langley, 102, 152
Launditch, 36, 69–70, 90
Launditch Hundred, 100, 110, 126–9
leets, 131–3
Letton, 85
Lindsey, 72
linear earthworks, 36, 69–70
Litcham, 135
Little Bittering, 182
Little Cressingham, 21
Little Melton, 154
Little Ouse, river, 6, 33, 38
Little Snarehill, 94, 100

Loddon, 21, 25, 55, 56, 64, 89–91, 100, 144, 145, 146, 153, 179
Loddon Hundred, 100, 128
London, 37
long barrows, 22
Longham, 110
Long Stratton, 42, 95, 103
Lopham, North and South, 93, 102, 124
Lopham Fen, 6
Lothingland, 183
Ludham, 101, 132
Lutting, thegn, 144

McKinley, J., 65
Malmesbury, William of, 83, 143 145
Mannington, 58
manorial organisation 2, 44, 114–26, 163–6, 174
Marham, 102
Markshall, 67
marling, 11
Marlingford, 97, 156
Marshall, William, 10
Marsham, 101
Marshland, 14, 125, 166
late Saxon settlement in, 111, 120
medieval settlement in, 169, 176–7
Middle Saxon settlement in, 91
Roman settlement in, 43
Martin, E., 72
Massingham, 17, 102
Matlaske, 141
Mautby, 108
Melton Constable, 85
Mendham (Suffolk), 106, 144
Mercia, 64, 76, 79, 105
Mesolithic period, 20
Metton, 85
Middleton, 85
Mileham, 87, 100, 111, 119, 123, 126, 153
minsters, 149–54

Mitford Hundred, 71, 99, 126, 128, 129
molmen, 165
monasteries, 143–9
moors, 167–8
Morley, St Peter and St Botolph, 97
Morningthorpe, 68, 95, 103
Morris, J., 72
Morris, R., 142
Morton, 87
Moulton, 85, 96
Mulbarton, 85, 169
Mundesley, 94, 95, 103
Mundford, 103
Myres, J. N. L., 50

Nar, river, 18, 36, 55
Narborough, 55
  hillfort at, 28
Narford, 55, 67
Neolithic period, 20–2
New Buckenham, 179, 180
Newton, 88
Newton, S., 74
Nomina Villarum, 164–5
Norfolk Archaeological Unit, 3
Norman Conquest, impact of, 162–7, 178
North Creake, 55, 61, 88
North Elmham, 3, 18, 53, 65, 81, 83, 92, 99, 123, 145, 148, 153, 155
North Erpingham Hundred, 101, 128, 130
'North Folk', origins of the term, 82–3
North Greenhoe Hundred, 100, 102, 126, 128, 131
North Repps, 95
North Runcton, 103
North Sea, 5, 47, 167, 183
Northumbria, 74–6
North Walsham, 152, 153, 179
Northwold, 103, 154
Norton (in Wymondham), 98–9, 133

Norton Subcourse, 85
Norwich, 1, 183
  Late Saxon development of, 134
  medieval development of, 178
  Middle Saxon settlement at, 79–80
  sacked by the Danes, 106, 134

Oby, 108
Offa, king of the Mercians, 76, 139
Old Buckenham, 87, 100–1, 102, 123, 166, 180
  Mere, 24, 58
open-field agriculture, 2, 172–7
  in north east Norfolk, 175–6
  origins of, 173–4
  on the southern claylands, 172, 176
  in West Norfolk, 174–5
oppida, 34–5, 41
Ormesby, 108
Oswald, puppet king of East Anglia, 105
Oswiu, king of Northumbria, 74, 76
Ouse, river, 14, 55, 69
Ovington, 87
Oxborough, 137
Oxwick, 89, 182

paganism
  Anglo-Saxon, 138–42
  Scandinavian, 107
pantiles, 183
Panworth Dyke, 69–70
Paris, Matthew, 63
parks, 123, 177
Pattesley, 182
Peddars Way, 38–40, 67
Pega, sister of Saint Guthlac, 64
Penda, king of Mercia, 75, 139
Pensthorpe, 103
Pentney, 55
placenames, 3
  Celtic, 54–5
  and Middle Saxon estates,

84–92
and pagan shrines, 140–1
and the Scandinavian
  settlement, 107–10
pollen analysis, 3, 23, 24, 58–9,
  113
Postwick, 89
Prasutagus, client king of the
  Iceni, 36–7, 38
Ptolemy, 32
Pudding Norton, 85, 102
Pulham, 154
Pye Road, 24, 38, 42

Quarles, 131, 182

Raedwald, king of the East
  Angles, 73–5, 77, 138
Ramsey Abbey, 101, 126, 180
Ravenna Cosmography, 32
Raynham, 130
Raynham estate, 11
Redgate Hill, Hunstanton, 21
Reedham, 144, 145, 146
Reepham, 158–61
Rendlesham (Suffolk), 76
Ricberht, assasin of king
  Eorpwald, 75
Ringmer, battle of, 106
Ringstead, 102
river names, 55–6
roads, Roman, 24, 38–40
Rockland All Saints, 108
Rockland St Mary, 108, 158
Rockland St Peter, 108
roddons, 43
Rogerson, Andrew, 28
Rollesby, 108
Roman
  coins, 42
  economy, 40–3
  forts, 36, 47
  period, 36–48
  pottery, 42
  roads, 24, 38–40
  settlement patterns, 42–5
  temples, 41

towns, 40–2
villas, 44
Roughton, 85
round barrows, 22–3
Runhall, 97
Ruston, 85
Ryston, 85

Saham Tony, 87, 100, 123, 126,
  153, 166
Mere, 58
possible early monastery at, 144,
  148
Saint Benet's Abbey, 148
Salthouse, 119
Sandringham, 84
Saxlingham, 103, 128
Saxlingham Nethergate, 123
Saxlingham Thorpe, 123
Saxon Shore
  Count of, 48
  forts of, 47
sceattas, 81
Scole, 38, 41, 103, 137
Sco Ruston, 85
Scratby, 108
Sea Mere, 24
Semer Green (in Dickleburgh), 151
settlement desertions, medieval,
  182
settlement patterns
  early Anglo-Saxon, 57–8
  late Saxon, 110–1
  medieval 8, 167–71
  Middle Saxon, 89–92
  Romano-British, 42–5
Sexburga, Saint, 139
Shadwell, 142
Schleswig-Holstein, 53, 167
sheep-corn husbandry, 8, 174–5
Shelton, 169
Shipdham, 70, 168
Shottesham, 123, 157, 159
Shouldham, 157
Shropham, 87, 101
Shropham Hundred, 71, 101, 102,
  107, 126, 128, 142

Sidestrand, 94–5
Sigeberht, king of the East
    Angles, 75, 83, 138–9, 143
Silfield (in Wymondham), 97, 133
Silvester, R., 82, 91
Smallburgh, 103
Smethdon Hundred, 129, 130
Snelling, Ulfketel, ealdorman of
    East Anglia, 106
Snettisham, 35, 102, 153
Soham (Cambridgeshire), 144
soils, 5
soke, 93–103
sokemen, 94–103, 116–21
Somerton, 85, 91
South Acre, 88
South Creake, 61, 88, 153
    hillfort at, 28, 30
South Elmham (Suffolk), 83, 145
South Erpingham Hundred, 101,
    128, 130
South Greenhoe Hundred, 71,
    126, 128, 128
South Lopham, 166
Southmere, 100
South Repps, 95
South Walsham, 87, 158
Spalda, 63
Spong Hill, Anglo-Saxon cemetery
    at, 3, 20, 53–4, 65–7
Stiffkey, 131, 158
    possible hillfort at, 30
Stiffkey, river, 18, 28, 182
Stigand, archbishop, 128
Stockton, 124
Stoke Ferry, 137
Stokesby, 91, 108
Stow Bardolph, 148
Stow Bedon, 101, 148, 152
    Mere, 58
'Strangers', 183
Suderbrarup, 53
Suevi, 17, 53
Suffolk, 6, 82–3
Suton (in Wymondham), 98–9,
    133
Sutton, 85, 110

Sutton Hoo, 74, 77, 78
Swabians, 53
Swaffham, 2, 153, 179
Swanton Abbot, 85
Swanton Morley, 36, 85
Swanton Novers, 85
Sweorda, 63
Swithelm, king of the East Saxons,
    76

Tacitus, 32, 34
Tas, river, 8, 18, 42, 45
Tasburgh, 96
    hillfort at, 28, 38
Tat, river, 182
Taverham, 87, 100, 142
Taverham Hundred, 100, 129
tenementa, 173–4
Terrington, 82
Testerton, 182
Thet, river, 18
Thetford, 1, 103
    hillfort at, 28
    Gallows Hill, 36–7
    Middle and Late Saxon town at,
        135
    sacked by the Danes, 106
    St Mary's church at, 151–2
Thetford Ware, 135, 169
Thomas, second bishop of the East
    Angles, 77
Thompson, 164
Thornham, embanked enclosure
    at, 37
Thorpe, 108
Thorpe Green, Weasenham St
    Peter, 110
Thorpe Parva, 158
Threxton, 36, 40, 41
Thrigby, 108
Thursford, 131
Thwaite, 108
Tibenham, 81, 96
Tiffey, river, 41
Tilney All Saints, 111
Tittleshall, 77, 110
Toftrees, 40, 67

torcs, 35
Tosny, Robert de, 180
Tottenhill, 103
towns
    Late Saxon, 133–6
    medieval, 178–81
    Middle Saxon, 78–80
    planted, 180
    'primary', 179
    Romano-British, 40–2
    topography of, 181
Tribal Hidage, 63, 80
Trimingham, 95
Trinovantes, 7, 33, 34, 35
Trunch, 55, 95
Tud, river, 18
tun, place-names in, significance
    of, 85–8
Tunstead, 100, 153
Tunstead Hundred, 45, 100,
    128–30
Tunstead Hundred Hill, 129–30
turbaries, 114
Tuttington, 101
Tydd St Giles (Cambridgeshire),
    82
Tytil, Tyttla, father of king
    Raedwald, 74

Ultan, brother of Saint Fursa, 138

Venta Icenorum, 32, 37–40, 47
Verulamium, 37
Vikings, 3, 105–10

Wacton, 96
Wade-Martins, P., 90, 110
Walpole St Peter, 82, 111
Walstan, Saint, 142
Warenne family, 166, 180
Warham, 131
    embanked enclosure at, 37
    hillfort at, 28, 30
warrens, rabbit, 11
Waterden, 182
watersheds, 15–17, 18, 121–3,
    124, 177, 182

boundaries on, 70–1, 128
water supply, 13, 15
Wattlefield (in Wymondham), 98,
    133
Watton, 81, 141, 180
Waveney, river, 6, 7–8, 13, 18, 24,
    25, 33, 42, 108
Waxham, 102
Wayland Hundred, 71, 126, 128
Wayland Wood, 141
Weasenham, 17, 110
Weha, ancestor of Raedwald, 74
Wellingham, 111
wells, holy, 141–2
Welney, 43
Wendover, Roger of, 63
Wensum, river, 13, 18, 36, 45
Wereham, 142
West Acre, 67, 88
West Dereham, 146, 147, 152, 159
West Rudham, 22
West Saxons, 105–6
West Walton, 82, 91, 111, 154
western escarpment, 13
Westerwanna, 53
Weston Longville, 85
Westwick, 89
Weybourne, 119
Whey Curd Farm, Wighton, 68
Whitlingham, 22
Whitwell, 159
wic, significance as a rural
    placename, 89
Wicken Farm, Castle Acre, 89
Wickhampton, 89
Wicklewood, 96–7, 159
Wickmere, 58
wics (Middle Saxon entrepots),
    78–80
Widsith, 74
Wighton, 102, 126, 131, 153
    embanked enclosure at, 37, 68
Wilby, 108
Wimbotsham, 101, 126, 180
Winfarthing, 132
Winterton, 85, 91
Winwaed, battle of, 76

Wissey, river, 18, 56, 69
Withburga, Saint, 99, 139, 141, 149
Witton (near Norwich), 22
Witton (near North Walsham), 42, 57–8, 85
Wolterton, 58, 103
Woodbastwick, 89
Woodcock Hall, Threxton, 41
woodland
    Domesday, 113–14, 121–3
    prehistoric clearance of, 20–8
    Romano-British and early
      Saxon, 60–2
Wood Norton, 85
Woodton, 85
Wormegay, 149
Worthing, 110

Wramplingham, 97
Wrenningham, 154
Wretham, 106
Wroxham, 56, 102
Wuffa, founder of the Wuffinga
    dynasty, 74
Wuffingas, 63, 72–9, 83, 91, 133, 139
Wulfhere 76, 80
Wymondham, 2, 71, 153, 166, 179
    Middle Saxon estate at, 96–9, 124, 133

Yare, river, 18, 45, 55, 108
Yarmouth, 1, 13, 18, 55, 126, 135, 178
York, 79
Young, Arthur, 11